Sexual Intelligence

The Groundbreaking Study That Shows You
How to Boost Your "Sex IQ"
and Gain Greater Sexual Satisfaction

Sexual
Intelligence

Dr. Sheree Conrad & Dr. Michael Milburn

CROWN PUBLISHERS
NEW YORK

Published by Crown Publishers, New York, New York.
Member of the Crown Publishing Group.

Random House, Inc. New York, Toronto, London, Sydney, Auckland
www.randomhouse.com

CROWN is a trademark and the Crown colophon is a registered trademark of Random House, Inc.

Printed in the United States of America

Design by Elina D. Nudelman

Library of Congress Cataloging-in-Publication Data
Conrad, Sheree D.
   Sexual intelligence : the groundbreaking study that shows you how to boost your "sex IQ" and gain greater sexual satisfaction / Sheree Conrad and Michael Milburn.
   1. Sex.   2. Sex (Psychology).   3. Sexual behavior surveys—United States.   I. Milburn, Michael A., 1950–   II. Title.
HQ23.C646   2001
306.7—dc21   2001017400

ISBN 0-609-60640-9

10   9   8   7   6   5   4   3   2   1

First Printing

To tdn, with love and thanks

and
To our research participants, for sharing
their stories and teaching us so much
—SHEREE DUKES CONRAD

To my three daughters, with love, Allison, Johanna, and Abby
—MICHAEL MILBURN

Contents

PART IV SEXUAL INTELLIGENCE IN ACTION

Acknowledgments

This book would never have been written without the help and support of a number of people. First, we want to acknowledge and thank our agents, Lane Zachary, Todd Shuster, and Esmond Harmsworth, for the tremendous contribution they made to this book. Todd believed in this project from the beginning, saw its potential, and spent countless hours with us, helping us to hone our vision of the book we wanted to write and helping us translate that vision onto paper. Lane's energy, commitment, and enormous talent made this book better than it could possibly have been without her contributions. She was agent, editor, critic, crisis manager, and always a source of help, guidance, reassurance, and on more than one occasion, sanity. Esmond worked tirelessly in many capacities, from agent to editor. We can never sufficiently acknowledge our debt nor express our thanks to these three extraordinary people.

We also want to thank our editor at Crown, Kristin Kiser, who from the beginning believed in this project enthusiastically. She brought to this book a keen intelligence that contributed significantly to the shape of the final product.

A project such as this relies on the efforts of many people. We benefited enormously from the diligence and hard work of our research staff, Eric Sundquist, Harry Nir, Lorrie Dellinger, Christina Jackson, and Elizabeth Wuehrmann, and from that of our clinical interviewers, Pat Song, Ethan Seidman, and Matthew Jakupchek.

John Yannis made an important contribution to chapter 12 in helping us to understand the legal issues raised by sexual harassment. Scott

Gold, at the Zachary Shuster Harmsworth Agency, contributed very significantly to framing chapter 13.

The first author, Dr. Sheree Conrad, would like to thank a number of people for their support and encouragement, first, and foremost, my mother, Thelma Dukes, whose love, support and example are the reason I have been able to do what I love—scholarship and writing. She worked twelve- and fifteen-hour days to make it possible for me to have the best education, and she has modeled for me the courage and fierce determination that have gotten me through more than one seemingly impossible task. She is the bravest person I know. My sister, Diane Bourque, has been another inspiration and model of courage, not to mention a companion in misery on days when the writing was going badly for both of us. My brother-in-law, Steven Bourque, has been a source of support and encouragement since we were teenagers. My nieces, Alissa, Aimee and Abby Bourque, are the light of my life; they constantly amaze me with their intelligence—they are so much smarter than I was at their age—not to mention their sense of humor and lovingness.

I want especially to thank Mary Kohák, Elizabeth O'Neill, Sheila Purdy, and Susan and Richard deCampo for sustaining me with their love, support, encouragement, advice, and sheer presence in my life for many years. You have each mysteriously been there, on so many occasions, when I needed a miracle, and I can never sufficiently thank you.

Finally, I want to thank several of my colleagues. Don Kalick has been a steadfast source of support through many trying times and a true friend, as well as a model of the type of scholar and teacher I want to be. My coauthor, Michael Milburn, has been mentor, colleague, and friend for many years. He did for me what he has done for so many students and junior colleagues—provided the guidance, support, encouragement, and example to make us into professionals who at least aspire to his own level of intelligence, integrity, talent, kindness—and patience! I also want to thank Deborah Kelley-Milburn and Allison Kelley, Johanna and Abby Milburn for their friendship and support over the years.

Both authors would like to thank Harvard University reference librarian Deborah Kelley-Milburn, who provided extensive research assistance and, through many readings of the manuscript, gave us the benefit of her fine literary sense and suggested a number of important improvements to the book. We would also like to thank Denee Hammond at UMASS-Boston, who is unfailingly professional, helpful, and kind, and without whose help, we would never have made the deadline.

The second author, Dr. Michael Milburn, would like to thank his wife, who is also Deborah Kelley-Milburn, for her love, support, encouragement, and thoughtful criticism that have enriched his life and this book in so many ways. My children, Allison, Johanna, and Abby, have also been unfailingly encouraging, as has family friend Andrew Reed.

There are so many people I should thank who have contributed to the fruition of this work of many years—I will name just a few. Old friends Ed Durham and Alan Teger gave me tremendous perspective on the topic, and psychologist Mel Schnall helped me considerably to develop my thinking. Also, the first steps along the path to this book would probably not have been written without the friendship of former students Jan Fay-Dumaine and Deb Kennedy. Finally, I would like to thank my parents, Thomas and Jo Anne Milburn, who provided such important guidance, encouragement, and role models for me as a social scientist and a person. For all this, and much more, I will always be grateful.

Sexual
Intelligence

Prologue: *Unsuspected Riches*

I had a dream. I've had it half a dozen times in the last few years. In the dream, I'm living in a small, dark, cramped apartment. There's a narrow hallway and just two rooms off either end. Each room is tiny: the bedroom is a box barely large enough for the bed. There are only two win-

> **Footfalls echo in the memory**
> **Down the passage which we did not take**
> **Towards the door we never opened . . .**
> —T. S. Eliot, "Four Quartets"

dows, blocked by dense foliage from trees growing too close to the building. It's odd—there's no kitchen in the apartment.

I *have* to find a better place to live; I search the city from one end to the other, going from rental agent to rental agent, each more phony and dishonest than the last. The spacious loft turns out to be in a dangerous neighborhood. The penthouse with the Jacuzzi is crawling with cock-roaches. The unique studio with a view turns out to be an attic room as cramped as my own apartment, and the view, a distant glimpse of the city skyline through a tiny slit between the surrounding buildings. In the end, I'm led over and over again by these hucksters to apartments as cramped and dreary as my own.

I come home one night to my apartment, defeated, hopeless, realizing that I'm stuck in this terrible place for the rest of my life. I go into the bedroom, toss my coat on the bed, and that's when I see it: a door on the back wall of the bedroom that I never realized was there: mute, wooden, coated with dust and grime as if it hadn't been touched in decades. I must have looked right at it a thousand times and never noticed it. Or simply concluded it led nowhere. Even now I assume it's locked or boarded up from behind. What good would it do to even try the knob? And what if the door did open onto some horror: a closet crawling with spiders, even a rotting corpse?

But curiosity finally overcomes fear and I turn the knob, pull the door open on its rusty hinges and step through the doorway—into a spacious room flooded with light. It's lovely, a sitting room laid with a beautiful pale gold carpet and furnished with Louis XIV chairs upholstered in white and gold. There's a doorway at the far end of the room which opens into another room, and then another, and another. Each room is different and exquisite, filled with the most varied, precious objects: one is hung with rich tapestries; in another there are jewels—emerald-encrusted necklaces, diamond earrings, gold bracelets—spilling over every surface. I pass from one room to the next—the succession of rooms seemingly endless—amazed and delighted at the richness around me, astounded to think it had been there all along.

That dream was told to us by Lorraine, a thirty-two-year-old woman who has been married for eight years and is thinking of getting a divorce. Her sex life is unsatisfying—a weekly ritual devoid of passion or excitement. Lorraine told us, "I love my husband, but I can't bear the thought that this is what my life is going to be for the next forty years, that I'll die without ever again feeling that thrill of anticipation and that aching need."

We have heard variants of Lorraine's dream from more than one person—men *and* women—that we've talked to in our research. Always, there is the central theme of a spacious, rich world that has existed all along, just beyond an unnoticed door in a cramped, dreary dwelling. It's an apt metaphor for a problem that afflicts millions of Americans: the vast majority tell pollsters and research psychologists that a good sex life is critically important to them, yet amazingly few people have satisfying sex lives. Not only are Americans dissatisfied with their sex lives, a startling number of them suffer from sexual dysfunctions—impotence, premature ejaculation, inability to achieve orgasm—that make it difficult for them to have a sex life at all. And it's not just the middle-aged or couples married twenty years who have such problems. Some of the highest rates of sexual dysfunction occur among *young* people.

When it comes to their sex lives, millions of people are merely existing in a cramped, dreary space that offers no nourishment—it's not surprising that the apartment in Lorraine's dream had no kitchen. When they do resolve to seek something better, *they go looking in all the wrong places*, sometimes exposing themselves to danger, constantly led on by false promises of the perfect sex life that always exists just outside of their reach, when, in truth, the possibility of a rich, varied, fulfilling sex life is closer at hand than they ever imagined. It's right there, within all of us, and has been all along. We only need to open the door.

PART I

A
New
Approach
To
Sexuality

chapter one

Passion's Fools?

At twenty-nine, Natalie was only months away from getting her Ph.D. in political science, a goal she had been working toward for seven years. She was being considered for

> It is impossible to love and to be wise.
> —Francis Bacon, *Essays*

a job at a prestigious university, and she and her fiancé were about to close on a house. Their wedding was planned for the week after graduation. After years of struggle and hard work, Natalie was finally close to having the life she had always wanted—and she was about to lose it all by sleeping with one of her students, an eighteen-year-old enrolled in one of her sections of Introductory Political Science.[1]

It was clear from the beginning of the semester that Mark, her student, had a crush on her. At first Natalie was amused and mildly flattered; he was tall, good-looking, and, at eighteen, already an accomplished jazz musician who played trumpet in a local band. By midsemester, her detachment had vanished. She thought about Mark constantly, even dreamed about him at night. He was in the habit of stopping by her office nearly every afternoon to chat; on the days when he didn't appear, she was miserable. Lately, he had once or twice mentioned a club where he was playing at night and suggested that she stop by. And if she did? What would happen at the end of the night? Natalie knew she was risking losing her job, her entire academic career, and her fiancé, whom she loved. "Some days I tell myself, this is crazy, *don't do it*," Natalie told us, "and other days I think I'll go mad if I can't touch

Mark, just once. I feel like I'm losing my mind. Why does sex have to be so *difficult?*"

Natalie is not alone in her despair over sexual feelings that seem unmanageable, perversely at odds with her own wishes—not to mention her best interests. Natalie is a smart woman and highly educated. If brains alone were at issue, she wouldn't have a problem. But so many smart people struggle either with passions that lead to disaster or with sex lives that are frustrating and disappointing—or nonexistent.

If you're like most people, sex is anything but simple. Most of us, no matter how liberated we are about sexuality in general, could name at least one sexual issue we are grappling with right now that is difficult, painful, and disruptive. You might be struggling with a powerful attraction to a person at work, an attraction that you know you shouldn't act on. Or be facing another Saturday night alone, wondering if you'll ever make love to anyone again. Perhaps you're in a happy marriage but the sex has become routine, and you're afraid that the price of a good marriage is the end of the kind of passion that makes you feel alive. Whatever you're struggling with, you probably have very few people you can talk to about it. Perhaps you haven't talked to anyone.

For all our society's apparent sophistication about the subject, sexuality is still treated as a disruptive force best not too openly discussed. We slow down to view the wreckage of other people's sexual misadventures, it's true, but we gossip about *them;* we don't talk about our own compelling and sometimes difficult feelings.

When it comes to sex, America today wears two faces. On the one hand, we seem obsessed with it. Wherever one looks—from men's and women's magazines to television talk shows to round-the-clock assessments of one president's interpersonal exploits—we are besieged by sexual images and sensational, superficial gossip about sex. Sex, it seems, is everywhere.

Yet, at the same time, there is a powerful force within our culture—in the form of old attitudes about sex—that enforces silence, shame, and repression. If we open the door to sexuality with one hand, we seem to slam it shut with the other. As a result, many people are left feeling confused and ashamed about their sexual desires and behaviors, as well as ignorant about their partner's.

For the majority of Americans, sex is not just important, it's an essential part of their lives. In poll after poll, the vast majority of Americans say that sex is a very important, even crucial, part of their lives. For example, when asked "How important is it to you to have a satisfying sex life?" 71 percent of American adults surveyed in a 1989 Harris poll said it is "very important" or "essential." At the same time, over half of Americans say that sex is the cause of stress in their lives, and 75 percent of Americans say they are concerned about having sex more regularly.[2]

There are plenty of signs that Americans are struggling and confused about sex, and have little in the way of guidance to help them. Consider just a few recent signs that all is not well in the sex lives of Americans:

- A popular president—reportedly a brilliant man and a former Rhodes scholar—risked his office and his place in history for the sake of oral sex in the Oval Office with a woman half his age.
- Last year, in a small town in upstate New York, thirteen girls—some as young as fourteen years old—were infected with the HIV virus by the same man. The local high school offers one day a year of AIDS education, which makes no mention of anal sex, oral sex, or condoms.[3]
- According to a major study recently conducted by sociologist Edward Laumann and his colleagues, of the University of Chicago, more than 40 percent of American women and nearly 33 percent of American men experience serious sexual problems such as lack of desire, difficulty maintaining an erection, or an inability to reach orgasm. Laumann found, contrary to popular belief, that some of the highest rates of sexual dysfunction are among young people.[4]

David is one of them. He is only twenty years old and he has had trouble maintaining erections and reaching orgasm:

> **With my girlfriend, sometimes I perform, and everything is going great, but then I can't finish the job—and I feel like, "Uh oh." I hate that.**
>
> **Me and a friend of mine always joke about it: "I know this guy, he couldn't get it up." And on TV they joke about it. I don't want to be that guy.**

In our long-term research program called the *Sexual Intelligence Project,* the results of our research show that, to have a satisfying sex life, we have to think about sex in a completely different way that transcends both repression and obsession with all things sexual.

To that end, we have formulated the powerful new concept of *sexual intelligence.* Being sexually intelligent means not only knowing all of the biological factors that affect how we behave sexually—neurons firing in the brain or hormones coursing through our bloodstream; the key to sexual intelligence is knowing *ourselves.* This means seeing beyond cultural myths that damage and distort our sexuality, uncovering our authentic sexual desires, and developing the emotional and social skills we need to share our *real* selves with our partners and maximize our chances for a happy sex life.

Specifically, we believe that each of us can be genuinely satisfied, and truly intelligent in our sex lives, only when we are intimately acquainted with our authentic sexual feelings—what we call the **secret sexual self**—and able to be honest with others about our sexuality. There is a way in which, despite our frankness, we don't really know ourselves sexually. We may have very tolerant attitudes toward sex on an intellectual level, but when it comes to our own sex lives and those of people close to us, there often remains much that is hidden: certain fantasies that we don't look at too closely—and don't talk about— moments of attraction or yearning that we brush aside, vague feelings of dissatisfaction or disillusionment that we have no way to address, self-consciousness or even shame about our bodies that makes us cringe.

We sabotage our own sex lives when, rather than looking within to discover our own sexuality, we allow so many things to obscure it: worries about what other people think, self-consciousness about our bodies, embarrassment that prevents us from telling our partners what really arouses us, guilt about *having* sexual desires. These inner demons and others like them can be conquered by becoming more sexually intelligent.

To really know ourselves, we each need to explore the unique pattern of desire and circumstance that has produced our secret sexual self. Each of us has built up over the course of our lives a history that has conditioned our sexual desires, overlaid our genuine healthy impulses with false desires, fears, mistaken beliefs, expectations, and hang-ups acquired from the culture around us, as well as our own negative experiences. These needs, desires, fears, and expectations are intertwined and layered over time and become the sexual identity we take with us into adulthood. The secret sexual self holds the key to the pleasures that transport us, the inexplicable attractions that hold us tyrannized in their spell, and the choices—wise and disastrous—that we make in our sex lives.

Our goal in this book is to encourage readers to discover the real inner landscape of their own desires, to become intimately acquainted with and to understand the nuances of their sexuality, and to use this knowledge to create a more fulfilling sex life.

People who have the courage to open the door onto their secret sexual self will find, amid the fear, doubt, shame, and confusion, a rich world of genuine desires and authentic feelings that hold the potential for finding real sexual fulfillment. We're convinced that sexual intelligence, the ability to know your own sexuality intimately and unflinchingly, gives people enormous power to transform their lives. It provides authentic knowledge we can rely on and trust, infuses our lives with a genuine source of passion, and frees us to make decisions about our sex lives that work for us, allowing us finally to be comfortable—and wise—in our own skin.

The Sexual Intelligence Project

In 1998, we launched the Sexual Intelligence Project to find out what makes the difference between a rich, fulfilling, conflict-free sex life and a disappointing or even destructive one. What is it that people with happy sex lives do? What attitudes and practices distinguish them from people who are frustrated and disappointed over and over again? In other words, what does it mean to be sexually intelligent?

We first distributed questionnaires to close to 500 people from around the country and around the world, ranging in age from eighteen to sixty-four, including men and women; homosexuals, heterosexuals, and bisexuals; married and single people; and virgins as well as those who've had as many as 150 sexual partners. In those questionnaires, our research participants answered questions about every aspect of their sexual lives, from their use of pornography and experiences with Internet sex, to their first sexual experience and the influence it has had on them, to the development of their sexual orientation, to what their parents taught them about sex, to whether or not they have ever cheated on a partner, to what they fantasize about. Because the questionnaire included demographic questions as well as a number of standard psychological tests, we are able to draw rigorous scientific conclusions in this book about the relationship between people's sexual attitudes and behaviors and gender, education, and personality characteristics.

We then conducted personal interviews with dozens of people who had filled out our questionnaire. We selected a wide range of participants and talked to them at length in conversations that revealed all of the detail, richness, and complexity of their individual struggles with sexuality.

Our research participants were primarily young educated people. Although we spoke to people as old as sixty, most of our participants were in their late teens or twenties. All of them had some college education, and the majority of their parents had attended college, too. Further, these people were not seeking help; most of them considered their sex lives within the norm. For all these reasons, you would think our research participants would be the most sexually liberated, the most knowledgeable, and the most savvy; that is, the people most likely to be enjoying trouble-free, exciting sex lives.

But they're not.

Our Results

We have learned from the Sexual Intelligence Project that despite the sexual revolution of the sixties, which seemed to offer the promise of replacing old repressive attitudes with a new openness, people today are just as unhappy about their sex lives and are just as unwilling to talk about their problems. The sexual revolution might never have happened for all the effect it has had on our willingness to confront sexuality directly. What we seem to be left with is not true openness, but rather a veneer of sophistication in the form of an obsession with sex in the media and popular culture. True freedom and frankness are as elusive as ever.

Pain and confusion about sexuality abound. Many, many of our research participants told us they struggle to find a happy, fulfilling sex life. They feel lonely, unhappy, and hopeless and suspect that everyone but them has a better sex life.

These are just a few of the surprising things we found:

1. Seventy-five percent of our participants said sex is very important or more than moderately important to them, but fewer than 25 percent claimed to have a very satisfying sex life. Almost half of the people we spoke to said they feel shame about some of their sexual desires or behaviors.

2. A startlingly high number of our participants suffered from sexual dysfunctions that can get in the way of even *having* a sexual relationship.
   - Forty-two percent of our participants reported experiencing a lack of sexual desire.
   - Nearly a third said there are times when they don't find sex pleasurable.
   - Fifty-seven percent reported being unable to achieve orgasm.
   - Half of young women between eighteen and twenty-nine reported finding intercourse physically painful.
   - Thirty-three percent of men between eighteen and twenty-nine said they had had trouble achieving or maintaining an erection, and 53 percent reported premature ejaculation.

Overall, nearly half of our sample reported less than satisfying sex lives.

Those people we talked to who are currently in a satisfying sexual relationship seldom got there easily; many of them recounted a trail of painful experiences along the way, and virtually all of them identified some area of their sex life that still poses problems.

Most interesting of all, we learned that people are starving to talk to someone about their sexual difficulties. Our research participants were extraordinarily candid with us about their struggles, and many of them told us how helpful the experience was. People *want* to talk about their experiences with sexuality; they just don't know how to begin—or they have no one to talk to.

Take, for example, one fifty-year-old man we interviewed who had *never* spoken to anyone about his sex life and some of the painful experiences he'd had—despite having been in therapy for years. When we asked him how it felt to finally talk about such things, he told us:

> I've said things here that I've never said to a breathing human being. It's embarrassing. A fifty-year-old man. I would love to be in here telling stories of all the sexual successes, or what a wonderful sex life I've had, but that's not the way it went.

One of our major findings is that as important as people say a good sex life is to them, a large number—in fact, fully half of our participants—say that their sexuality has no importance for who they are as a person. It's tragic that people yearn for better sex lives, without realizing that the key to finding one is to look inside—to uncover, accept, and learn from their secret sexual selves.

The Three Components of Sexual Intelligence

The results of our research suggest that the answer to a range of problems lies in a whole new approach to sexuality. The answer is not to repress our sexual desires, nor to become more "liberated" sexually. The answer isn't in learning new techniques, or even in the kind of knowledge that people can acquire from books about human sexuality. It certainly doesn't consist in becoming more seductive or learning how to manipulate others. The answer from our research is to become more sexually intelligent.

A satisfying sex life is not an unattainable ideal. But the idea that one can have a satisfying sex life *without effort, thought, or understanding* is, we would argue, an illusion. One of the first steps toward developing sexual intelligence is to be aware that sex is not something magical, effortless, or available only to the young. Each of us can attain a rich and rewarding sex life by doing the hard work it takes to acquire the necessary information and insight—about sex in general, about how other people (including our sex partners) experience their sex lives, and above all, about our own sexuality.

As part of our survey, we developed a test that quantifies a person's overall level of sexual intelligence. We have found that a person's score on our Sexual Intelligence Test is a powerful—often the single most powerful—predictor of how satisfying the person's sex life is and whether or not the person suffers from sexual dysfunctions.[5] Later in the chapter, we explain this test in greater detail.

Sexual intelligence is made up of three components, each component involving a distinct set of skills. There are key differences between people who develop enriching sex lives and those who are disappointed—even damaged—again and again. Sexually intelligent people *do* things differently. Being sexually intelligent—and having a better sex life—doesn't depend on luck, beauty, or innate sex appeal. It depends on skills that people can acquire, develop, and master over time. Thus, sexual intelligence is something that everyone can reasonably hope for and work toward.

The three crucial components of sexual intelligence are (1) sexual knowledge, (2) awareness of the secret sexual self, and (3) the ability to connect with others.

Sexual Knowledge

One of the key differences we've found among people is that those who are sexually intelligent possess accurate scientific information about human sexuality that they use to guide their decisions and sexual behavior. The first step, then, toward becoming more intelligent about our sex lives is obtaining accurate knowledge that can serve as a foundation for the new behaviors we need to practice.

Acquiring that knowledge—*and being able to put it into practice*—is not a simple matter. It requires, first, that people develop the skill of spotting and challenging myths about sex that are entrenched in the culture. Whether it's what they have picked up from popular culture, the media, their families, religious authorities, or what they have overheard on the playground or in the locker room, much of what people learn about sex is based on misinformation, unexamined assumptions, even superstition, which is more harmful than helpful. Until we identify these myths and free ourselves from them, we're unlikely to really absorb and benefit from more accurate information.

These myths are so thoroughly embedded in the culture that they form an unexamined belief system within which we unwittingly live out our sexual lives. Take just one example: the myth of the instant sexual connection, the spark felt across a crowded room that guarantees not only sexual fulfillment but total happiness. Many people take such instant attraction as a sign that the other person might be *the one:* the person they have been waiting for their whole life. But sexual attraction isn't necessarily a guarantee of happiness. Having that small bit of perspective, that ability to look with a critical eye at a romantic belief woven into the culture, helps people to become more sexually intelligent and to find sex lives that are genuinely fulfilling.

One of the benefits of freeing ourselves from myths about sex is that it opens up to us a world of information that *works*, that really can make our sex lives better, and having that information increases our self-confidence and self-esteem. Another crucial benefit is that we remove a veil of illusion from our lives so that we can each see *ourselves* more clearly. When we uncover our true sexuality, we become much better able to set aside messages from the media, our families, and society, and to take control over our own sexual lives.

Awareness of the Secret Sexual Self

Once we have freed ourselves from the myths about sex that surround us, the second step toward a better sex life is to become acquainted with our own individual sexuality—what arouses us, what presents difficulties for us, what we are drawn to, what we prefer. Sexually intelligent people know themselves. They have insight into their secret sexual self, the pattern of desires, needs, preferences, fears, even hang-ups that drive their sexual behavior. They are able to tell, for example, when their sexual desires are substituting for emotional needs that are not sexual, such as the need for self-esteem, for security, or for power. They know when they are having sex simply because they're lonely.

Our secret sexual self is a tremendously valuable part of our personality. It is a map to the landscape of our unacknowledged desires, unexplored emotional conflicts, and unexamined assumptions about ourselves and our bodies. As we mentioned earlier, it is the guide that can point the way to a healthier, happier sex life and personal life. Sexual intelligence means, first and foremost, knowing the truth of what the secret sexual self has to tell us about both our healthy, genuine desires and the way in which those desires have been overwritten by false media images, negative body concepts, inhibitions taught within the family, and other negative messages about sex—from the culture around us and, sometimes, from our own painful experiences. Our secret sexual self holds the truth that will set us free to pursue a more rewarding sex life.

Sexual attractions are often based on a complex, tangled set of associations built up by past experiences and learning. Sexual desire can be colored by past experiences and unmet emotional needs in a way that often leads to disastrous sexual relationships. Exploring our own sexuality can eliminate obstacles to sexual happiness and reveal our genuine desires and preferences.

Knowing the secret sexual self is the most important component of sexual intelligence: without knowing ourselves, we are often unable to put into practice the scientific knowledge that we've acquired. For example, the person who is motivated, in part, to have sex in order to get approval from another person may be unable to say no to unprotected sex despite knowing that he or she could become infected with HIV. The secret sexual self is also the key to acquiring interpersonal skills necessary to relate to others. Without knowing ourselves, we can't share our sexuality with a partner and forge satisfying relationships.

Connecting with Others

Sustaining an enriching sexual life involves other people. For that, the sexually intelligent person needs a third set of tools: social or interpersonal skills, including the ability to talk to our partner about our sex lives as well as the ability to understand our partner's sexual self. For many people, simply summoning the courage to talk to their partner about their sex life is terribly difficult. Nonetheless, it's crucial. One of the things that most people learn very early on, in their families, is not to talk about sex. The notion that our own sexual feelings are, literally, unspeakable is one of the myths that serve as a barrier, both to knowing those feelings and talking about them. Once we can get beyond that code of silence and we open up to our partner, talking is a powerful way of challenging sexual myths, further discovering our genuine sexual feelings and becoming intimate with another person. Sexual intelligence involves learning how to be honest with ourselves, and our partners, about who we are sexually.

Once you become more familiar with your sexual self, there is nothing more freeing, and reassuring, than sharing it with your partner. Whether you are negotiating sex in a current romance, trying to understand what went wrong sexually in a relationship that ended, sharing sexual concerns with a friend, or teaching your children how to manage their own emerging sexuality, talking about sexual feelings is crucial to making smart decisions about our sex lives—ones that are right for us, and respectful of others. We have discovered from our research just how transformative and healing talking about sex can be, especially with our sexual partners—and what depths of trouble and pain people can get themselves into by *not* talking with their partner about their sexual needs and feelings. Just as we talk to our loved ones about our emotional needs and conflicts, we must also learn to talk about our sexual feelings. Everybody has a sexual self that needs to be explored and expressed. When we repress and hide this part of ourselves, the results are as destructive as when we keep our emotions locked inside. We lose a sense of who we are and drain our lives of authenticity and passion.

People who are sexually intelligent have the interpersonal skills to talk to their partner about their sexual needs and to imagine vividly how their sexual behavior may affect their partner's feelings. They also know how to listen to their partner's sexual concerns, needs, and insecurities, and how to have sexual empathy for their partner.

The Sexual Intelligence Test: Measuring Your Own Level of Sexual Intelligence

One of the most important things to come out of our research is the Sexual Intelligence Test, a way to quantify sexual intelligence in general, as well as the three components that make up sexual intelligence. By taking this test, you can see how far you've come in acquiring the skills and attitudes of sexually intelligent people and how far you have to go. Plus, your score on any one item on the test helps you pinpoint where your strengths and weaknesses lie, and what you need to know or do to increase your level of sexual intelligence. Throughout the book, you can compare your responses to specific items on the Sexual Intelligence Test to the responses our research participants gave.

The Sexual Intelligence Test consists of fifty-two multiple-choice and true-or-false questions that inquire about everything from how often people talk to their partner about their sex lives, to how people handle conflicts in a sexual relationship, to how people feel about their sexual fantasies, or how they would react if their partner wanted to try something new in bed. The items on the test were carefully culled from over a hundred different questions we developed based on our knowledge of the scientific literature on sexual behavior and our own hypotheses about what makes some people more sexually intelligent than others. There are three types of questions: (a) ones that measure your knowledge of human sexuality and your ability to put that knowledge into practice, (b) ones that assess your awareness of your secret sexual self, and (c) ones that assess your interpersonal skills with a sexual partner. While there is no one definitive right or wrong answer to each of the questions on the test, some answers are more sexually intelligent than others. The possible answers for each item are assigned a point value that reflects how sexually intelligent—or unintelligent—the answer is. Here's one example:

The first item on the Sexual Intelligence Test asks:

In your current relationship (or in your last long-term relationship), approximately how often do you (did you) talk with your partner about your sex life?

The possible responses you can choose are listed here, each with its attached point value.

a) Once a week (+3)

b) Once a month (+2)

c) Once every six months (+1)

d) Never (−3)

All the research literature shows, as we'll see, that talking to your partner about your sex life is extremely important and that people who talk to their partner regularly have better relationships and better sex. Since talking to your partner *at all*—even as infrequently as once every six months—is a step in the direction of sexual intelligence, if you answered c) to this question, you would receive 1 point. The more people talk with their partner, the better, so if you had answered "once a month" you would receive 2 points and if you said "once a week," you get 3 points. If, on the other hand, you *never* talk with your partner, you would receive a *minus* score on this question. In general, the more sexually intelligent your response on any one question, the more points you earn. In the appendix, where you can take the Sexual Intelligence Test, we show you how to convert your overall Sexual Intelligence score to a letter grade, from A to F. We also show you how to assess your skills in each of the three areas of sexual intelligence.

In each chapter of this book, you will learn more about the various items on the test and what they predict: for example, what the benefits are of talking with your partner about your sex life. You will also see, in the stories of people like Natalie, *how* to put the attitudes and skills of sexually intelligent people into practice in your own life. As you read, you can go back to the test and reevaluate your initial responses in the light of what you've read.

In addition, you can test the new skills and attitudes you've discovered, with exercises at the end of each chapter. Some of these exercises give you the opportunity to learn more about your own sexuality, and some of them allow you to try out your sexual intelligence on everyday dilemmas.

How to Increase Your Sexual Intelligence

The three components of sexual intelligence—being able to spot sexual myths and replace them with scientific knowledge about human sexuality, becoming acquainted with your own sexuality, and learning to relate to others sexually—require people to practice different behaviors and acquire new attitudes.

Natalie, the graduate student we met at the beginning of the chapter who was tempted to sleep with one of her undergraduates, serves as an example of someone who, at a crucial juncture in her life, successfully employed the three components of sexual intelligence and, as a result, went on to have a more satisfying sex life—and a loving relationship.

Natalie's dilemma came to a head when, after months of flirting with her student, Mark, she finally—against her better judgment—succumbed to his repeated invitations to come hear him play in a jazz club. This is what happened:

One night, Mark's band was playing at a club just down the street from me. I decided to go just for a little while, just to hear him play, I told myself. But I changed into a short skirt and put on makeup just the same. I think in the back of my mind, there was the possibility that I'd leave with him at the end of the night.

I got there and found a seat at a table out of the way. They were just finishing up the first set. Mark was good, even better than I'd imagined. Watching him play, the way he held the trumpet between his palms, the way he leaned his whole body back on the high notes, he was so hip, so confident. He was irresistible.

When they broke after the first set, he was mobbed by women—he must have been stopped five or six times as he made his way over to me.

He seemed delighted to see me, took me in his arms, gave me a long hug, then dragged me over to meet his friends, at a table down front. He introduced me to each of them. Finally, he turned to the last one, a very pretty girl who looked about nineteen, and said, "This is my girlfriend, Alix."

Natalie was devastated. She had to face Mark the next day, and she could barely look at him, never mind answer his questions after class. She felt deceived and betrayed by Mark's flirting, his small seductive gestures, the way he touched her arm to emphasize a point, the way he had stopped by her office every afternoon, even invited her to hear him play. She was angry and hurt and felt like an idiot.

The next time Mark stopped by her office to chat, Natalie couldn't get the girlfriend out of her mind, couldn't help herself. She was curt with him and cold. The look on his face shocked her: he was hurt, she could tell, and he looked so young. Natalie told us:

That's when I got it. <u>This is a student.</u>

In my mind, I had gone over a million times what could happen to <u>me</u>—losing my job, being charged with sexual harassment, all the scandal and the disgrace—but the one thing I never considered was the effect on Mark, the possibility that <u>he</u> could get hurt.

It was the thought of hurting a student over whom she had power that ultimately stopped Natalie from acting on her feelings. She became convinced that she couldn't have sex with him. Having come to a decision, she thought there'd be an end to her turmoil; instead, she went through a period of intense grief, a reaction that seemed out of all proportion to the actual situation.

It made me start to wonder—why was Mark's spell so powerful? I'd been attracted to men before—even after I got engaged—but never like this.

For a while, I was just miserable. Then, I remembered something that happened when I was in high school. One summer I worked in a pizza parlor, and the manager was this guy who seemed to me so cool—he was older, a lot of girls liked him, they were all having sex with him. Plus, he drove a Trans Am. So he seemed to have something special.

> I had a terrible crush on this guy. He dated every girl in the place but me. I was definitely a misfit in that town. I didn't have the right kind of hair, the right clothes, the right interests. Finally, it came to be my turn. He asked me to go to the movies, and we dated a couple of times. After two weeks, he dumped me. I was devastated.
>
> That fall, I went away to school. In the spring, at Easter, I was home for break, and I ran into him in the supermarket. I'd been away to college; you know, in my mind, I was now a woman of the world. I decided to get even with him. So, I slept with him.

Contrary to Natalie's expectations, the guy with the Trans Am didn't come begging for more, allowing her to spurn *him* this time. After she slept with him, Natalie never heard from him again. She was left feeling rejected once more. What the pizza parlor manager and Mark had in common was that they were both "cool"—they had some allure that made them irresistible, the allure that she lacked. Each of them, she felt, had the power to transform her, to supply what was missing in her. If they wanted her, she would no longer be a "misfit"; she might even be the person she had always secretly longed to be:

> When I saw that connection—saw how I had tried to be someone else vicariously, by getting involved with a man who had the qualities I wanted for myself, it suddenly hit me: Why couldn't I be a bit more cool on my own? What was stopping me from listening to jazz, going to clubs, dressing differently? In other words, from being any person I wanted to be?

Powerful forces, such as unmet emotional needs originating as early as childhood, can drive a fascination with someone who is unattainable or inappropriate. In Natalie's case, the needs that became entangled over time with her sexual desires and fueled the obsession with Mark were more recent, dating from her adolescent self-doubt.

Painful as it was, the process of self-examination that Natalie went through after she decided not to sleep with Mark in time produced a shift in her feelings. When we spoke to her six months after our initial interview, the feeling that Mark was *the one* had faded. She was back to working on finishing her Ph.D. and planning her wedding. She looked like a different person. At our first interview, she had worn a pleated skirt and shapeless sweater, her hair pulled back in a barrette. Now her hair was loose and straight, professionally cut and streaked with blond highlights. She wore a black leather jacket and boots with her jeans and turtleneck. The effect was young and hip, compared with her earlier dowdiness. She told us:

> It's funny—at this point, I'm not obsessed with Mark anymore. That feeling that I <u>have</u> to have him is gone. He's attractive—don't get me wrong—I'd love to have sex with him if I had met him at a different time, in other circumstances, or if I could do it without any complications. But I don't feel now that it's a tragedy if I don't.
>
> In one way, this whole thing was useful. I learned a lot about myself, about my own insecurities and needs.

Natalie stands out among the people we interviewed as someone with a fairly high level of sexual intelligence. Not that she didn't experience a great deal of pain and confusion over Mark; but the way she handled her dilemma is very different from the majority of the people we talked to. For one thing, Natalie didn't act on her sexual attraction to Mark right away. She was able to tolerate those feelings long enough to make a decision about what she really wanted to do and what would be best for her. Second, she was capable of having empathy for others: she could imagine vividly what the effect of sleeping with Mark would be on him—and on her fiancé, Greg. Third, Natalie had the courage to look within herself, to examine her own sexuality and how it had developed, to look at some of the unmet emotional needs connected with her sexual desires. What Natalie got out of the struggle over Mark—rather than one night of sex that might have had terribly destructive consequences—was self-knowledge, confidence, and peace of mind. There was also another important payoff, in the form of a more fulfilling sex life:

> Before the whole Mark thing, sex with my fiancé was pretty ho-hum. We'd been together for four years and, I guess like most people, we'd settled into a routine. Then, in the period when I was obsessed with Mark, sex with Greg was nonexistent. It was hard for me to have sex with one man when I was thinking about another.
>
> Our sex life has definitely improved. For one thing, Greg, my fiancé, thinks my new look is sexy. Changing my appearance—silly as it may sound—somehow

helped me to free up something that was there in my personality all along—
some edge. I don't know how to express it, exactly, some more adventurous side,
maybe. But the main thing is, all those days and nights of all-consuming sexual
fantasies about Mark taught me that sex is important to me. I don't take it for
granted anymore or think of it as something that you do once in a while if you're
not too tired or preoccupied.

If one thing stands out, again and again, in the stories we've heard,
it's that people who are less sexually intelligent suffer a great deal of
pain and confusion in their sex lives, much more so than people who
score high on the Sexual Intelligence Test. People who are more sexually intelligent seem to be able to move forward in their lives while the
less sexually intelligent often seem stuck in some fundamental way,
either haunted by a powerful sexual disappointment or playing out the
same painful conflict over and over.

Take Frank, for example, who, unlike Natalie, was unable to employ
any of the components of sexual intelligence and thus, after one painful
disappointment, ended up living a life devoid of passion, human contact, or hope.

The minute we sat down, before we'd even had a chance to put a
question to him, Frank announced, "Currently, I do not have a partner,
nor do I wish to."

Frank is thirty-eight years old; Italian on his father's side, Irish on his
mother's, devoutly Roman Catholic on both sides. He is one of a large
family. He and his four brothers and two sisters grew up in Brooklyn.
Frank was the first of his family to go to college. Though a delightful
research participant in some ways—funny, self-deprecating, intelligent,
charming—Frank was also bitter and very cynical about life. As a
young man, he had majored in journalism and intended to become a
writer. While still an undergraduate, he won an award for his fiction
and published several short stories. In those days, his life seemed full of
promise. But then he got involved with a woman.

When he was twenty, Frank began dating, and soon moved in with
Patty, a girl he had grown up with:

I had known Patty since sixth grade. I felt bad for her, knowing her family situation. She came from a very rough background—alcoholism in the family, drug
abuse. But I thought she was a good kid, I trusted her.

Patty had been with this guy for seven years before she started going out with me. She had a child with him. Patty told me that he had raped her, beat her, and did all these things to her. Supposedly, he wasn't in the picture because of what he had done to her. Plus, he wasn't paying child support or taking care of the baby in any way. When I first met the baby, Heather, she was two. I was the one she called "Daddy"—I was basically her father.

I caught him there about four times alone with her—she didn't think it was any big deal. She denied that anything was going on. Hell, he had raped her, taken advantage of her—I said don't let him in. I couldn't figure out why she was doing it; it was supposed to be for the kid, so I let it go. Because it would have made me the bad guy if I said the father couldn't be there. I wasn't the jealous kind of guy, so I let Patty do her thing, basically trusted her. It took me a while to figure it out.

In the meantime, I lost touch with my family and my friends. They were telling me Patty was trouble, but I wouldn't listen. I wanted to believe her—so I shut them out.

Then Patty became pregnant. So, okay, we were going to have a baby. We were on the way back from a hospital visit one day, and Patty tells me that her ex-boyfriend did something to her and she thought the child might be his. I think she was basically just sleeping with him all along. At that point, I started asking questions: did he use a condom? No, he didn't, and all this time, I'd been having a sexual relationship with her. She was kind of putting my life on the line, not caring. That was it for me. I stopped seeing her.

I would have done anything for her, her and Heather. I was supporting them both. Jeez, I was making Patty's car payments. So now I'm stuck with a 1995 Dodge Dart which is a piece of crap. She got one over on me pretty good.

I miss Heather. I was definitely that baby's father for two years. It was not easy dropping that.

Frank's experience was very painful, it's true, but the full extent of what it cost him didn't become clear until later in the interview, when we discovered that Patty is the only woman he's ever had sex with. He hasn't had one relationship since her betrayal, sixteen years ago. Frank has basically given up—not just on women but on many of his other passions, too. Since Patty's betrayal his life has become impoverished and constricted in so many ways. When he met Patty, he was in college, majoring in journalism, writing award-winning fiction, and planning on a career as a writer. When the relationship with Patty ended, Frank dropped out of college and went to work for his father's construction firm. He now works long days putting up dry wall. Most nights he comes home and flops on the couch with a six-pack and watches a movie on video. Once in a long while, he stops for a few beers on the way home from work with a couple of the guys—most of them much younger—on the construction crew. He no longer writes fiction or even reads much. While Frank's brothers and sisters have married, had children, begun careers, he has stayed in the same holding pattern for the last sixteen years. He's now the bachelor uncle existing on the fringes at family gatherings.

At the end of our interview, Frank told us wistfully:

> **Marriage is something I had always looked forward to. Spending the rest of your life with someone. I always expected to have that, but I'm not looking forward to it any time soon because of the emotional risk.**
>
> **I just know that if it happened to me again—what happened with Patty—I would be devastated. When someone that you love—and someone that you <u>think</u> loves you—does that, cheats on you, it destroys all hope and trust.**
>
> **You could say that sex is a weapon, one of the most powerful weapons in the world, as far as emotional ties go. Patty definitely used sex as a weapon, and I got burnt—bad.**

Frank was so devastated by one woman's betrayal that he came to view sex itself as dangerous. By swearing off sexual relations with women altogether, Frank thought he could avoid being hurt again; instead, he has isolated himself from warmth, companionship, and physical pleasure. Perhaps even worse, by trying to banish his sexuality altogether, Frank has drained away his former creativity, passion, and hope. His life has fallen into a narrow routine: work, drinking on the couch at night, occasionally a beer with the guys. Rather than looking within and trying to understand why he got involved with Patty and how it ended so disastrously, Frank decided that sex itself is just too risky.

Frank's life did not have to turn out so bleak. He could have handled things differently—in a more sexually intelligent way—so that the painful experience of losing Patty would not have destroyed his entire life.

For one thing, Frank could have honestly confronted the pain and betrayal he felt at Patty's duplicity. Second, he could have chosen in the wake of that betrayal to look within, at himself and the reasons why he denied the evidence of his own senses for so long, why he convinced himself that the presence of Patty's ex-boyfriend was innocuous. He persisted in this denial long after most people would have asked some hard questions. In order to continue his denial, he cut himself off from his family and friends. He could have examined unmet emotional needs in his life that may have complicated his attraction to Patty. He seems to have been drawn to her in part because of her unhappy past and a need to be the knight in shining armor for her and her little girl. Talking to others about his experience, exploring his own past and any associations he found there between being a man—being sexual—and being compassionate toward women, could have helped Frank to see how much he had to offer another woman. Taking a hard look at the way Patty treated him and talking to others about his experience could have convinced Frank that he deserved better and that he had the power to find a better relationship, that his compassion for people, his capacity for love and loyalty, didn't have to set him up again to be used by a woman with overwhelming problems.

Perhaps then he might have had the confidence to keep himself open to meeting another woman, someone with whom he could have had a more honest and fulfilling relationship. If Frank had had the ability to challenge some of the romantic myths about chivalry in our culture, if he had been willing to go through the painful process of self-examination to clarify his motives for becoming involved with a woman like Patty, and if he had let his friends and family in and continued to talk to them, he might now have a very different life.

By developing the skills of sexual intelligence, we can lead lives of passion and self-discovery. In Frank's story, you can see the consequences of a lack of sexual intelligence. Developing those skills takes work. Examining our inner selves, in particular, can be very painful, but we don't have to do it alone, and we can anticipate a powerfully rewarding payoff—the kind of sexual life we've always wanted.

The Journey Toward Sexual Intelligence

This book is divided into several parts, each of which will bring you closer to the goal of leading a more intelligent—and fulfilling—sex life.

In Part I, we introduce a new way of thinking about human sexuality and discuss the benefits of an active sex life.

Part II is devoted to stumbling blocks that get in the way of improving our sex lives: early learning in our families and religious communities, and messages about sex in popular culture, specifically the media. By the time you finish Part II, you will have encountered—and challenged—some of the most powerful myths about sex that prevent us from acquiring accurate knowledge about human sexuality.

In Part III, we look in detail at the secret sexual self, the cornerstone of sexual intelligence, and all the factors that contribute to its development.

Part IV brings sexual intelligence into the everyday world, by looking at how sexual attraction works, how you can cope effectively with sex in the workplace, and the challenge of maintaining fidelity in committed relationships.

Finally, in the Epilogue, we describe our vision of a new, sexually intelligent generation—our children—and how we can help them to avoid some of the painful learning about sex we have acquired by trial and error.

The Promise of Sexual Intelligence

Our findings from the Sexual Intelligence Project offer hope to people suffering from sexual problems, as well as those who are dissatisfied with their sex lives. The concept of sexual intelligence holds the key to the origin of many sexual problems. What's more, it provides concrete answers to people who want to know how to improve their sex lives. *People who possess what we call sexual intelligence are far less likely to suffer from sexual dysfunctions than those who lack sexual intelligence.* Specifically, they are less likely to report:

lack of sexual desire

difficulty becoming lubricated

physical pain during intercourse

difficulty achieving or maintaining an erection

premature ejaculation

being unable to achieve orgasm

not finding sex pleasurable

Our research shows that, for both men and women, their level of sexual intelligence is a powerful predictor of these sexual dysfunctions, a better predictor than anything else we've found. For example, a lack of sexual intelligence is even more damaging to a person's ability to function sexually than harboring tremendous guilt about sex. And possessing sexual intelligence is an even better indicator of whether a person can function sexually than having been in therapy.[6]

Sexual intelligence is also a key predictor of whether people report being <u>satisfied</u> with their sex lives. We've found, for example, that the lack of sexual intelligence is even more of an obstacle to sexual satisfaction than having been sexually abused in childhood.

Sexual intelligence is not simply a matter of knowing facts about reproductive biology; it is not a matter of knowing exotic techniques or maneuvers in bed; and it is not an inborn ability or talent that a few lucky people possess. The notion of a special kind of intelligence that can be developed and honed may sound vague and difficult to put into practice. What's groundbreaking about our work is that we've found it is possible, not only to specify what sexually intelligent people *do* that makes them different from the less sexually intelligent, but also to quantify just how sexually intelligent a person is and what he or she needs to do to become more sexually intelligent. In that respect, we would have to argue with Francis Bacon's contention that it is impossible to love and be wise. Rather, we're convinced that sexual feelings *intelligently understood and managed* can enrich our lives enormously and make us whole.

How Sexually Intelligent Are You?

As mentioned earlier, in our research, we found a way to measure sexual intelligence. We developed the Sexual Intelligence Test, which quantifies a person's level of sexual intelligence, and we have administered the test to hundreds of people. You can test your own level of sexual intelligence by taking the test now, which is included in the appendix at the end of the book. Read on after taking the test to learn more about how to increase your sexual intelligence.

chapter two

The Secret Sexual Self

At thirty, Julia found a wonderful man. Sam treated her with respect, he cared about her, he obviously loved her. And she loved him. Plus, the sex was great. But then something disturbing began to happen when they had sex:

> Make it thy business to know thyself, which is the most difficult lesson in the world.
> —Miguel de Cervantes, *Don Quixote*

> For some reason, sometimes when we're having intercourse, I just start crying, sobbing, as if my heart would break. Then, lubrication stops and it stops being pleasurable, and we end up breaking off right in the middle. . . . Whatever it's about, it has nothing to do with Sam. He's very sweet about it, but it wounds him. I feel awful about this. I don't know why this is happening to me: it's the first time I've felt happy in so long. I love Sam. I don't know why I would be crying now, because I feel so safe with him.

Like Julia, most of the time we assume we know who we are sexually. It seems obvious: we're gay or straight or bisexual; we're attracted to people who are outgoing or more reserved; we prefer blonds or brunettes; we like to do certain things in bed and not others. That's all there is to it, we assume. It's only when things go inexplicably wrong, as they did for Julia, that we realize there may be more to our sexuality than we know.

That is a signal that we need to explore our sexuality more closely. The primary key to being sexually intelligent is knowing and coming to terms with the secret sexual self. Why do we call it *secret*? Because it is a part of our selves that we don't truly know. Although popular culture has been telling us for the last three decades that sex is fun and liberating, no one has ever told us that sex is also highly individual. Because of our own as well as society's residual discomfort with sex, we've never been encouraged to look inward at our own desires, to locate our own compass that points the direction to what we really want sexually, and when we feel safe, at ease, and ourselves in a sexual encounter. When we come to know and understand our unique sexuality, we become able to navigate sexual relationships with clarity, confidence, and self-acceptance.

Each of us has a secret sexual self that is as unique as a fingerprint. It consists of our genuine, healthy impulses and personal preferences plus all that we have learned about sexuality from our families, from the culture around us, and from all of the experiences we've had with sex in the past. Because many of the messages people absorb about sex are inaccurate, painful, or even destructive, the secret sexual self is a complex, multilayered, sometimes contradictory web of yearnings, associations, assumptions, and apprehensions that, when seen clearly, unerringly point us to the *truth* about our own sexuality. We have each built up over the course of our lives a unique history of sexual interactions that have conditioned our desires; created fears, insecurities, beliefs, and expectations; and deposited layers of guilt and shame. All these factors unwittingly shape our sexual desires and determine our behavior.

Take, for example, the woman who, without even being fully aware of it, has absorbed from the culture the belief that it is the man's role to initiate sex. On top of that, she may feel insecure about her own attractiveness, comparing herself with unrealistic images of female beauty in the media. Together, those two things may prevent her from ever taking the lead sexually, and she may end up frustrated, unfulfilled, and even at odds with her partner. Or consider the person who has never received approval, warmth, or emotional support growing up and tries to meet those emotional needs through sex, going through a succession of sexual partners without finding either emotional *or* sexual satisfaction.

The secret sexual self holds the key to dilemmas such as these. By investigating the complex inner world of our sexuality, we can uncover our genuine, authentic desires and free ourselves from assumptions, beliefs, expectations, fears, and accidental associations that can hold us back from finding a fulfilling sex life.

So much of the confusion our society suffers over how to lead healthy, fulfilling sex lives derives from the fact that when it comes to sex, as a society, and as individuals, we so often focus on *behavior* alone and not on the thoughts, feelings, and emotions that accompany behavior.

The key to a great sex life is not what we *do* in bed—anyone can learn a new technique—but rather what is going on in our minds, often without our clear awareness, while we are engaged in sexual behavior. We seldom pay close attention to whether we have positive, emotionally comfortable associations with sex or not. As soon as our associations with sex become negative or uncomfortable in any way—because we have been taught to be ashamed of having sexual desires, because we have been hurt or humiliated by past sexual encounters, because we've internalized media images that lead us to feel self-conscious about or even loathe our bodies—sex that could be pleasurable and life-sustaining becomes problematic and dissatisfying.

Consider an example: imagine being in bed with the most attractive, sexually desirable person you know. If your mind doesn't cooperate—because of worries about work, because you're self-conscious about your body, or otherwise preoccupied—the sex isn't going to be great. That's because satisfying sex depends on neurochemical reactions in the brain, and, in our example, the part of the brain that controls sexual arousal is receiving inputs from two sources: the physical stimulation to your body, but also other parts of the brain that process memories, emotions, beliefs, and so forth. The end result is that the pleasurable physical stimulation may be outweighed by painful memories, distressing emotions, or beliefs about what you should or shouldn't be feeling or doing.

We urge you to begin the important process of exploring your own sexuality. Because people's secret sexual self includes fantasies, propensities, and memories or fears that are disturbing, many people turn their back on it, ignore it, or try to repress it entirely.

But it is only by casting off the shame surrounding these elements of our sexuality, gathering the courage to look at them squarely, without judging ourselves, that we become free to choose what we want and how we will behave sexually, free to choose a sexual life that lets us feel good about who we are and enjoy sex unencumbered.

Knowing ourselves is crucial to becoming more sexually intelligent because

past experiences can influence our sexual behavior in ways we don't understand,

unmet emotional needs can get in the way of having the satisfying sex life we want, and

unexamined beliefs about what we are supposed to feel or want or like can obscure our genuine sexual desires.

How do we come to know our secret sexual self? It is as close as our thoughts, feelings, and sensations; yet it is all too often obscured by experts who offer a statistical composite of the "average" person that becomes normative for everyone, and by popular accounts that claim to have all the answers for this statistical "Every man and woman." Getting to the truth about our sexuality entails paying attention to our *own* feelings and reactions, the quiet voice within that knows when we are headed down the wrong path.

Let's look at how some of the people in our study came to terms with their secret sexual selves.

Banishing Ghosts: When the Painful Past Buries Our Secret Sexual Self

One of the clearest examples of the way painful past experiences can get in the way of people's genuine sexual desires is the experience that Julia described to us: inexplicably, in the middle of making love to a man she loved and trusted, she found herself breaking down, sobbing, and unable to continue having sex. The very word Julia used to describe how she felt with Sam—*safe*—was the tip-off to understanding her secret sexual self. It made us wonder whether Julia had had a previous sexual experience in which she felt unsafe. Indeed, it turned out that she had been raped years before. Julia had not thought about the experience in over a decade; it was so painful that she put it out of her mind and never suspected the link between her painful past and her present dilemma with Sam. In our interview, Julia remembered that painful experience:

> It was freshman year in college. This guy was a very good friend of my roommate. He was also a born-again Christian. When I first met him, we got to talking, and he told me his dad had died, and my immediate reaction was, "You poor thing." I told him, "Oh, I'm so sorry. If you ever want to talk about it, I'm here."
>
> So one night, he called me, wanting to talk. He was a resident adviser in the dorm; he had to be in his own room in the evenings, so I went there. We were just sitting and talking. And then, I don't know what happened exactly, but then he started to take his pants off. I said, "No, I don't want anything to happen." But he got on top of me, and I'll never forget what he said, he told me, "Just say, yes." I screamed at him, "Nooo!" And then, then, he just did it.
>
> It was so bizarre. He was an RA at the school, and he was a Christian. I couldn't believe it was happening. I just waited for it to end. I think I pretended to enjoy it. I don't know why I did that. I was trying to make it okay for myself, to say that I did like it, so it wouldn't be so bad. I was scared of him. I was seventeen and he was twenty-two, and he was a lot bigger than me. He had been in the Marines. I didn't tell anyone what happened. I was so embarrassed because I didn't try to fight him off.

The rape in college held the key to Julia's mysterious sorrow during sex with her current lover. Because she felt safe with Sam, she was able to let down her guard. When she did, the wonderful sex she had with Sam served, by contrast, to bring into sharp focus the brutality of that sexual assault in college. All of the grief she had never let herself feel at the time of the rape poured out. Seeing that connection helped Julia to understand her puzzling behavior and reassured her that there was nothing wrong with her current relationship. Had she not explored the past and the effect that one experience had in distorting her sexuality, she might have run from the love and warmth that Sam offered her. Because of her insight, and Sam's love and support, Julia was able finally to mourn that traumatic experience in college. As a result, her sex life with Sam has gradually become as good as it used to be—better, actually.

Julia's story highlights the way in which an experience from the past can obscure our genuine sexual desires and accidentally condition our present sexual behavior, creating mysterious dysfunctions. But there is more to the secret sexual self than that. Our unexplored sexuality holds more than the answer to mysterious dysfunctions. Much of what is hidden is very positive. The fact is, the richness and full extent of most people's sexuality goes unnoticed and uncharted. If we were able to look beneath the surface past the false beliefs, unmet emotional needs, and negative experiences that have conditioned our sexual behavior, we could uncover our genuine sexual preferences and feel—perhaps for the first time in our lives—genuinely fulfilled. That was what happened in Bethany's experience.

How Unmet Emotional Needs Can Mask Our Secret Sexual Self

Bethany, a twenty-seven-year-old banker we interviewed, is a perfect example of someone who found real sexual fulfillment—a sex life that felt right for *her*—only through the process of discovering the unmet needs and unexamined beliefs that had kept her in a relationship that wasn't right for her. On the screening questionnaire that inquired about her current level of sexual satisfaction, Bethany checked off 5 on a scale where 7 represents the maximum. She is currently involved with a man she cares about and, in her words, "Each lovemaking session is great. I never knew that two hours was a possibility." As great as her sex life is now, it took time and painful learning for Bethany to get out of a long-term relationship that was very unsatisfying, even destructive.

Bethany's story really begins with her early family life. Her mother died when Bethany was five years old, leaving her completely dependent on her father. But in a short space of time, she lost him, too, in a way that had a terrible impact on her later self-esteem:

Daddy remarried six months after my mother died.

My father didn't tell me they were getting married. One day I went with this lady, Daddy's "friend," to try on a dress; it was a fancy dress, and I thought that was neat. Then, on the day of their wedding, they woke me up at 7 and just told me, "You have to wear this dress and go to church." They didn't sit down beforehand and say, "We're getting married." I was surprised somewhat.

Then my father decided it would be best for me to go and live with my grand-

mother. He was working all the time, and it wasn't convenient for my stepmother to take care of me.

Not surprisingly, later in life, Bethany found herself gravitating to older men for the acceptance and attention she never got from her own father.

I've had a difficult time drawing lines. Because there was the absence of a male figure in my life, there wasn't that boundary, like "He's old enough to be my father!"

My first lover, Alex, was forty-two and I was nineteen. There were a lot of things that I was uncomfortable with, right from the start. Because I was so much younger than he was, I thought they must be okay. Because what did I know? And I tried to believe that these things were okay with me.

For example, Alex would buy me lingerie: garter belts, red lace. I never felt good in it, I just felt cheap. He would buy hard-core porn videos, and I was never aroused by them. I thought I was supposed to be, and I assumed that something was wrong with me. And he liked to role-play. He wanted me to play the innocent schoolgirl. He wanted me to call him "Daddy," and he would spank me a lot.

I was in college, and I wanted to be open-minded. I didn't want to be judgmental. I had my own fantasies, and tried to respect his, but I would feel sick afterwards. They weren't the kind of torrid evenings that I could tell to a best friend and feel good about. I was very secretive about our sex life: the truth is, I felt degraded and humiliated a lot of the time.

After being in a relationship with Alex for so long, sex for me was defined in terms of what <u>Alex</u> liked, what turned him on. After that ended, for a long time it was really hard for me to stop being in a degrading position sexually. The guy I'm with now is not particularly into kinky sex, and I prefer our relationship. We don't have to role-play now, or use accessories; it's just us.

Being in a relationship that was that unhealthy helped me to recognize a healthy relationship when it was presented to me. I learned a lot about being independent and knowing what my needs are in a relationship, and knowing what I'm comfortable with in bed.

Bethany stayed in the relationship with Alex for four years, despite the fact that she didn't share his sexual tastes: she wasn't aroused by dressing up in red lace garter belts, or by playing the naughty schoolgirl and being spanked by Daddy. What kept her in the relationship, in part, was her need for attention and approval from a father figure. That need to be accepted and wanted by her own father had gone unmet for a very long time. Plus, she was young and inexperienced and had little with which to compare her sex life with Alex. Over time, though, as Bethany became more conscious of her own preferences, it became clear to her that she needed a different kind of sexual relationship, one in which she felt more herself. The sex life she was having with Alex went against the grain of everything she genuinely desired.

Bethany came to know her secret sexual self—both her authentic sexual tastes and the way in which they had been overwritten by a powerful need for love and acceptance from a father figure that she mistook for sexual desire. Bethany became sexually intelligent as she saw how her unmet early need for attention from her father actually held her back in key relationships with men.

Our genuine sexual desires can be obscured by past experiences that have left traumatic associations, by unmet emotional needs that get in the way of discovering our real preferences, and by unexamined beliefs. The latter often stem from cultural norms that set up expectations for everyone within the culture, expectations that may fit some individuals better than others.

When Cultural Norms Clash with Our Authentic Desires

Knowing our own sexuality also requires us to distinguish between what our culture tells us is "normal" and what feels right to us, as individuals. Take Carlos, for example. He is a twenty-two-year-old medical student from Cuba who has had sex with only one woman, his girlfriend of four years. In some ways, that goes against what he perceives as expectations for men in his culture. It certainly makes him different from his friends. Listen to how Carlos has struggled between what seems "normal" to him, based on the culture he was raised in, and what feels comfortable for him as an individual:

Men in my culture are expected to be more sexual. It's considered good for a man to have some experience before he gets married. What is the expression? "Sow

wild oats"? But it's not fair because it's not the same for the women. In my culture, the women stay virgins until they get married.

There were times I felt jealous of my friends, because they were hooking up
with lots of girls. I did think about doing that, but my girlfriend and I cared
about each other, so I didn't. Being raised around my girl cousins and my aunts, I
saw how they got hurt, and I didn't want to do that to someone I cared about. I
admit there are times when I see a good-looking woman and I think about her,
but that's all I do.

It's not that you need a lot of different people, it's just that you need to do different things.

For Carlos, the cultural stereotype that a man isn't a man unless he
has multiple partners, even though he is in a relationship, doesn't work.
It isn't him. His genuine desire isn't for multiple partners, but for variety with his current partner. In discovering this, Carlos has, at least in
this one regard, found his true sexual preferences underneath the cultural expectations he was raised with.

The ramifications of not exploring one's secret sexual self can be pro-
foundly destructive. Brad, a successful tax attorney we interviewed, is
in his late forties, over six feet and built like an ex-linebacker, all of that
bulk squeezed into a very expensive suit, and nearly bald, with wisps of
gray fringe left on the sides. Brad answered our questions with affable
good humor, seemingly at ease. When he started to talk about his wife,
however, he began shifting in his chair. Beads of sweat appeared above
his upper lip and, from the expression in his eyes, it was clear that this
wasn't going to be easy for him. Here was a man who was feeling terrible pain and confusion. This is what he told us:

I've been living a lie, sexually, for twenty-five years, and now it's caught up with
me. I wish Nora and I had talked more about what was happening in our marriage.

I met Nora in college. She was the one woman I truly loved. I never wanted to
be with anyone else. I was very inexperienced when we married. Nora had styled
herself as this incredibly sensuous person, before we got married, so even though
we didn't have sex until our wedding night, it never occurred to me that we'd
have any problem in that area. But, once we were married, as far as actual sex
goes, she was just paralyzed.

Sex has always been a problem with us. I wanted sex much more often than
she did—I think she would have been happy to just forego the whole thing. It

got to the point where I felt like that little boy in the movie <u>Oliver</u>—you know, "please, may I have some more?" It was humiliating. So, I'd shut down. I figured, if you don't want it, fine. And we never talked about it. I told myself, after all, marriage is about more than just sex. It shouldn't matter so much to me.

Brad's marriage went increasingly downhill until he and Nora were barely speaking. Finally, they decided to go for counseling. But, by then, Brad had a secret:

I'm sitting there in couple's therapy with my wife, talking about how things aren't good between us sexually, and, meanwhile, I'm involved with this woman at work, Jeanne. One day, we were in my office, discussing a case, and suddenly I was kissing her. Before long, I was going to her place on the way home from work two or three times a week.

Purely from the sex standpoint, it's incredible with Jeanne. I had no idea how good sex could be. But it's created a lot of guilt and that has caused an awful strain on me, physiologically. I had a heart attack not too long ago—had to have heart surgery.

So, now I'm having sex three times a week with Jeanne—even though it's damn near killed me—and, at the same time, sitting there with a therapist, saying to Nora, you know, "let's work this out." And I want to work it out—I love Nora. But how am I ever going to tell her the truth? These days I get in the car in the morning to drive into the city, and I just want to keep on going until I end up in Phoenix or someplace.

Brad's first mistake was to bury and ignore his sexual desires. If he had been more honest with himself and able to acknowledge how important an active sex life was to him, he could have gathered information that would have let him know that wanting sex is perfectly healthy. Perhaps then he would have been able to respect his needs and to discuss the matter openly with his wife. Because Brad was unable to look honestly at his sexual needs and share that part of himself with his wife, he set himself up to become involved in an extramarital affair and placed his marriage in serious jeopardy—to say nothing of the toll his conflict about having an affair has taken on his health. The sexually intelligent approach would have been to confront his dissatisfaction with his sex life and to have discussed it with his wife much earlier, perhaps with the help of a therapist. That's not to say it wouldn't have been very difficult for Brad to do that—as he told us, he felt humiliated by being the sexual supplicant in his marriage; but by *not* doing so, Brad created an even more difficult situation for himself. He has backed himself into a corner and now feels that his only option is to leave the one woman he has ever loved. In Brad's case, a conflict over how frequently he and his wife had sex might have been worked out if they had talked honestly about their sex life; when Brad kept his sexual needs under wraps, the conflict grew and festered in silence into a potentially catastrophic situation.

Our secret sexual self is a critical part of who we are. It is essentially a map to the landscape of our unacknowledged desires, unexplored emotional conflicts, and unexamined assumptions about ourselves and our bodies. It is the guide that can point the way to a more fulfilling sex life. Sexual intelligence means, first and foremost, knowing the truth about both our genuine desires and the way in which those desires have been distorted by media messages, painful past experiences, cultural expectations, and inhibitions taught within the family.

Knowing one's own tastes and preferences is crucial to becoming more sexually intelligent. Without that self-knowledge, all the scientific knowledge we acquire about human sexuality, the new sexual techniques we learn, even the best interpersonal skills won't make sex more satisfying. Without knowledge of the powerful motivations that may have shaped our sexual behavior, we can't apply any of the scientific knowledge we acquire. Without knowing what we really prefer sexually, the best interpersonal skills in the world may still not get us what we want.

You can assess your own self-awareness by going back and looking at your answers to several questions on the Sexual Intelligence Test that measure knowledge of the secret sexual self. For example, if you answered yes to Question #5, "Have you ever kept a sexual secret from a partner over a long period of time?" you, like Julia, may have a past painful sexual experience that is getting in the way of enjoying sex in the present. Or, like Brad, you may be living a double life that could lead to painful consequences.

If you answered "frequently" to Question #40, "Do you ever feel shame about some of your sexual desires or behavior?" you may, like Bethany, be involved in sexual activities that run contrary to your genuine preferences and desires.

These, and the rest of the items on the Sexual Intelligence Test that evaluate your awareness of your own sexuality, are a good starting point for investigating your genuine sexual feelings and whether or not you are currently respecting them.

In addition, before engaging or refusing to engage in a sexual act, we suggest that you check in with your secret sexual self and ask the following questions:

1. Am I being true to my genuine needs, desires, and preferences?
2. Am I being really honest with myself about what I want in this situation?
3. Will this particular sexual act hurt me by going against my genuine desires?
4. Will engaging in this act deepen self-destructive patterns that have already shaped my sexuality in a negative way?
5. Will this experience genuinely bring me joy?
6. Will it strengthen and affirm my healthiest impulses?
7. Will it honor my partner's genuine sexual self?

The answers to these questions are important because they go to the heart of who we and our sexual partners really are, and what makes us happy, sexually. It's important that we regularly check in to see if we are honoring and cultivating our sexual selves. When we come to believe things like "I'm too fat for anyone to want me," or "I could never share my true sexual feelings with my wife, so why bother to try?" or "I'm too old to act 'sexy' anymore," we squash our sexuality and, over time, deny ourselves one of life's essential gifts.

However difficult it may be to look squarely at our own sexuality, it's worth it. The truth really will set us free to uncover our own tastes and preferences, and to find a more authentic, fulfilling sex life at last. To begin understanding your secret sexual self, try the following exercise.

What You Can Do:

Write out your sexual history. When you have a quiet hour or two, sit down and write out a narrative of your sexual experiences. Begin with the first sexual experience you had, describe what happened, how it felt, and what you thought about it at the time. Do the same for the major sexual experiences and relationships you've had since then. It's important to write this out rather than simply thinking about it. There's something about seeing an honest account of your sexual experiences on paper, in black and white, that often helps you to spot patterns that you might want to change—for example, having sex in order to please another person or to try to strengthen a relationship. Seeing your experiences down on paper also helps to spot patterns of feelings about sex and attitudes toward sex. Most people are surprised by what they discover about themselves in this way. Writing your sexual history is the first step to discovering your genuine sexual self.

chapter three

Why Have Sex?

Why have sex? Why not? You may be wondering why we even ask. As we've seen, the vast majority of people say a good sex life is critically important to them. Yet, given the complications and difficulties of the average person's sex life, many of us might be tempted at times, like Frank, to give up on sex altogether. That is a terrible mistake.

Our sexuality is an essential part of us, as fundamental as our emotions, intellect, or personality. When we bury it, we cut off an important part

> The omnipresent process of sex, as it is woven into the whole texture of our man's or woman's body, is the pattern of all the process of our life.
> —Havelock Ellis, *The New Spirit*
>
> One hour of right-down love
> Is worth an age of dully living on.
> —Aphra Behn, *The Rover*

of ourselves. One of the prerequisites to sexual intelligence is to accept that we are sexual beings and to prize and cultivate our sexuality.

The truth is, sex is good for you. Susanne, one of the women we interviewed, put it well:

I think sex is a good thing, physically. I often find myself thinking about it, imagining having sex in exotic locations, just thinking about sex in general because it feels really good and I enjoy it.

Susanne isn't a scientist and doesn't have all the latest research findings at her disposal, but she instinctively recognizes what the scientific evidence in fact shows: an active sex life makes us happier people; what's more, it can improve our physical as well as mental health, and even extend our lives.

Many people want better sex lives, but our research shows that they are doing surprisingly little about it. The majority of them devote more time and effort to doing chores and pursuing their hobbies than they do to finding—and sustaining—a fulfilling sex life. They might behave differently if they knew that putting effort into their sex life is as important as exercising, eating right, and otherwise taking care of their health.

The first thing that sexually intelligent people do that distinguishes them from the less sexually intelligent is recognize that sex is fundamentally good for their health, offering a number of remarkable benefits, physically and mentally. Though some people still see sex as dangerous, it is actually a failure to cultivate sexual intelligence that is truly hazardous. Negative attitudes toward sex, or a fear of sex itself, can lead people to be dishonest about their desires, to have sex in a surreptitious, shame-ridden way, or in a compulsive way—without admitting to themselves what they are doing and without taking appropriate precautions to prevent disease and pregnancy—or to forego sex entirely. Neglecting the sexual part of oneself and excluding sex from one's life entirely means losing out on the many significant health benefits of sex.

Given all of these benefits of sex, it would make sense for people to invest energy and commitment, first, to do whatever they need to do to establish a sexual relationship, and, second, to keep it alive by continuing to have sex regularly. But many don't.

Among the questions we asked our research participants were whether or not they were currently in a sexual relationship, how frequently they had sex, and how committed they were to finding a sexual partner. Most of our participants were relatively young—between eighteen and thirty-nine years old. You'd imagine that they—if anyone—would have vigorous sex lives. Nonetheless, many of them are having sex less frequently than we would have thought. Nearly a third of them have sex once or twice a month or less. Fourteen percent have sex only once or twice a year. Only a third of the people we surveyed have sex once or twice a week—the frequency that research shows is optimal for taking advantage of one physical benefit of sex—increased immune functioning.

People fail to cultivate an active sex life for many reasons. For one thing, there is a powerful, ubiquitous myth in our culture that suggests sex is *in itself* dangerous—that it poisons one's mind, weakens one's character, destroys one's moral fiber, or saps energy for "higher" cultural achievements. That is far from the truth.

Nevertheless, a surprising number of people, young people included, see sex itself as inherently dangerous to their mental and physical health. Consider the views of one of our research participants, Gary, a young student:

I don't masturbate anymore, really, because I believe that masturbation is self-destructive. Any guy can tell you—if you're masturbating on a day-to-day basis—think about it. I hurt my body physically, right, plus mentally and emotionally. I know a lot of people, when they masturbate, and they're done with it, they always feel disgusted or used, and you're the person who did that to yourself.

Gary is mistaken. Neither sex in general nor masturbation specifically have any negative physical effects. He is not alone in his belief, though.

We were amazed at the number of the people we talked to in our Sexual Intelligence Project who shared the belief, to one degree or another, that masturbation has negative physical or mental consequences. Over 40 percent of the people we talked to agreed to some extent that masturbation is wrong and shouldn't be practiced, and "will ruin you."[7] They scored significantly lower on both overall sexual intelligence and scientific knowledge about sex than people who rejected that archaic view.

Aside from the influence of such myths, there are other reasons for the lack of effort people put into their sex lives. The fact that the people in our study have sex relatively infrequently may be due, in part, to lack of knowledge about the health benefits of sex. We asked people, "Do you think that having sex, like exercising and having good nutrition, can actually make you more healthy and live longer?" Forty percent told us either that a regular sex life has no benefits for physical health or that they were skeptical of such claims, believing them to be unsubstantiated by science.

That sex is healthy is based on a great deal of scientific evidence.

The Benefits of Sex for Physical Health

Regular sex with a partner—as long as proper precautions are taken—provides a range of substantial benefits for people's physical and mental health.

For one thing, having sex can actually provide significant cardio-vascular exercise. If you have sex three times a week, you can burn as many as 7,500 calories a year—the equivalent of jogging seventy-five miles. Sex also lowers your cholesterol and tips the ratio of good cholesterol to bad cholesterol in a positive direction. Having sex increases oxygen to your tissues and organs, and boosts testosterone, which in turn fortifies bones and muscles and enhances your sex drive. Put simply, having sex regularly makes us stronger, and thus more capable—as well as more interested—in having yet more sex. There are a number of other health benefits of a regular sex life, ranging from reduced prostate problems to lower stress, and less chance of succumbing to heart disease.[8]

For women, sex can help increase overall levels of estrogen, protecting the heart and keeping vaginal tissues supple, reducing irregular menstrual periods, and decreasing the pain and psychological stress of PMS.[9]

There's even evidence that having sex regularly can improve immune functioning, helping us to resist colds and flu. In a 1999 study, psychologist Carl Charnetski of Wilkes University in Wilkes-Barre, Pennsylvania, asked 111 college undergraduates about their sexual activity in the previous month and also measured their immunoglobulin (IgA) levels from their saliva. IgA is a component of the body's immune system that attaches to foreign intruders, such as viruses, and then calls on the immune system to destroy them. Charnetski found that students who had sex once or twice a week had IgA levels 30 percent higher than those who were abstinent.[10]

Specific health benefits are associated with a hormone called dehydroepiandrosterone, or DHEA, which is released at orgasm. DHEA is a hormone produced in the adrenal gland from cholesterol. Recent research shows that DHEA can sharpen your thinking, increase immune system functioning, inhibit the growth of tumors, promote bone growth, and even function as an antidepressant.[11] DHEA is one of the newest health-fad supplements on the market. Taking the commercial hormone has some potentially serious risks, but, as it turns out, such supplements may not be necessary—Dr. Theresa Crenshaw maintains that DHEA levels peak at three to five times normal levels just before orgasm. In addition, studies have shown that DHEA levels are significantly higher among individuals who remain sexually active.[12]

Can Sex Make You Live Longer?

Many of the health benefits that a regular sex life provides would be expected to increase a person's life span: for example, DHEA inhibits tumor growth, potentially preventing cancer. Having sex regularly has also been linked with reduced heart disease, one of the top deadly diseases in America. A 1998 study following men for twenty years found that those with above-average levels of DHEA were 15 percent less likely to die from heart disease.[13]

There is now definitive evidence that having sex regularly can actually increase one's life span. A 1997 study in the *British Medical Journal* concluded that, for men at least, having regular sex reduces the risk of dying. The study, conducted by researchers at Bristol University and Queen's University in Belfast, looked at 918 men between the ages of forty-five and fifty-nine who lived in the South Wales town of Caerphilly and five nearby villages. Men who reported having an orgasm twice a week or more had half the mortality risk of those who were less sexually active. The death rate among less sexually active men was 2.2 times greater than that for the sexually active. The effect of regular sex was particularly striking when it came to heart disease. What makes this study so significant is that the researchers controlled for a range of factors known to affect health and longevity, such as smoking, cholesterol levels, blood pressure, and preexisting heart disease. Now we know it is not simply that healthy people both live longer and, because they are healthy, are more likely to be sexually active. Rather, having an active sex life makes a difference in how long men live, even aside from their general health.[14]

Finally, sex may make the inevitable processes of aging easier to bear. Testosterone, which is released during sexual activity, is one of a class of hormones known as corticosteroids; among their other effects, they reduce the joint inflammation and pain of arthritis.[15]

The Benefits of Sex for Mental Health

Regular sex also has benefits for people's *mental* health. Sex increases bloodstream levels of endorphins, naturally occurring painkillers that can help reduce stress and provide feelings of relaxation, contentment, and overall well-being. Regular sex should also improve our relationships, because of increased oxytocin levels, which are very high at orgasm. Oxytocin is the chemical that has been called the "bonding hormone" because it is associated with affectionate feelings and a desire to be close to another person. Studies of married people show that they are happier and healthier than their single or divorced counterparts, suggesting that regular sex plays a role in emotional well-being.[16]

Research both in the United States and abroad has consistently found that when people's sex lives are unsatisfying, their overall quality of life suffers, too. For example, Soren Ventegodt of the Quality of Life Research Center in Copenhagen, Denmark, did a representative survey in 1998 of 2,460 Danish citizens comparing people with satisfying sex lives to those suffering sexual dysfunctions. The quality of life for people with sexual dysfunctions was almost 10 percent lower than for those with a good sex life.[17] The same link between sexual satisfaction and quality of life has been found in other countries, too.[18]

Ruth Matthias and her colleagues at the UCLA School of Public Policy and Social Research found a direct link between sexual satisfaction and mental health in a study they published in the *Gerontologist* in February 1997. They reported research on 1,216 elderly people (the average age was seventy-seven years old). Almost 30 percent had had sex in the previous month, and 67 percent were satisfied with their current level of sexual activity. There was a clear, statistically significant link between individuals' satisfaction with their sex life and high scores on psychological tests of mental health.[19]

More of a Good Thing

We've seen the physical and mental health benefits of a regular sex life. It turns out that a committed relationship in which a sexual partner is readily available translates not only into more sex, but better sex. (And that, of course, is a good thing for one's health and longevity.)

Dr. Linda Waite, a professor of sociology at the University of Chicago, recently reported the results of research from the 1992 National Health and Social Life survey to support the argument that married people have more sex—and better sex—than single people do. Specifically, married men reported having sex twice as often as most of the single men surveyed, and married men reported more satisfying sex lives than did single men or those living with a partner. Dr. Waite argues that married people are more willing to invest in skills to please a partner with whom they are heavily emotionally invested in a long-term relationship. Sexual happiness may hold other benefits, too; according to Dr. Waite, divorced men were more likely to abuse drugs and alcohol and more likely to suffer depression than men who were married.[20]

What Would You Do for a Better Sex Life?

Even people who know the value of a good sex life may still find it difficult to summon the time, energy, and self-confidence to do something about it. We asked our research participants how committed they were to establishing a satisfying, regular sex life. *Less than half* said they put as much effort into finding a partner as they do into their hobbies and daily chores. In fact, nearly a third told us that, by the time they're done with the tasks of daily life, they don't have the energy to think about how to improve their sex lives. Six percent told us they were so embarrassed by how bad their sex life is that they try not to even *think* about the possibility of having sex. It doesn't help that cultural myths suggest Prince or Princess Charming will simply show up on our doorstep one day. That myth is one that many people accept unthinkingly: 40 percent of the people we talked to had a helpless attitude toward improving their sex lives, believing that "a good sex life is not something you can work at—it either happens or it doesn't."

Evelyn is one of the few people we talked to who overcame that attitude and made a conscious decision to pursue a better sex life, even though it wasn't easy for her. Evelyn is an attractive forty-seven-year-old who divorced seven years ago. She assumed that she would soon get back into the swing of dating and find the right person for her, but it turned out to be more difficult than she thought:

I guess I was naïve. I thought once I'd gotten over the grief of the divorce, you know, I'd date and have fun, and a year or two later, I'd be married again—happily this time. Well . . .

I can't tell you how many dates I've been on. It's not that I'm not willing to kiss a few frogs. . . . I just never thought there'd be so many of them. It got to the point where I just gave up. I couldn't stand another blind date, another evening with a guy you know you never want to see again after the first five minutes, or another dinner with a guy who seems wonderful and you think you really click together—and then he never calls back.

So I stopped dating. I figured "maybe I'm trying too hard; maybe if I'm meant to be with someone, it will just happen." I don't know about other people, but that strategy didn't work for me. I just spent a lot of time alone, and a lot of time complaining to my friends about how miserable I was. Finally, I decided, this is nuts: if I'm not willing to do something about this problem, I have no right to whine about it all the time. So I made a deal with myself that I'd pick out five ads from the personals every week and answer them—and just see what happened. That felt like a reasonable amount of effort.

It didn't happen overnight, but Evelyn met a man whom she cares about enormously and she reports that their sex life is great:

It took courage to hang in there, and keep making those five phone calls a week. But it was worth it. You can't imagine what a relief it is—and a gift. To be touched again, to have that passion. It doesn't seem to matter that I'm forty-seven and he's fifty-five—it's pretty incredible.

It's particularly important that people not give up on sex when they're young because of the effect it can have as they get older.

Sex Throughout the Life Span

If people aren't enjoying the benefits of an active sex life when they're younger, there's a good chance they won't be having sex when they're older. Research studies have shown that one of the strongest predictors of being sexually active at an older age is the frequency of sexual intercourse when one is younger. But understanding the importance—the very possibility—of having a sex life when one is older requires sexual intelligence. We asked respondents to our Sexual Intelligence Test what they thought their sex life would be like when they were in their seventies. The results were very revealing.

People who said that they couldn't imagine themselves being sexually active in their seventies scored significantly lower on the test than any of the other respondents, averaging nearly an F. People who answered that it was pretty unlikely that they would be sexually active in their seventies scored a little higher, but still in the D range. People who said they wanted to be sexually active in their seventies scored significantly higher on sexual intelligence and those who said they would do "all they can" to be sexually active then scored higher still.

Why the pessimistic attitude about having a sex life when we get older? When men and women age, their bodies change, and many of the people we talked to have serious fears about the consequences of these physical changes for their sex lives. Lydia, an attractive woman in her late fifties with silver hair, was particularly candid about her experience:

It was somewhere in my forties, I think, that I began avoiding mirrors. I went gray early—everyone in my family does—but for a long time, I colored my hair, so I could deny what was happening. By about forty-five, though, I started to notice these tiny lines around my eyes. And my skin didn't glow the way it used to. On a good day, my skin looked the way it would have in my twenties after a week without enough sleep.

I used to have beautiful skin. It sounds immodest—I know. Beautiful skin, and a nice body. Really nice breasts, and great legs. At least, men said so. I got spoiled, I guess. I was used to men—this was in my twenties—looking at my legs or sneaking a look at my breasts, and doing a double-take. And being interested. I never doubted that there would be a man who was interested.

In my forties, whenever I did catch a glimpse of myself in a mirror, I couldn't avoid seeing that my breasts were just a little saggier, my waist was thickening, so were my thighs, there were these creases where I used to have spectacular cleavage. You don't have to be particularly vain, I don't think, to feel regret, even a certain amount of horror, when you see irreversible signs of aging. Right around the time I started going into menopause, around fifty, I started losing interest in sex. It got to the point where we'd go a month or two sometimes without having intercourse. It wasn't that I loved my husband any less; my feelings about my body had really affected my sexual desire. I couldn't stand the thought of him undressing me and seeing my body, and I couldn't understand why he didn't feel the same revulsion about my body that I did.

Our sex life is much better now. I'm through menopause, the kids have finished high school and moved out, but the most important thing is that over time, I did come to terms with my body. For one thing, I work out now, so I feel more healthy, though it hasn't produced any miraculous change in the way my body looks. I guess I've accepted that my body is aging—not, mind you, without going through a real grieving process. It helps that my husband is very accepting. Now, when he wants to unbutton my blouse and kiss my breasts, I just try to enjoy it. I tell myself, he's not getting any younger either—and I still love <u>his</u> body. I just try not to think too much about all those thin, gorgeous twenty-year-olds in the movies and on television!

Growing older doesn't have to mean the end of sex, but it does mean finding a way to come to terms with changes in the way our bodies look and function. For almost everyone, changes in physical appearance as we age can be very difficult to integrate into our identity as sexual beings. We need to be able to let our vision of who we are sexually change as our bodies change. As you read this book and learn how to develop your sexual intelligence, you will see that the sexually intelligent person knows how to disregard cultural stereotypes, such as the idea that sex is only for the young or beautiful or for people with unwrinkled and perfectly toned bodies. As the number of older people in the United States continues to grow, it is more important than ever before to be sexually intelligent about aging, to accept the biological changes that happen to men and women and see the bigger picture: that having an active sex life at any age will help keep you physically healthy.

Sexually intelligent people make sex a priority in their lives. Far from being dangerous, sex is good for us, physically and emotionally. Feeling and acting sexual is not itself dangerous. To the contrary, denying one's sexuality at any age can exact a high price in lost energy, passion, and creativity—even in one's overall physical health. For health reasons alone, it pays to invest time, energy, and thought into having a sexual relationship—and a satisfying one. Whether it comes to finding a sex partner or finding time for sex with your partner, all the research shows that the health and psychological benefits you stand to gain make it well worth neglecting the housework or foregoing the occasional poker game.

People who see sex as healthy and good, and who cherish their sexuality, radiate warmth, vitality, and sex appeal. The vibrancy of their sexuality may carry over into other areas of life, too—in the form of warm interest in their friends, love for their families, enthusiasm and commitment in their work, a greater sense of humor, and increased humanity. They may actually live longer than other people, too. Therefore, it's in our own interest that we develop the sexual intelligence that holds the key to an active sex life.

How Sexually Intelligent Are You?

Try out your sexual intelligence by considering how you would handle this dilemma:

> The last few sexual relationships you had ended painfully—so much so that for the last six months you haven't dated at all. You would love to have a sexual relationship, and you tell yourself that you're going to make an effort to meet someone new, but instead of calling that attractive person you met at the gym, answering a personal ad, or joining a group to meet people with similar interests, every weekend you end up either calling a friend to go to the movies or staying home alone.

Questions to Consider

1. Why is it that, despite wanting a sexual relationship, people may have trouble taking steps to find one? If you have ever been in this situation, what was it that stopped you from getting out and looking for a new relationship?
2. If you were in this situation, how could you motivate yourself to find another sexual relationship?
3. Are there ways you could get your friends to help motivate you to find a sexual partner?
4. In this situation, how much effort would you be willing to put into finding a new relationship—compared with the effort you put into work, chores, and hobbies?
5. If your previous sexual relationships have ended badly, what could you do to explore what went wrong and how would you use that knowledge to find a happier sexual relationship?
6. What kind of assumptions might hold you back from finding a satisfying

sexual relationship? For example, in this situation, would you assume that the right sexual opportunity will show up on your doorstep "when the time is right" without any effort on your part—the way it often does on TV or in the movies?

Bear in mind the following principles of sexual intelligence.

Scientific Knowledge

The benefits of an active sex life go far beyond physical pleasure. Regular sex improves the functioning of your immune system, reducing the chance of colds and flu.

Sex may also make you live longer. It certainly reduces men's chances of dying from heart disease.

It is particularly important to have an active sex life when you're young, because it means you're likely to continue an active sex life as you age— and sex can make the aches and pains of aging easier to bear.

Sex has benefits for your mental health as well as your physical health.

Put as much effort into finding a satisfying sexual relationship as you would into preventive health measures such as exercising, eating right, meditating, and so forth.

Sexual problems such as performance anxiety, lack of desire, or premature ejaculation are very common and don't have to prevent you from getting involved with someone. See your physician first if you have problems such as these, and make sure that they are not caused by a medical problem.

Don't compare your sexual relationships to the perfect or trouble-free ones that you see portrayed in the media or that you imagine others have.

Awareness of Your Secret Sexual Self

Confront emotional problems that may have hampered you in past sexual relationships.

When you find yourself hesitating to take a chance on a new sexual relationship, weigh the cost of disappointment against all the benefits for your health and even longevity.

If you are no longer twenty—or even thirty—and your sex life isn't what it once was, consider whether that may be due to negative feelings about yourself or your body and challenge those negative perceptions.

Connecting with Others

Have compassion and patience with yourself as well as your partner if either of you have problems such as performance anxiety, lack of desire, or inability to maintain an erection.

Consider getting professional help, from your doctor or a therapist, if problems like these are getting in the way of your sex life.

PART II

Stumbling

Blocks

On the

Road to

Sexual

Intelligence

chapter four

Silence, Shame, and Fear:

Early Learning in the Family and the Church

Maggie, a twenty-eight-year-old who recently returned to school to complete her nursing degree, never had a conversation with her parents about sex while she was growing up. The one thing she *did* learn from them, she remembers still:

> The stoical scheme of supplying our wants by lopping off our desires, is like cutting off our feet when we want shoes.
> —Jonathan Swift,
> *Thoughts on Various Subjects*

In my home, sex was never talked about. One time—I was about eight—my sister and I were playing with our Barbies. We had a Ken doll, and we had a vague idea, from watching the soaps at a babysitter's house in the afternoon, that there were grownups who were boyfriend and girlfriend, and what they did together was lie on top of each other. So, we had Ken on top of Barbie. My father walked in, and saw that—he didn't say a word. But we weren't allowed to have Ken dolls anymore after that. So then we had to cut the hair off one of our Barbies really short.

Although Maggie's father might have thought he was protecting his daughters from knowledge they weren't ready to handle, what he actually communicated to them is that sex is something forbidden—never to be mentioned or discussed.

One of the key components of sexual intelligence is having accurate scientific knowledge about human sexuality and being able to use that information in a way that improves our sex lives. Just as important is the ability to know our true sexual selves and to share that part of ourselves with our partner. The mastering of these two skills can lead to a life of great joy, expression, and freedom. Unfortunately, there are powerful stumbling blocks that routinely prevent people from putting into practice the knowledge they gain from scientific sources and experiencing the confidence, strength, and authenticity that come from knowing their true sexual identities. Among these stumbling blocks are family dynamics and religious dogma, which we discuss in this chapter, and negative messages about sexuality in the media and popular culture, which we look at in the next chapter.

Once we have learned to spot some of these stumbling blocks, we can move on to a life of sexual fulfillment that *we* choose, rather than acting out cultural or family scripts.

Silence and Shame: Learning About Sex in the Family

Our earliest opportunity to learn about sexuality is within the family. Most children are curious about sex and have questions about it at a fairly young age. Parents can have a tremendous influence on their children's later sexual attitudes and behaviors, depending on how they handle these early questions—or they *could*—if they ever talked to their children about sexuality.

Difficult as it is to believe, close to 60 percent of the people we surveyed in the Sexual Intelligence Project reported that their parents told them *nothing* about sex. Another 13 percent said the only thing their parents told them about sex was not to have it, while an additional 14 percent received some information from their parents about reproductive biology and the need for safe sex. Again and again, we heard how little our research participants had received from their parents in the way of useful guidance about sex—amazing, given that the majority of people we surveyed were between eighteen and thirty, meaning their parents lived through the sexual revolution of the sixties. Consider just a few of the responses we got to the question "What did your parents tell you about sex?"

- "My parents did not tell me anything. We never had a talk. They never sat me down and told me anything about it. They told me not to do it, and that was it."

- "When I was 18, my parents were like, 'Let's talk about sex,' and my brother and I said, 'What do you want to know?' "
- "What did my parents tell me about sex? Not to have it."

That last response came from a thirty-nine-year-old man who, by his reckoning, has had between 100 and 150 sexual partners.

Only 7 percent of the people we surveyed had ever had a meaningful, open discussion with their parents about sex, one that covered not just reproductive biology and diseases, but the whole range of emotional and interpersonal issues that sex raises.

From the perspective of cultivating sexual intelligence and developing healthy sex lives, failing to talk to one's children about sex is a grave mistake. Our research shows that people whose parents talked to them about sex are far more sexually intelligent in adulthood than those whose parents never said a word. Given that sexually intelligent people have fewer sexual dysfunctions and more satisfying sex lives, talking to young people is critical for their ability to function sexually as adults.

People whose parents communicated openly with them about sex are not only more sexually intelligent overall, they are better able to talk openly and honestly about sex with their partners, as well as with others. In contrast, the adult children of noncommunicative parents don't talk to their partners about their sex life, don't communicate when a problem comes up, and are unwilling to talk to a friend, confidante, or counselor in order to work out sexual problems. As a measure of how difficult it is for them to talk about sex, consider just two of our findings:

- Nearly a third of the people we surveyed said that if a problem came up in their sex life, they would do *anything* other than talk to their partner directly, including giving the situation some time and hoping things would change, or even looking for a different partner.
- Over 40 percent said that if a problem came up in their sex life they would never feel comfortable talking to a third person—such as a friend or counselor—about it, or would do so only as a last resort.

A 1995 study conducted by scientists at the Research Triangle Institute in Washington, D.C., confirms our finding that people have more difficulty talking about sex than anyone imagined. James Gribble and his colleagues developed a new computer-based survey technique in which adults aged eighteen to forty-five were interviewed either by a computer or a human researcher. What they found is astounding—and sobering: when asked by a human researcher, 29 percent of respondents said that they talk with their partner about their sex life less than once a month; when the interview was administered automatically, by computer, fully 50 percent of respondents admitted that they talk to their partner less than once a month. And 15 percent admitted to the computer that they had *never* discussed their sex life with their partner. This research confirms that people not only have great difficulty talking openly with their partners about sex, they even have trouble admitting how little they actually communicate![21]

There are many possible reasons for parents' failure to talk to their children about sex: parents may fear that bringing up the subject of sex may encourage teenagers to experiment, or they may lack information about human sexuality themselves. But one of the primary reasons why people don't talk to their children about sex, we found, is that their *own* parents were uncomfortable talking about the subject. As Lloyd, a forty-two-year-old doctor we interviewed put it:

> **I'm not much better at the discussion part than my parents were. I don't know if I have the tools. Talking about sex here, to you, is a completely dispassionate situation. I have nothing on the line here, and, still, it's hard. When I try to talk to my kids about sex, I feel like I have everything on the line. How do you do it?**

A recent study by psychologists Bruce King and Joann Lorusso confirms what we have found: more than half of the university students King and Lorusso surveyed said they had never had a meaningful conversation with their parents about sex. Interestingly, 60 percent of the parents of those students believed they *had* had such a conversation. One father who thought that he and his son had communicated in a meaningful way about sex—the son disagreed—elaborated on what he meant: "We have always stressed our view [that] if he is to succeed in his education and career, he must keep moral and celibate."[22] King and Lorusso also found that when parents had had a meaningful discussion about sex with their own parents while growing up, they were much more likely to initiate such a discussion with their teens. One mother in King and Lorusso's study put it poignantly, "I always hoped I would be able to handle such topics with my children, but I guess I was unable because it was never really discussed with me."[23]

One of the obvious results of silence within the family is that people learn not to talk about sex. That alone is a major stumbling block to a healthy, fulfilling sex life in adulthood. Shame and guilt also grow out of silence about sex. What can't be openly discussed—even named or acknowledged—children assume must be bad or shameful.

Despite the fact that the parents of most of our participants gave them little or no explicit information about sex, they often implicitly communicated very negative messages that created fear or a sense that sex is something dangerous, illicit, or shameful. These are some of the messages our research participants received from their parents about sex:

- "My mother should have talked with me about sex and not said that it is bad. My father cheated on her, so she is very negative and has passed that on to me."
- "Pretty much I learned to be afraid of having sex and, when the time came, I wasn't prepared."
- "I was getting to the age when my mother had to tell me about the birds and bees. She said to me, 'Okay, well, in a few years from now you're going to start bleeding from between your legs for a week, and it's going to happen every month until you die, and it hurts.' It scared the crap out of me. I remember wanting to kill myself, because I couldn't understand living like that."

Another way in which parents created shame was by overreacting to evidence of their teens' emerging sexuality. For example, the parents of one woman we interviewed responded to an adolescent fantasy as if it were a horrible crime:

I remember having this dream when I was like fourteen or fifteen, and I wrote about it in my diary. I was with a boy from school—he was a very gentle, loving person, and I had had a crush on him forever. In the dream, we were making love.

To me it was a beautiful dream, and I wanted to write about it. My parents read my diary, and they freaked. They said, "Who is writing this? Who is this devil? This is awful, awful."

They took something beautiful and turned it into something disturbing. It made me feel bad and dirty.

The type of sexual beings our children become depends heavily on the way parents view sexuality and the attitudes about sexuality they convey—often without saying a word. Parents' implicitly communicated beliefs and attitudes about sex can instill shame and guilt that are particularly damaging for their children's sexuality in adulthood.

It's Not So Much What Parents Say As What They Do

One of the most important things we've learned is that it is not just the things parents say or don't say that influence their children's sex lives in adulthood, it's also the way they *treat* their children. Parents who raise the healthiest adults are those who have positive attitudes toward sex, who talk to their children about sex, who provide firm guidelines without being punitive and harsh, and who are available and involved in their children's lives.

Previous research has shown that intolerant, strict attitudes toward teenage sexuality actually backfire. In one study, teenagers whose parents were overly strict and "had a lot of rules about sex" tended to rebel and be much more promiscuous than teenagers whose parents were moderately strict.[24]

In our own research, we found something much more surprising. People whose fathers were punitive *in general*—even about such things as tracking mud into the house, failing to clean one's room, or "talking back"—experienced more guilt about sex in adulthood and reported less satisfying sex lives; at the same time, though, they were more likely to rebel and become promiscuous. Parents who are strict and punitive do more than instill shame and guilt. They paradoxically accomplish just the opposite of what they intend to do, that is, prevent their teens from becoming sexually active.

When parents are rigid, controlling, and punitive—in some cases, even physically abusive—children learn to respond to external controls on their behavior rather than developing their own internalized sense of right and wrong. But the most serious consequence of harsh, punitive parenting, we have found, is that it produces adults who have very little insight into their genuine sexual selves. They don't know what their real sexual desires and preferences are, and they don't see that their motives for having sex are complicated by a need to oppose their parents' control. Rather than look within, they simply do the opposite of what their parents tell them.

Take Joseph, for example. He is a twenty-year-old student who was born in Chicago. Listen to the way he describes his upbringing and the effect it had on his behavior once he got out of the house:

> **My dad's kind of a strict father. His attitude was always, "You can't do that, got to stay home." My parents used physical punishment. Instead of being grounded, I was spanked with my parents' hands or a belt. It was painful. It would leave welts.**
>
> **I was a virgin until I was eighteen. When I went to college, something happened—it just let loose. I was out of the house, and I went wild.**

Joseph reports that he "has a lot of sex" and is "not sure" how many sexual partners he has had. Currently he estimates he has sex twelve times a week.

But it isn't just punitive parenting that is linked to promiscuity. Overly permissive parenting also has negative effects—in fact, exactly the *same* negative effects. It is not simply repressive attitudes that lead to sexual acting out in adolescence. The same study that found sexual intercourse rates high among teenagers whose parents were very strict also found high rates of promiscuity among adolescents whose parents were very *permissive*. In a more recent, 1994, study, Carol Metzler and her colleagues at the Oregon Research Institute in Eugene, Oregon, found that risky sexual behavior among adolescents is linked with parents' failure to monitor their children's behavior, and the unavailability of parents or parental figures.[25] When teens don't receive the attention they need from parents, they may go looking for it in early sexual relationships. The combination of treating teenagers harshly and punitively—communicating implicitly that sex is dangerous or shameful—and then neglecting them is a recipe for disaster. As adults, people who have grown up with these mixed messages are likely to be promiscuous, to put themselves into dangerous situations, and even unwittingly gravitate toward violent relationships.

Take the example of Chloe. She is a bright, independent twenty-two-year-old, just beginning law school. Chloe's parents are both highly educated professionals. Chloe's mother is a psychiatrist, with both a private practice and an appointment at a prestigious teaching hospital. Her father is an architect. From the outside, they look like the perfect family, but behind closed doors, Chloe's father abused her and her sister:

> When we were little, my father would take off his belt and threaten us and spank us. We were terrified of him. Dad would come home, chase me around the house, trying to hit me. There were times when he would drag me upstairs, throw me in my room, and hit me. He would buy sticks, whipping sticks, and we would find them and break them, but he kept on buying them.

Both parents were rigid and strict about dating. They feared the day when Chloe, the oldest, would become sexually active, and they accused her of having sex when, in fact, she wasn't:

> They thought I was doing all these awful things when I wasn't. Finally, after my parents kept on accusing me, I was like "Fuck it, they think I'm doing it, might as well."

Although Chloe's parents were controlling and strict, at the same time, they were largely unavailable: they had no time for her. Chloe's father was struggling with his own demons and trying to keep a job; her mother was preoccupied with her psychiatry practice and with trying to hold the family together and pretend that everything was normal. Chloe described the combination of intrusiveness and neglect this way:

> They would be completely overprotective and call the cops if I wasn't home by 6 o'clock on summer evenings, even when I was a teenager, but they were never home because they were both working.

Chloe rebelled against her parents' strict control by having sex early, at fourteen, sneaking out of the house to have sex with a boy they disapproved of:

> I was fourteen, and I had a boyfriend whom I was forbidden to see. We would sneak out at two in the morning, and we would meet halfway between our houses, in the woods behind the old elementary school we used to go to. We had sex right there on a bench.

It felt so good to be in love with him. He wouldn't even look at other girls. The bad part was he would get real jealous if I talked to other guys, and like threaten them. At the time, it made me feel like, "He loves me so much."

He was actually kind of an obsessive personality. One night, I was babysitting, and he had called me, I guess, a dozen times, and didn't know where I was. I didn't get home until after midnight, and I went right to bed. He stopped by my house and he was throwing rocks at my window to try to wake me up. I was so exhausted, I didn't hear a thing.

So he broke into my house. The first thing I knew, I heard my father downstairs shouting, "What's your name? What's your name?" And then I heard my boyfriend say, "Alan," and I was like, "Nooo." I went downstairs and my father said, "Go look out the window." There was my boyfriend, handcuffed, being put into the backseat of a cop car.

In the eight years since Chloe became sexually active, she has had twenty-five different partners. Now, in adulthood, Chloe is repeatedly drawn to violent men and has a hard time staying with a man for more than a few months at a time:

It's not sex that is the biggest problem for me, it's relationships—I just can't seem to have a long relationship. I don't know if it's that I'm picking the wrong men . . .

Any relationship I've been in, for the first couple months everything is great, I'm like totally high, it's wooo, everything is wonderful—and then I start feeling smothered.

Maybe it goes back somehow to my parents. They would hit me and then tell me they loved me. That might have something to do with why I get involved in a relationship and then become ambivalent about it after a couple of months.

People whose parents alternately neglect them and treat them harshly—even physically abuse them—may learn to equate love with violence: on the one hand, gravitating to familiar signs of possessiveness and control that they mistake for love; on the other hand, avoiding extended relationships or real intimacy because of their fear that love must necessarily turn to violence in the future.

So Where *Do* People Learn About Sex?

In the absence of explicit information about sex from their parents, many children acquire a haphazard education from their peers—a case of the woefully ignorant being led by the largely uninformed—or from the culture around them, often from the media. Not all of it is positive or helpful. Consider just a few of our research participants' experiences:

- "The way I found out about sex was my father worked for a plumbing supply house, and there were usually degrading comments made about women, and *Playboys* were lying around open, and I would look at them occasionally. Nothing was said to me when they would see me looking at them. They were all guys, and I think they thought this is the way a boy evolves into manhood."

- "I first learned about sex in my friend's basement when I was in the third grade. In sixth grade, we had sex education in school—three years too late."

Raising Sexually Healthy Adults

As we've made clear, very few of the people we interviewed in the Sexual Intelligence Project had received any guidance at all—never mind helpful guidance—about sex from their families. But twenty-three-year-old Eric, an engineering major, had a different experience. His story serves as an illustration of what parents can do to raise sexually intelligent adults. Eric's mother grew up in a very punitive, non-communicative family. She determined not to treat her son the way she had been treated. As Eric tells it:

My mom grew up in a very religious family. Her father is a minister. He had these rigid, strict rules, and she always felt it was wrong. She's always been very open to making sure that I was doing what I wanted to do. Not forcing something on me. That's kind of when people decide to rebel, and do things that maybe they don't want to do just to go against their parents. She's always been very honest with me, and said, "I want you to do what you want to do, what feels right to you." I think she knew that I would make the right decision.

Neither Eric's mother nor his father, however, simply left him to his own devices. They set firm limits for him and his sisters:

> **The big thing with them was parental involvement. They knew where I was going, who I was with, what time I would be back. So I definitely had a sense of "I am answering to someone higher than me or my friends."**
>
> **And they definitely had rules. I had to be in by a certain time. They wouldn't let me go to this concert or that concert because I wasn't old enough. It was the same with my sisters. If they wanted to go off camping for a weekend with a bunch of guys, my mother would say, "You can do this, but you might want to make sure you're not putting yourself in a situation where something bad can happen." So my sisters had to think about it and realize that maybe that wouldn't necessarily be a very safe situation.**

Eric's parents also talked to him, and to his sisters, openly about sex—not simply the biological aspects of it, but the emotional and interpersonal implications involved:

> **My mom and dad never had a negative attitude toward sex—they said they thought sex education was a very positive thing. I had friends who had it enforced that sex was a very negative thing, but my parents never portrayed it that way.**
>
> **My mother and my father, too, would explain things to me in a warm manner. I remember, once, my dad and I were driving in the car. I was just starting to go out with my first serious girlfriend, and I think my dad knew that it was approaching the point where I was probably going to start having sex, if I hadn't already. He asked me, "Have you had sex with her?" and he asked me if we were using birth control. Then he told me, "Just be careful; be sure you don't hurt this girl. Don't mix up feelings with sexual desires." I got it that you don't mess around with people's feelings.**

Parents have unlimited potential to promote healthy discussions about sexuality with their children. These discussions provide safe, loving opportunities for children to express and overcome their confusion about sex. When these discussions do not occur, when silence reigns within the family and children learn to equate that silence with shame and fear, as adults, they not only will spend a lifetime unable to communicate with their partners about sex, but they also will be trapped by destructive, negative attitudes that leave them feeling ashamed of their authentic sexual desires. The remedy is simple, if not always easy: we can talk to our children honestly, answer their questions with accurate information, and communicate a positive attitude toward sexuality.

Deadly Passion: Organized Religion and the Fear of Sex

As young children, we first learn about sex—directly or indirectly—in our families. Our next introduction is usually through organized religion. Indeed, some of the attitudes toward sex that parents teach us, implicitly, come from their religious beliefs and training. Although spirituality can provide depth and meaning to our relationships, punitive religious doctrine can send the message that sexual desire itself is dark and deadly. Such messages contribute to fears that prevent people from valuing their sexuality and being free to pursue an active sex life, with all its health benefits. Religious dogma can leave people confused and torn between their desire for a spiritual life and connection to a religious community and their healthy need for a satisfying sex life.

What's amazing is the extent to which organized religion—and not just Christianity—still inculcates fear of sex as a dangerous, unruly force and attempts to control passion by insisting on abstinence outside of narrowly prescribed limits, specifically marriage and procreation. In fact, over the last two decades, we've seen an increase in fundamentalism, particularly Protestant Fundamentalism, that has underscored traditional sexual prohibitions.

Protestant Fundamentalists in America have defined a political agenda centered around what they call "family values," which includes a whole range of sexual prohibitions—against premarital sex, abortion, and homosexuality. What's more, they have had considerable success in influencing national politics with their agenda, as we showed in our previous book, *The Politics of Denial*.[26] The dogma of the Religious Right, like that of many other fundamentalist religious groups, views sexual passion as a force independent of rationality, an autonomous evil within us that can prompt us to act against our own best interests and that must be strictly controlled.

While parents may invoke a variety of negative consequences to forestall premarital sex, it's organized religion that has the *really* impressive threat at its disposal—eternal damnation. It's through such images as the threat of spending eternity burning in hell that religion communicates the attitude that sexuality—outside of narrowly prescribed limits—has terrible consequences. Many people have picked up that message, whether in their families or in church. Among our research participants, for example, over 40 percent agreed with the statement "There is always a price to pay, sometimes a very high price, for sexual passion."

Our research in the Sexual Intelligence Project shows that there is a significant difference in sexual intelligence between people who belong to religions that take a restrictive, punitive attitude toward sex and those who belong to religious groups more tolerant of human sexuality. People who listed themselves as Protestant, Jewish, or having no religious affiliation scored significantly higher on sexual intelligence than did Roman Catholics and Fundamentalist Protestants and Muslims. (In our sample, the majority of Jews were non-Orthodox and the majority of the Muslims were Fundamentalist.) For example, the Fundamentalist Protestants scored, on average, a D in sexual intelligence, Roman Catholics scored, on average, a C, and non-Fundamentalist Protestants scored a B–. People who reported that their parents were highly religious while they were growing up were significantly less sexually intelligent than those who said their parents were less religious. Our guess is that participants who reported their parents as being "highly religious" may have been remembering strict or rigid beliefs communicated by their parents, as opposed to their parents' level of spirituality.

One of our research participants described the heavy-handed way in which her religion attempted to inculcate its sexual morality:

Hearing the church's view of sexuality pissed me off. When you're little, and you're in your little uniforms, you look up to the priest and the nuns and you think it's great because you sit around and sing songs all day. But when you get older and they start teaching you about sex and sexuality and making choices— it's all a contradiction. They're teaching you to make their choice, not to make your own choice. They showed us actual videos of women having abortions, live, which is sort of like, you're sitting there thinking you are in some sort of

war camp, they're showing you these videos, trying to brainwash you. It was disgusting. You ask questions about something and they can't give a legitimate answer.

Such attempts at indoctrination are not without consequences, whether people end up accepting or rejecting the doctrine itself. Consider what one young woman told us about the results of her religious education:

I went to Catholic junior high and high school, and there was a lot of talk of abstinence and premarital sex being a mortal sin. I never got the logistics of sex, just that it was bad. The sexual education I got probably gave me more dilemmas to face than someone with healthier sexual attitudes.

When Beliefs Don't Match Behavior

One of the most interesting things researchers have found is an apparent discrepancy between what highly religious people believe—for example, no sex before marriage—and how they actually behave. Professor Joseph Donnelly, from Montclair State University, and his colleagues, for example, looked at the relationship between religiosity and sexual behavior among 869 middle-school students. They found that how religious the students claimed to be predicted their *attitudes* toward sex, but not their *behavior.* Highly religious students were more likely than less religious ones to disagree with the statement "It is all right for two people to have intercourse if they are in love." When it came to behavior, though, equal numbers of highly religious and less religious kids had already had sexual intercourse.[27]

Attitudes toward sexual intercourse don't necessarily predict behavior. In a study done by Erika Pluhar at the University of Pennsylvania, along with colleagues at Cornell University, which looked at the link between religion and sexual attitudes and behaviors among college students, highly religious students expressed the most disapproval of premarital sex; nonetheless, close to a quarter of them had in fact engaged in sexual intercourse. Those highly religious students who *did* have sex were likely to rely on withdrawal rather than any other form of birth control. As Pluhar and her colleagues point out, withdrawal is not a very effective means of contraception, nor does it protect one from sexually transmitted diseases.[28] Previous research has found that young people who can't accept the fact that they have sexual desires *do* sometimes act on those desires, but they have a tendency to do it furtively—behind their own back, so to speak—denying to themselves that sexual activity is a possibility and taking no precautions against pregnancy or sexually transmitted diseases.[29]

Faith, Fear, and Sex

The difference between people who have a strong religious faith that sustains them and those whose religious training has crippled their sexual intelligence was illustrated for us dramatically by the contrast between two of our participants, both raised in the same faith, by parents whose religious views were, in one case, strict and inflexible, and, in the other, more loving and tolerant.

The first participant is Gary, a tall, handsome twenty-year-old history major, whose blond hair was cut extremely short, almost military style. In fact, we soon discovered that his father is a retired army colonel. Gary's parents were originally from Georgia, but the family moved to the Boston area before Gary was born. Gary was raised Protestant and, like his parents, identifies himself as a "born-again Christian." According to him, "Sex is only allowed once you are married."

Despite his current beliefs, Gary has engaged in oral sex, which at one time he did not define as "really having sex"; he has also used pornographic magazines and videos and visited a strip club. In the last year, however, he has disavowed all sexual activity, including oral sex and even masturbation.

Gary's father demanded strict adherence to Fundamentalist Protestant views forbidding sex before marriage. The religious doctrine he espoused was completely at odds with the teen culture Gary was a part of, and, initially, Gary rejected his father's views:

> There was always a culture clash, between the things I'd learn at home and in church and the things you did in high school to be "in." You know. Half the stuff I was doing I wasn't supposed to do. . . . My parents always taught me those things were wrong, like . . . using drugs, drinking alcohol, sex before marriage. But since I was a teenager and wanted to fit in, I went along with it. The world I was living in, it was all about dating, getting as much play as you can. I figured, "When I go to college, all I'm going to do is bang, bang, bang."

As a teenager, Gary experimented with oral sex, and he had one glorious week of freedom, in high school, when he was allowed to go on a senior class trip to Montreal:

> I loved it. I was away from my parents for five days with eighteen kids from my high school. We went to strip clubs and met girls, had some hookups there, so to speak. In those clubs they had lesbians on the stage for you, stuff like that. There were even hookers around. To me, that was a great time.

What started out as a young man's vision of heaven, however, by the end of the week proved disillusioning. As Gary describes it from his current perspective:

> After all, it was just a big alcoholic haze of sex and the smell of lust everywhere. We blew hundreds of dollars just so girls would . . . the strippers didn't even like us, it was part of their job to pretend like they're seducing us so we could slip 'em some money. Get a little kiss on the cheek.

Gary ended up feeling tricked by women who exploited his desire for them in what seemed to him a cynical, even crass way. It left him with a bad feeling about himself and his sexuality. That theme of being degraded by his own sexual desires reappeared again and again in the interview.

For example, Gary now believes that the oral sex he had with several girlfriends was wrong:

> I look back and realize it was a mistake, the oral sex, I mean. I was misled and astray back then. I didn't have any real relationship with these girls. They were just party hookups, or girlfriends of a few months. I felt like an animal. The girls had no sense of dignity or honor.

Gary fears his sexual impulses so much that he won't even be alone in the same room with a woman:

> I'm not going to sit in a room with a girl alone. I'm not going to go over to her house if nobody's home, to study or whatever, because you never know. Alone in a room, anything could happen. The situation itself is disrespectful toward her, as well as to me. I'm protecting her dignity and her honor and her chastity.

Gary has not only given up oral sex and being alone with women, he has also stopped masturbating. We have already encountered his views on the subject, in chapter 2. His feeling, expressed in that chapter— that masturbation is self-abuse—seems to be based on his fear of what he sees as his potentially excessive desires:

> There are times, like, you go on like rampages: you get a porno video, and it's a really good one, and you got the house to yourself. I got a friend, his highest number was masturbating thirty-six times in one day. I was like, "What? That's crazy." As opposed to my four. And four was like too much for me, too. It came to a point where I'd watch a movie and one nipple would make an appearance, and right there, I was off. It just came to a point where it was animalism.

Here the same theme appears, again, of being degraded or used by his own sexual desires and being somehow damaged by sex, which Gary sees as, in itself, dangerous or toxic.

It appears that Gary's return to the church doctrine of total abstinence is a way both of guarding himself against the feeling of being degraded and exploited and a way of controlling what he fears are excessive sexual desires—a way of ensuring that masturbating four times in a day never turns into thirty-six times. Use of pornography *can* be tied to addictive or compulsive sexual behavior, although in Gary's case that seems more a fear than a reality. His fear about the dangers of sex and the need to strictly control his sexuality are more related to the sexual repression that is a central theme of Protestant Fundamentalism.

Having forsworn all sexual activity and returned to the religious views of the church and his parents, Gary believes he has found a new peace and a proper view of sexuality and its place in life:

> Basically I look at sex now, it was a gift from God, and when we reproduce, he made it pleasurable for us, so that we'd want to have children. But people have taken this and taken advantage of it. It's just obvious—we're not doing something right because we're devolving into animalism and we're just worshiping our passions and desires.

Gary is sure that the future holds the promise of an ideal woman who is waiting for him out there, and that their sex life together—once they're married—will be wonderful:

> I plan to marry a virgin. It's important because you're supposed to be a virgin before you get married. A friend of mine, he's like, "But I need a wife who's good in bed. I got to make sure she's good in bed, or I'm not going to want to marry her."
>
> And I told him, "If you've never tried a stack of buttermilk pancakes, and I put syrup and butter all over it, I know that you're going to like it. If I gave it to you and you tried it for the first time, you're going to like it. You're going to love it and it'll be special for you. That's going to lead you on to wanting to try blueberry and chocolate chip and strawberry, and even waffles and toast." I know it would be special.

It's a lovely image, but a deceptive one: Gary is further misleading himself in thinking that someday the perfect woman will come along and effortlessly solve all his conflicts about sexuality.

Contrast Gary's experience with that of twenty-year-old Tamra. She, too, was raised in a Fundamentalist Protestant family by parents who do not believe in premarital sex. But her parents were very different from Gary's in the way they communicated their beliefs to Tamra:

> My family are really, really strong Christians, and they definitely believe in not having sex before marriage. That's something I've struggled with a little bit. . . . But at the same time, my mom has always been, "Listen, if you are going to have sex before you are married, I may not agree, but I'll take you to the doctor, I'll get you birth control—even if I disapprove." So even if I make a decision she doesn't agree with, I know she's there to support me. And my dad is the same way.

Tamra is currently in a relationship in which she is very happy, and she reports a high level of sexual satisfaction. Tamra has certainly struggled with her beliefs and wondered if what she is doing is right. In fact, for a time, she and her boyfriend stopped having sex because she wanted to be clear about what she was doing and why:

> I've struggled with whether or not it is a sin for me to be having sex before marriage. That's strictly based on my religious beliefs, and wondering, "Well, if I ask for forgiveness," and go do it again, am I . . . Or should I be asking for forgiveness, because it feels good and I don't want to be forgiven.

And that's part of the reason I asked my boyfriend, "Can we back off for a little bit, because I want to figure this part out. It's nothing to do with you. It's all
figuring out what I believe and why I believe it."

For Tamra, despite her period of struggle, there is none of the tone
that we heard in Gary's story, no fear of her own sexual desires or strict
attempt to control those desires, nor the sense that sex is animalistic or
degrading. Her parents' openness and their ability to tolerate the possibility that Tamra might have different beliefs, seem to have spared
Tamra the negative associations that sex has for Gary—associations
that are not likely to disappear once he marries and that may well cause
problems for his sexual life then.

Embracing the church's doctrine seemed to be the way Gary found to
protect himself from sexual desires that felt too threatening. Gary
reverted to the church teachings he grew up with during adolescence
when his first sexual experiences produced pain and confusion. He
opted for abstinence until marriage because of his fear of his own
sexual impulses. He substituted a rigid rule for the painful process of
examining his reasons for having sex, his own values, and his past. No
one can say that the decision he made is right or wrong. In fact, one
could say that the church's ready-made rule about abstinence provided
a safe haven for a young person who desperately needed at least a temporary moratorium from sexual activity. It is not so much any particular doctrine—for example, the belief in abstinence until marriage—that
represents a stumbling block toward sexual intelligence. Rather, it is
the *way* some religious groups enforce those doctrines—by invoking an
old, very damaging vision of sex as something, *in itself*, malignant and
dangerous—that is less than sexually intelligent. The unfortunate thing
for Gary is that he identified with religious doctrines that portray sex as
something to be controlled at all costs, as an impulse dark, dangerous,
and shameful that can exact a terrible price.

It takes courage to discard these myths. They are so much a part of a
religion for which we may feel great love and respect. But these myths
deny us sexual happiness, something that we each deserve and that is a
part of a healthy life.

How Shame and Fear Prevent Us from Integrating Our Sexuality into Our Identity

We could not end this chapter without discussing the destructive myths about homosexuality that are closely associated with the doctrine of some religious groups in America. These myths run rampant through our society and cause many people to suffer. For gays and bisexuals, discovering their sexual orientation and integrating it into their identity is complicated considerably by homophobia among those around them.

The pain, shame, and confusion that gay and bisexual people often experience in the process of discovering their sexual preference is largely due to societal homophobia, which too often encourages them to deny or distort their genuine sexual desires. Sex is healthy; cutting people off from their true sexual selves is not.

Despite the fact that there is no evidence that homosexuality is pathological, many social institutions—organized religion, for one—continue to propagate this view. Many religious denominations consider homosexuality a "sin." The Religious Right continues to mount its own peculiarly paranoid campaign against homosexuality.

There is also a fair degree of prejudice against homosexuals among the American public. A June 1994 telephone survey of 800 adults for *Time* magazine found that 53 percent of the adults questioned said that homosexual relationships between consenting adults "are morally wrong," and 39 percent said that homosexual relationships are "not acceptable at all." The survey was repeated in 1998 and found very little change in attitudes: 48 percent of adults felt that homosexuality is morally wrong, and 33 percent felt that homosexual relationships are not acceptable. In the 1998 survey, 51 percent of the respondents believed that homosexuals could change their sexual orientation if they wanted to.[30]

Don't Ask, Don't Tell

Homophobia has recently taken a slightly more subtle, but equally damaging, form. The military, some religious denominations, and many individuals, in a peculiar attempt to avoid open prejudice against homosexuals, have tried to make a distinction between people's sexual orientation and their public identity. In the military, for example, gay men and women are promised that no one will ask about their sexual orientation, but warned at the same time that they must not tell. For them, that means hiding a central part of their identity from the people they live and work with—and may well die with. The Catholic Church has taken the position that one can be homosexual and still remain within the church—as long as you don't act on your sexual desires.

In our research, we asked participants, "How do you feel about individuals who identify themselves as 'gay'?" Thirteen percent said that homosexuality is morally wrong, 56 percent said that it would be wrong for homosexuals to deny their sexual identity, and 31 percent said it is acceptable for a person to be gay, as long as he or she doesn't "flaunt it," in other words, as long as individuals keep their sexual orientation hidden. Those who said it would be wrong for homosexuals to deny their sexual identity scored significantly higher on sexual intelligence, overall, and on the Scientific Knowledge component of sexual intelligence, than did people who said being gay is acceptable if it isn't "flaunted." While people who believe that homosexuality is acceptable as long as it's kept hidden may seem open-minded, they are essentially demanding that people hide and compartmentalize an important part of who they are.

This is a problem, not only for gays in the military, but for most individuals, gay or straight, in this culture. The identity that we show to the world most of the time is a desexed self that is difficult to sustain. People do this for many reasons: because they have learned, from their parents, religious authorities, or the culture around them, that sexuality is something to be ashamed of and to hide, or because they are afraid of their sexual desires and of the possible consequences of acting on them inappropriately. To be sexually intelligent, it is necessary to integrate your sexuality into your identity.

This does not mean necessarily broadcasting private moments to the world. The issue is entirely internal, a matter of integrating who we are sexually into a coherent self-image so that we feel ourselves all of a piece. We don't have to split off part of our personality—namely, our sexuality—and hide it from *ourselves* or from the people we are closest to. We don't have to pretend to be someone we're not, put on an act, or remember which lies we've told to whom. Mainly, it means not lying to ourselves.

For gays and bisexuals, integrating their sexuality into their identity is particularly difficult because they have homophobia to contend with. They may have difficulty coming to terms with the social reaction to their sexual orientation. Some come from families in which homosexuality is unacceptable on religious grounds; some face expectations that they live up to social scripts concerning marriage, having children, and fitting in to a conventional heterosexual lifestyle; some face discrimination and even violence from homophobes in the community.

Consider Megan's experience. She is thirty-two and grew up in a close-knit Irish Catholic neighborhood that is famous for banning gays from marching in the annual St. Patrick's day parade. Megan began her story with an understatement:

> **Being gay in my neighborhood was not good. I basically was in the closet until I was old enough to get out of there.**

Megan grew up poor in the projects, the sixth child in a family of seven. Her mother worked nights in a factory and her father drove a city bus. In the environment in which she grew up, being gay simply wasn't an option, and so it never occurred to Megan that she might be:

> **There just were no gay people in the community. It was like they didn't exist. If you were, you were dead. My neighborhood is the kind of place, if a black person walked through, they'd beat the crap out of him. If you were gay, they would kill you, literally kill you. It never crossed my mind; I wasn't a lesbian.**

So Megan never made a connection between the crushes she had on women, beginning with her second-grade teacher, and the possibility that she was gay. She was a tomboy, who hung out with the guys, which in a way, worked for her:

> **I remember liking my second-grade teacher, it was like a crush, when your heart goes pitter-pat. I also had a crush on Olivia Newton John.**
> **I hung out with all the boys until I was like fifteen, when I went to high school. It was me and sixteen guys that hung out. I liked what the boys did. They were**

good to play hockey and basketball with. And I liked what they liked. They liked to look at pictures of naked women, and I did, too. <u>Playboy</u> or whatever.

When Megan was fourteen, her mother, concerned that she was turning into a tomboy, sent her to an all-girls Catholic school. Megan laughed as she told us:

My mother was trying to get me to stop hanging around with boys. I had never really been exposed to a lot of girls. But when I went to this school, I really started getting big-time crushes. I had crushes on all my teachers, I had crushes on all the girls in the class, and then I realized that my crushes were sexual. But I kept everything on a nice, platonic level. Nothing deep. Not that people in the neighborhood were really deep anyway—you never sat around and talked about your feelings.

So I never realized, until I was fifteen or sixteen, that I was gay. Around that time, I remember, one night I was watching a movie with my family, and there was a lesbian in the movie. And my mother was like, "Oh, my God, I would disown my daughter if she was ever a lesbian." And I'm like—to myself, of course, "Oh, my God." And I started thinking about it. I never really thought about it, I just, innocently, never gave sex any thought. Probably because I knew that feeling sexual toward women was wrong.

Megan didn't dare tell the friends she'd grown up with:

I knew, if I had ever come out to my friends in the projects, I would have been killed. I grew up in the projects—I'm telling you, if a black person had walked in, they would have killed him. Beat him with a baseball bat and not think twice. Gay kids, they kill. Because all gay people are pedophiles as far as they are concerned.

Previous research confirms Megan's and so many other young people's experience with obstacles to revealing their sexual identity—in school and even to those they are closest to. For example, Dr. Susan Telljohann and a colleague at the University of Toledo found that 42 percent of the women and 30 percent of the men they studied said their families responded badly when they revealed their sexual orientation. Only about 25 percent felt that they could talk to school counselors about their sexual orientation. Half of the women and over a third of the men claimed that discussions of sexuality in their classes communicated negative messages about homosexuality. Sadly, fewer than 20 percent of the students had found even one person who was supportive to them.[31] Other studies have found the same lack of support in the schools for students who are struggling with their sexual identity.[32]

The homophobic reactions that some gays and bisexuals encounter when they reveal their sexuality can be devastating: Dr. Scott Hershberger and his colleagues at the University of Kansas, in a study of 194 gay and bisexual teenagers, found that losing friends because of one's sexual orientation was one of the most important factors that predicted suicide attempts.[33] Homophobic attitudes among a person's peers, teachers, and family are particularly destructive in the light of a finding, reported by Dr. Andrew Boxer and his colleagues in the Department of Psychiatry at the University of Chicago, that coming out is an important part of increasing the self-esteem of people who are gay or bisexual.[34]

An important part of discovering our genuine sexual self is knowing whether we are primarily attracted to the opposite sex, our own sex, or both. That process is made much more difficult—and painful—by social attitudes that condemn homosexuality. In some cases, those attitudes can be potentially deadly. Take Paul's case as an example.

Paul: Coming to Terms

Paul is a twenty-seven-year-old marine biologist. He knew he was gay by age three or four, and even had a crush on Luke Skywalker. Like so many of the gay and bisexual people we talked to, Paul encountered homophobic attitudes from both his parents and in school. His parents told him nothing about sex until he asked for information at the age of thirteen:

> They gave me a book to read about sexuality and puberty. It contained <u>nothing</u> about homosexuality, which was a problem since I'm gay. Both of them were pretty homophobic and regularly made hostile remarks about that whole community.
>
> In high school, the typical insult for someone was to call him a "fag" or call him a "girl" or something like that. There were a couple of people who were per-

ceived to be gay, and they had a substantial amount of physical violence brought upon them. Teachers would often take part in jokes, make comments about people, turn their eyes when things were happening to people.

Paul never engaged in any of the sexual experimentation typical among teens:

I didn't do anything with anyone until after I came out, when I was nineteen. It was probably some degree of homophobia, that if I did anything I would have to acknowledge I wasn't straight, and I wasn't ready to deal with that yet. . . . I was aware that I was horrified by the fact, when I put a name to it. I just tried to repress it.

That attempt to deny his sexuality led Paul into a phase of his life that could have ended tragically:

I got into drugs—everything from pot to Ecstasy to crystal, coke a little bit.

It was something I was doing to avoid problems. I remember thinking for some twisted reason, that doing acid after school would somehow make me either forget or lose the whole queer aspect of myself. And when I realized that that just wasn't working, I started thinking, "I'm probably screwing my life up doing drugs, and exposing my self to physical harm, and it's not helping, so . . ." So I stopped, but the problem of my sexual orientation was still there—I couldn't run away from it—and now there was no way to avoid it.

I ended up taking a bunch of sleeping pills. I took them, and I was in my room, and my mom came home. She came into my room and said, "Hi," and told me she loved me. She began talking about random stuff or whatever, and she went into her room. I started thinking how bad she would feel when she found me the next morning, so I went into the bathroom and made myself throw up, and got a friend to take me to the hospital.

At that point, Paul realized that he needed help. For a time, he saw a psychotherapist, but the man was less than helpful because he didn't seem to understand the pressures Paul felt about coming out. It was the Internet that proved to be Paul's salvation. There, for the first time, he encountered information about being gay that didn't fuel his self-hatred:

When I got online, for the first time I was coming across things related to gay and lesbian issues. That was the first time I had ever seen it in a positive light. That sort of transformed my whole concept of the thing, and I thought maybe there was some way I could manage to live with myself as I am. Seeing that started to evoke a little anger about the stuff I realized I was going through all this time.

At the same time, I was still crippled by internalized homophobia, and very much ashamed of the whole thing and not wanting to . . . wishing I wasn't that way and not wanting to tell people. Eventually, I told a couple of friends first, and then ended up telling my parents.

Paul was amazed to find that his friends were understanding:

I was pretty much expecting to have all of my friends leave me, but all of them were very supportive.

His parents were a different matter:

My mom's initial response was to ask me if I wanted to have an AIDS test, or if I had been messing with any of the kids in the neighborhood. My dad hasn't really said anything. Basically not a single word transpired between him and me after I came out.

And then, I started taking things off the Internet that I was finding and giving them to my parents to educate them to an extent. My mother ended up actually being very supportive.

Paul is now in a relationship with a man he cares about very much, a relationship that is both sexually and emotionally satisfying.

Paul demonstrated a great deal of sexual intelligence in actively working on integrating his sexuality into his identity and finding a sexual life that is satisfying and enriches him as a person. He somehow found the ability to talk to people—a therapist, his family, his friends—about his sexual identity, despite the fact that his parents and peers had previously made it clear that they had very negative attitudes toward homosexuality. Though he did for a time try to escape through drugs, Paul had the wisdom to recognize that he needed to confront his secret sexual self and he had the courage to do so. Paul also has the intelligence to know that discovering one's sexuality and integrating it into a coherent identity is a lifelong process:

I don't think homophobia is something I will ever be free of. But when it does manifest itself, I can recognize it now as that, so I don't feel so much personal strife from it. And it's something I actively try to address and combat in myself, and something I try to make other people aware of too. I feel like I'm doing much, much better with it.

I think there's still more to discover about myself. I don't think I would say, "I'm done." Maybe when I'm on my deathbed I'll say that, but until then I'm not going to limit myself and say, "That's as far as I'm going to go with this."

While the challenges for gay and bisexual people in discovering their sexuality and integrating it into their identity are often greater than for straight people—largely because of homophobia in this society—the bottom line, regardless of a person's sexual orientation, is the question of whether or not he or she is sexually intelligent. The same principles that apply to straight people also apply to gays and bisexuals. Sexually intelligent people are able to integrate their sexuality into their identity in a meaningful way. As a result, they have more satisfying sexual lives and are less likely to suffer from sexual dysfunctions.

To achieve sexual intelligence, we believe, we must strive to be honest with ourselves about our genuine desires and examine the ways that negative messages—whether from our families, religious doctrine, or the culture around us—can inculcate shame and fear and breed silence that leaves us alone with those feelings. Paul's story is one that we've found particularly inspiring because it illustrates the point that, despite the negative, repressive attitudes about sex that still exist, despite the negative messages we may have picked up along the way, from our families, from organized religion, we don't have to give up our sexuality *or* our families, friends, or religious faith. We can be who we are sexually and there is the hope of finding acceptance—hope that only increases as our own sexual intelligence, and that of the people around us, increases.

What You Can Do

The first step in identifying implicit messages about sex you learned growing up in your family that may still influence your sex life is to try answering some of the questions we asked participants in the Sexual Intelligence Project:

- What did your parents tell you about sex?
- Did you ever have a meaningful conversation with them? What did your conversations cover? Reproductive biology? Diseases? Safe sex? Abstinence?
- What is the one thing that you think your parents could have done differently to prepare you for a healthy sexual life in adulthood?
- Did you have formal sex education in school? What was the content of the instruction? Anatomy and reproductive biology? Scary films about venereal disease?
- Did anyone talk to you, while you were growing up, about emotions and human relationships, as well as reproductive biology?
- Do you feel that what you learned from your parents or in school about sex was helpful to you when you first became sexually active? Did you learn anything that was not helpful?

Just as it can be important to identify implicit messages about sex that you learned early on in your family, it is important to look at the messages about sex that you may have absorbed from your religion. Asking yourself the following questions may help you to examine what you learned, either directly or implicitly, from your early religious training:

- Do you remember receiving any explicit messages about sex in religious education classes? What were those messages?
- Do you know what the doctrine of the religion you were raised in is in regard to sex? For example, is premarital sex considered a sin? Is divorce acceptable? Is sexual pleasure considered a natural and acceptable part of being human? Is it limited to certain types of relationships or goals: marriage, for example, or procreation?
- Did your parents communicate religious messages about sex to you when you were growing up? Did they consider certain types of sex or sex in certain circumstances (e.g., premarital sex, homosexuality) "a sin"?
- Do you currently feel that your sex life is at odds with the teachings of the religion you belong to or that you grew up in?
- Do you ever feel that you have to choose between your religion and the sexual life that feels true to you? Have you given up one or the other: stopped attending religious services, for example, or restricted your sex life to practices approved by your religion?

chapter five

The Magic Cure-All:

Portrayals of Sex in the Media

Twenty-three-year-old Becky, a tall, stunning woman with beautiful dark skin, watches popular television shows and films, nightly, that leave her feeling that a fulfilling sex life is hopelessly out of her reach. When we

> **The love you give to me**
> **will free me . . .**
> **It's Sexual Healing.**
> —Marvin Gaye,
> "Sexual Healing"

asked her one of the standard questions in our interview, "How does your sex life compare to those you see on TV and in the movies?" she laughed, bitterly, and told us:

> It doesn't—<u>at all</u>. For me, it's just not as enjoyable as it is for the people you see on TV.
>
> The love scenes that they show—that never happens to me. The way they portray people having sex—I've never had any of those feelings. Just the physical things they do seem unreal to me, the passion they have, or the way they are just so excited. Why doesn't that happen to me?

Popular culture communicates a set of myths about sexuality that are so ubiquitous we hardly even notice them. These myths become so ingrained in people's thinking—in the form of unexamined assumptions about the function of sex, how we should behave sexually, what is "normal" or "abnormal"—that we often respond automatically within the framework of these assumptions.

Television, the movie playing at the local cinema, fashion or teen magazines, and pornography all sell us messages about sex that, even though they directly contradict the repressive, fearful attitudes we examined in the last chapter, can have an equally disastrous effect on people's sex lives. These messages reach millions and can torpedo people's chances for sexual happiness. Often, they make people feel bad about themselves, their bodies, and their sex lives. They also encourage people to treat sex as a consumer product that can solve any problem. Media messages about sex alienate people from their genuine sexual desires just as much as old repressive attitudes toward sex do. To become more sexually intelligent we need to be able to spot media myths and break free of their influence so that we can hear and respect our own authentic sexual desires. So much happiness awaits us once we have learned to discard these myths.

Media Myths about Sex

Learning how to place media images of sexuality in proper perspective is perhaps one of the greatest overall challenges to sexual intelligence. All too often, popular culture offers a distorted view of sexuality that has a potent negative effect on the way people judge their bodies and appearance and on how they behave and treat each other sexually.

We look at the following four myths in detail in this chapter:

- Everyone else is getting more than you are.
- Your body isn't good enough.
- Sex—if you could get it—would solve all your problems.
- If necessary, get it by force.

These messages are not unconnected. The same media images that suggest that everyone else is getting more sex than you are offer an implicit answer to *why* your sexual life is so much less exciting than that of the characters you see on TV and in the movies: your body isn't good enough. Which is too bad, because—the media suggests—if only you could get it, sex would solve all your problems. Taken together, these media myths suggest that sex is the ultimate consumer product, the magic cure-all that can change your life but that, unfortunately, for many people remains just out of reach. In this chapter, we look at these negative messages, how they originate, and the consequences they have for people's sex lives.

Everyone Is Getting More Than You Are

If we took television or the movies as our guide, the conclusion would be inescapable: just about everyone is getting more sex—and better sex—than we are. One of the biggest and most harmful myths disseminated in the popular media is that everyone, everywhere, has a fantastic sex life. Prime-time television, movies, and music videos constantly suggest to us that life is something of an orgy, that for *everyone else*, particularly those who are young and physically attractive, sex is as basic and uncomplicated as breathing or eating, and that having a satisfying sex life requires nothing much beyond showing up. Though most of us see through this myth to some degree, still, when one gorgeous twenty-something character on television confides to a friend, "We had *great* sex last night," it's difficult not to wonder whether the sex we're having could be called "great."

Characters in television and films not only have sex constantly but, apparently, effortlessly every time. They spontaneously land in bed and the sex is incredible. The media's portrayal of sex makes it seem that sex is something magical—you've either got that instant connection or you don't; and if you do, the sex is great. A surprising number of people we surveyed in our research have bought into this media myth: 40 percent of them agreed with the statement that "A good sex life is not something you can work at—it either happens or it doesn't." While it may be true that people occasionally experience that instant, effortless over-the-top connection, for most people, most of the time, it doesn't work that way. Good sex requires getting used to a partner physically, learning to communicate about what you want or don't want, and developing trust and familiarity.

What's more, with rare exceptions, the sex portrayed in the media occurs in a world free of AIDS or other sexually transmitted diseases, and one devoid of emotional consequences. In a recent study by the Henry J. Kaiser Foundation that looked at 1,351 randomly selected prime-time TV shows, *not one* of the scenes showing sexual intercourse in these programs made any reference to the risk of sexually transmitted diseases or the need to practice safe sex.[35] Certainly not the episode of *Ally McBeal* that had her coupling in literally steamy ecstasy with a total stranger in a drive-through car wash.

While prime-time television, movies, and music videos show a world locked in constant embrace, even *more* sexual imagery—and more varied and extreme images—are available in pornographic magazines, videos, and websites. Such images are not consumed simply by the odd "sex fiend." Millions of Americans use pornography. A national survey done in 1987 found that 61 percent of Americans reported having seen an X-rated movie, either in a theater or on video.[36] In our own research, fully 84 percent of our participants had at one time in their lives watched an X-rated movie. Approximately 52 percent of the participants said they had seen an X-rated movie in the last year, 40 percent had looked at pornographic magazines, 31 percent had used the Internet to access pornography, and 19 percent had been to a strip club.

Pornography is a multibillion-dollar-a-year industry. The types of images available have expanded tremendously over the past decade. In particular, images of sexual violence against women (and men) in pornography have become increasingly frequent, and the Internet has advanced the availability of pornography far beyond what was once the case. The availability of pornographic images on the Internet has solved the problem that keeps some people from using pornography.

With all of the sexual content readily available, as close as the television set in the living room, the local video store, the cinema, or the computer on our desk, we are exposed to sexual images everywhere. Next to the glorious images on screen, whose sex life could withstand scrutiny? Even though many viewers may understand intellectually that the level of sexual activity they see in the media is exaggerated, it would be hard for the ordinary person not to compare his or her sex life with media images and conclude that everyone else is getting more—and better—sex.

The Influence of Sexual Content in the Media: Living Up to Impossible Standards

And that is exactly what many people conclude. Take Becky, for example, the woman we met at the beginning of the chapter who wonders why the incredible sex she sees on the screen doesn't happen to her. We went on to ask Becky whether she thought the sex scenes portrayed on television and in the movies were at all realistic; she told us, yes, she thought that level of passion and ease was realistic "for other people"—but not for her. When we asked her if she felt any disappointment with her own sex life after watching television, her voice dropped as she told us sadly, "Yeah."

Or consider another example: Harry, a twenty-five-year-old participant in our research who—ironically enough—met his girlfriend at the movie store renting a video. Harry told us he worries about his masculinity because, unlike the characters portrayed in those videos, he isn't necessarily ready for sex twenty-four hours a day, every day. He told us:

> **Sometimes my girlfriend will ask me to have sex with her, and I don't really feel like doing it. Sometimes, I'd rather just relax, and then I think: what is it? Most guys are supposed to want to have sex all the time. Then I think something's wrong with me.**

We've found that people compare their own sexual experiences with those on screen, often to their disappointment. In our research, 16 percent of the people we surveyed compared themselves with characters on television and in the movies and concluded that their own sex lives were disappointing or told us that they had only once or twice in their lives had sex that could equal on-screen passion.

Even if people don't consciously compare their sex lives to torrid encounters at the car wash or other media images of ecstatic sex, such images may subtly influence our estimation of what everyone else's sex life is like. When we asked people to compare their sex life with what they imagined "most people's" to be, 15 percent were quite sure their own sex lives were "not nearly as exciting" as most people's. As we mentioned in a previous chapter, 6 percent of the people we talked to said they were so embarrassed by how bad their sex life is that they try not to even think about the possibility of having satisfying sex!

Dolf Zillmann and Jennings Bryant, scholars at the University of Alabama, have done extensive research on the effects of pornography on the way people perceive their own sex lives. Zillmann and Bryant exposed a wide range of people, both men and women, to either one hour a week of nonviolent, X-rated videos, or one hour a week of situation comedies devoid of sexual content. They found that the people who watched the X-rated videos were significantly less satisfied with their sex lives. Interestingly, the effect of the videos was not to make people doubt their own sexual performance. Rather, in comparison to the sex scenes on video, they found their *partners* sadly lacking—both in their willingness to try new sexual activities, and in their overall sexual performance.[37]

Take Ron, for example, a twenty-year-old student from Jamaica, who has been frustrated and disillusioned by the fact that sexual images in pornography don't always translate well into real life. He told us, "I use pornography pretty much all the time—magazines, the Internet, looking for hard-core stuff. More than one guy with a girl. I see different things that I want to try." He and his cousin went on a quest to act out some of their favorite scenes, but it just wasn't the same:

> **We've had a lot of escapades, when me and him and two girls were together in the same room. Or me and him with three girls, two of them bisexual. In reality it didn't come off as well as in my fantasies. I imagined there would be more noise, that the women would be happier.**

People who are sexually intelligent have a perspective on the misinformation fed us by the media. They're aware that, for many people, simply having sex is a feat. We know, from national survey data, and from our own research, which found similar numbers, that at least one-half and as many as three-quarters of Americans are dissatisfied with their sex lives. Depending on whether we are talking about men or women, and which age group we look at, at least one-third and as many as over 40 percent of Americans suffer serious sexual dysfunctions that interfere with a satisfying sex life—or may prevent them from having a sex life at all. That conclusion comes from both Edward Laumann's national survey data and results from our own Sexual Intelligence Project.

Given the statistics, four out of ten people riding the bus with you every morning suffer some sexual dysfunction, whether lack of desire, premature ejaculation, or difficulty maintaining an erection, that seriously impairs their sex life. If you turned to the person sitting next to you and asked, "How's your sex life these days?" (we don't recommend this, by the way), three-quarters of the people on that bus, if they were honest, would have to say, "Not as satisfying as I'd like."

But that's not the reality the media shows. When people see ecstatic, effortless sex happening all around them in the media, it is bound to contribute to shame and confusion, compounding the pain that people experience when their sex lives fall short of the mythical ideal. It's natural that they would wonder, in the words of one of the people we interviewed: "Why isn't my sex life like that? What am I doing wrong?" As it turns out, the media has an answer for that, too.

Your Body Isn't Good Enough

One of the ways in which media myths create a disappointing gulf between on-screen images and sex in real life is by portraying impossible standards of physical attractiveness that many people will never reach—and don't need to, in order to have a fulfilling sex life. Television, films, videos, and pornography all suggest to viewers that constant, ecstatic sex is the norm, leading us to conclude that our own sex lives, by comparison, are pretty tame—even lacking. If we wonder why, the media implicitly suggests an answer: we're not young enough, thin enough, muscular enough, attractive enough.

The media bombards us with images that are supposed to mimic reality, but those images generally have more to do with peddling products and fantasies than reflecting the world we actually live in. In advertising, films, and television, women are always thin and young; men are lean, muscular sex machines. These images surround us and form a cultural matrix that is impossible to escape. Television, film, and Internet images are sent out across the globe every day, magazine covers shout at us from every newsstand and supermarket checkout, billboards are everywhere we look. The images that surround us define what we should look like if we expect to have sex at all.

Every woman who shopped in a grocery store, bought cough syrup at the pharmacy, stopped by a newsstand for the evening paper, or browsed through her local bookstore in April 2000, for example, would have been confronted by an array of fashion magazines. In that month, the cover of a single magazine whispered the insidious question "Still Single?" and implicitly offered a remedy for that condition, going on to ask "Is Your Hair Making You Look Fat? Old?" and promising to reveal "Our Little Secret: What Men Think About Your Orgasm Face— Guys Compare Notes."[38] It is no longer enough to be thin, physically attractive, and young to succeed sexually; you also have to have the right hair and the winning facial expression at the moment of orgasm.

And that was just one magazine cover. Multiply that by all the fashion magazines, all the teen magazines and men's and women's magazines, all the television programming, movies, and pornographic materials, and what you have is a parallel universe in which everyone looks a lot better than you do. Even the Internet now delivers the message: at this very moment, in the middle of typing this paragraph, an e-mail came in from Women.com asking: "Are you a '10'?"

Images of physical perfection can lead people to loathe the way they look and provoke them to go to great lengths to try to live up to an unrealistic standard of attractiveness. One way to begin to break free of all this propaganda is to take a look around you at the people you encounter in everyday life, few of whom have perfect bodies or faces but are attractive nonetheless.

The Consequences of Media Images of Physical Perfection

There is now a great deal of research showing that images of women in the media have destructive consequences for the way real women feel about themselves and see their bodies. For many women, seeing images all around them in the media and advertising of thin, beautiful, perfect females creates depression, anxiety, and self-consciousness about the way they look, including dissatisfaction with their bodies and concern about their weight.

In our own research, we heard, again and again, that same obsession with appearance and weight, a perpetual, painful self-consciousness among women that is fed by media images.

Consider just a few examples. Cara, a twenty-five-year-old woman, has had concerns about her appearance since she was a child:

It started early, maybe when I was nine or ten. I used to watch <u>Days of Our Lives</u>. Now, I watch <u>Friends</u> or one of those shows and it's always the same thing. Monica, from that show, she's really skinny, and I feel so bad, thinking, "They always get the guy"; "Guys are always looking at them, they never look at me."

Sometimes I think I'm overweight because of them [she is, in fact, quite thin]. They are so ideal: beautiful, skinny, funny, witty, perfect hair all the time. Every woman feels that way. I think men know that that's not real, or, at least, they accept that. There's a TV woman, and there's the woman by their side—only remotely related. That's why they like to look at the magazines.

Or listen to Patrice, who compares herself with the supermodels she sees in the media:

My brother will be watching <u>Baywatch</u> and I walk by and my heart sinks when I think about going to the beach. Why can't I look like that? If only I had a nice tight butt and tight abs and big boobs, I'd look so much better in a bathing suit. But I'm just not built like every supermodel in the world.

Then there is Eva, who is five feet, six inches tall and wears a size 6:

Sometimes, when I've watched a movie the night before, and I get up in the morning and look in the mirror, I feel bad and think, "These jeans are only a size 6."

Only a size 6? This is a woman of average height who feels bad about her body because she can't fit into a size 4 or a 2.

It's not just women, however, who are confronted with media pressure to live up to exaggerated standards of physical perfection. Though the media still sends men the message that money, power, and status can ensure them sexual success, there is a new emphasis on a standard of physical attractiveness for men that is unrealistic. Remember the Diet Coke commercial some years back that had a group of women office workers congregating at the window of their high-rise office building at the same time every morning to watch a gorgeous young construction worker strip off his shirt, displaying a flat stomach and impressive chest muscles, in preparation for his Coke break—Diet Coke, that is?

Research shows that impossible standards of attractiveness in the media lead to distorted body images and self-concept among men, just as they do among women. Jane Ogden and Kate Mundray at the University of London found that *both* men and women who viewed pictures of the ideal thin body felt more dissatisfied with their own bodies—that is, they felt fat and less attractive.[39] Kristen Harrison and Joanne Cantor, at the University of Wisconsin in Madison, found that exposure to images of thinness in the media was associated with a range of negative consequences for women, including a drive to be thinner, dissatisfaction with their bodies, ineffectiveness, and symptoms of eating disorders. Men who were exposed to the same media images were affected, too: they were more likely to endorse the ideal of thinness for themselves and also for women![40]

According to Harrison Pope at Harvard Medical School, because the media now frequently portray men as big hulklike figures, many men become obsessed about not being muscular enough. Some of these men become so insecure about their bodies that they spend hours at the gym each day, not leaving a lot of time to actually have a sexual relationship.[41]

Listen to the painful dilemma of one forty-eight-year-old man we talked to whose only source of information about sex growing up was pornography, with its exaggerated images of physical attractiveness for both women and men. After a long, unhappy marriage and a painful divorce, Pete has recently gotten involved with a woman he cares about. His girlfriend, Audrey, an attorney, is blind. Pete met her one evening when he helped her negotiate a busy intersection and found they lived two blocks from each other. Even though the relationship seems promising, Pete still has his doubts:

I always felt so unattractive as a kid, that I didn't think I was capable of getting a date. So I had a very limited sexual life as an adult. Now, you see most of these male actors on TV, they are big and so on. I'm not big; I'm fat. Then, too, you have to compare, you know, he's got a bigger penis, probably, than I do . . .

This relationship, it's kind of close to the first normal relationship I've had in my life, as far as the sexual end of it. So that's good. It's good. It's a little . . . it's a little confusing, because this lady is blind, and with my own sense of unattractiveness, I keep coming back to, "Yeah, but would she be spending time with me if she could see what I look like? And if she were able to go out and socialize freely—have her pick of guys?" And I don't know the answer to that. I honestly don't.

Somewhere in my mind I've come to the conclusion, maybe not, but this is where we are, and it's working, so stop asking questions. But, still, there's that small sense of doubt.

Working through the divorce, one of the things I said to myself was, "Okay, now, are you going to be attractive, are you going to find the normal relationship, is this going to be okay?" And I guess there is still that one little element where I say to myself, "But, would this actually be happening if she knew what you looked like?" I may never get to find out.

The irony is that Pete is, in fact, a very attractive man. Unrealistic images of physical perfection in the media create self-consciousness that can't help but have an inhibiting effect on people's sex lives or even discourage them from seeking a sex life altogether.

Our research participants, both men and women, made it clear that such media-induced self-consciousness about their bodies has a definite effect—and not a salutary one—on their sex lives. Several of the items on our Sexual Intelligence Test asked people if concerns about their appearance interfered with their sex life. Five percent of the people we asked said, flat out, "I'm not attractive enough to have a good sex life." Another 31 percent said they believe that their physical appearance affects their chances for a good sex life. When we asked specifically about weight, more than half of our respondents said they could be happier with their bodies in that regard. Five percent responded, "I'm too overweight to have a good sex life," and nearly one and a half percent said, "I'm not muscular enough to have a good sex life."

Media messages place us in an impossible bind by suggesting, not only that constant, ecstatic sex is the norm, but that constant sex could solve all your problems—assuming, that is, that you were thinner, younger, better looking. No one need be lonely, sad, lacking in self-esteem, confused, or depressed if only they were getting the kind of sex that TV and film characters take for granted. The media's obsession with sex sends a message that has the potential for creating an addictive approach to sexuality. Such an approach to sex not only fails to solve people's problems, it can create additional ones.

Sex—If You Could Get It—Would Solve All Your Problems

Remember the old Marvin Gaye song, "Sexual Healing," which promises that "whenever blue teardrops are falling," all you have to do to feel better is have sex? It's just one of the many examples of the myth widespread in American popular culture—expressed in music, films, and literature—that sex can cure any ill and heal any pain. Perhaps the starkest example we've seen is in the film *Prince of Tides*. The main character, played by Nick Nolte, is a man who is clearly in trouble.

Something has gone very wrong in his life, but he doesn't know what until his sister's psychiatrist (played by Barbra Streisand) asks him to come in for a consultation about his sister, who has made repeated suicide attempts. Nick Nolte uncovers a terrible secret from their past: both he and his sister were brutally raped as children. When Nick Nolte's character has this revelation, he is overcome with anguish and grief. The psychiatrist first holds him in her arms to comfort him and then sleeps with him. Presto—he's cured. The problem with this scenario is not simply that a short-lived affair—even with Barbra Streisand—is unlikely to heal thirty-year-old wounds; it's the fact that having sex with your psychiatrist is more likely to inflict additional damage than to cure anyone.

As unrealistic and even destructive as it is, the media myth of sex as a magic cure-all is powerfully attractive. The result is that many people use sex as a sort of drug, to deaden emotional pain and substitute for other things that are lacking in their lives—self-esteem, happiness, meaningful activities.

Consider Arielle, one of the participants in our study, who has internalized the media message that more sex is better, and that sex is a magic cure for any problem. Arielle first had sex at the age of thirteen, and since then, she has had twenty-three partners. She's currently nineteen.

Arielle learned about sex early, from pornography:

My parents really taught me nothing about sex—worse than nothing. School was more mechanics of bodily functions than of interpersonal relationships. By the time they got around to that, it was too late for me. I got most of my learning from my brother's hidden pornography. My brother was older, and he had a lot of pornography in his room. My sister discovered his big pornography stash, so she would bring them in our room, and we would read them. That was where I first learned—reading these things. I guess I realized my parents weren't going to be a source of information. Then as I got older, I would read all the typical girl magazines like <u>Cosmopolitan</u>.

Arielle had sex at the age of thirteen, with a cousin's friend, who was twenty-one at the time. Psychologists consider sex under the age of sixteen with someone at least five years older to be sexual abuse, because the older person has so much more power and influence—by virtue of the age difference—someone under sixteen can't really genuinely consent. Arielle, however, is blasé about the experience, even a little proud of it. She told us, "Yeah, there was quite a bit of age difference. Maybe it's a little cocky, but I think I was maybe a little mature for my age. I felt like I could handle it. Not physically, I didn't get my period until I was fourteen, but I felt like I could handle it."

Arielle answered yes to fifteen out of twenty-four items on a scale that asks questions such as "Do you often find yourself preoccupied with sexual thoughts?" and "Has sex been a way for you to escape your problems?"

She described frequently using sex to avoid confronting problems in relationships, and especially to avoid the painful process of ending a relationship. For example, with one boyfriend:

There were times he would want to have sex and I wouldn't. Especially toward the end, I lost my sexual desire for him. The relationship really should have been over, but I would have sex just because it would delay having to talk about our problems and delay having to deal with the fact that we were going to have to break up and it was going to cause a lot of pain. A lot of times I would have sex with him, not because I had any desire to—it was easier at the time instead of dealing with the problem.

But Arielle also has used sex as a way to escape the problems of daily life:

This summer I got back with my first boyfriend, from a way long time ago, Lars. He is into drugs, and he is such a burnout.

I was definitely doing it for stress release. I was working as a courier this summer, and I had to drive all the time, and I was in a terrible car accident, so driving sort of freaks me out. Driving was very stressful for me; it still is.

I would go to Lars's house at night, sleep over, and leave in the morning. It was kind of weird. I would go over there thinking, "Tonight, not going to do it, just not going to do it, just going to go home." It was a purely sexual relationship. I definitely used it. I felt it would make me happy and would take my stress away.

Despite the number of sexual partners Arielle has had, it doesn't seem as if she has experienced a great deal of sexual pleasure. She reports suffering from multiple sexual dysfunctions, including being unable to achieve orgasm and not finding sex pleasurable. Nor has sex solved her everyday problems—her nervousness about driving, for example. When we talked with Arielle about the number of partners she has had, at first her tone was jaunty, unconcerned: "I don't think I've had a promiscuous past at all," she told us, laughing. (We hadn't used the term "promiscuous.")

> I think that the last few years, I've chalked up a little bit of a list. I'm okay with it. I don't think there's anything wrong with being promiscuous if you're not hurting yourself or anyone else. I don't think I'm particularly promiscuous . . . I don't see it as a negative or a positive, either way.

As she continued to talk, though, her tone became doubtful, even uneasy.

> I mean, a lot of times you sit around with friends talking, and you say, "I've had sex with this number of people or that number of people," and they tell you how many guys they've slept with and it would seem a lot lower; but if I think back in my head, going through and counting them up, the number of them—twenty-three since I was thirteen—so that's actually, what, over seven years? But I don't think it's bad. So it's really not a lot, I don't think, personally, . . . [here her voice dropped] . . . when you look at it in that sense.
>
> Sure there's been a few times when you don't really know someone as well as you know the other people, but most of my relationships have at least been . . . maybe there were a few that I didn't really know the people that well. Obviously you want to look at it as something a little more special than just sleeping with someone. . . .

Arielle is by no means alone in using sex to avoid conflict or escape problems. When it comes to avoiding conflict in a relationship, 40 percent of our respondents told us they have had sex with a partner to avoid talking about a conflict that they feared might end the relationship. And it's not just relationship problems that people use sex to avoid. Thirty-one percent of the people we talked to initiate sex when they are feeling bad about something like work. Close to a quarter said they deliberately use sex to escape their problems—some even said if it weren't for sex their problems would overwhelm them.

Given powerful and pervasive media messages that sex can solve all one's problems, it is not surprising that people would grasp at that solution avidly. Sex is presented as the magic cure-all, and pervasive media messages encourage us to obtain it at any cost, in any way we can. Many media messages go so far as to suggest that it is all right to obtain sex by using physical force.

If Necessary, Get It by Force

One common myth propagated by pornography that concerns us greatly is that violence, including rape, is something that the victim in the end enjoys. There are economic reasons for this: it's hard to imagine that there would be much of a market for graphic rape scenes that show the actual terror and pain that victims experience. The problem is that such media messages suggest to men—perhaps young men, in particular—that a woman's protests against being forced aren't genuine.

Media images that blend sex with violence against women reinforce the notion that women really want to be raped, or enjoy it, despite their protests. These, along with the belief that no really means yes, constitute myths about rape held widely in this culture, even by men who have never raped a woman and probably will never do so. These "rape myths" can have a very destructive effect on sexual relationships between men and women.

Dozens and dozens of experiments have investigated the effects of violent pornography, and the overwhelming weight of the evidence is very clear: watching violent pornography increases men's acceptance of rape myths (beliefs that women are asking for it or that they want to be forced); increases men's willingness to commit rape; and actually produces changes in their arousal patterns, so that they become physiologically aroused by scenes of violence against women.[42]

Viewers also become habituated to the violence in pornography over time, choosing increasingly violent themes.[43] The experience of one man we interviewed illustrates these points. Scott, a lawyer in a prestigious firm, was well dressed, with a thick mustache that he stroked on occasion in the pauses during speaking.

My interest in pornography started in adolescence. My father had issues of _Playboy_ hidden in his desk drawers. My mother would throw them out periodically,

and I would retrieve them from the trash. I would masturbate while looking at the women—this was long before I had the courage to approach an actual girl. As I got older, <u>Playboy</u> seemed pretty tame. In college, I bought magazines with pictures showing people having intercourse. Other guys in the dorm had the same kinds of magazines, so it didn't seem wrong or unhealthy. Then, when I was in law school, that type of pornography wasn't as arousing as it had been; I began buying magazines and videos with more extreme themes, principally bondage scenes, with women tied up and helpless.

I got to the point where I masturbated looking at those magazines every day. Then I got my wife to do some of the things that I saw in the magazines. She did it for a while, but then she got tired of it and didn't want to have sex that way. I got angry when she refused, and it created some real problems in our relationship. Plus, I started to get nervous because I had moved on by then to pornography containing violent scenes—the women weren't just tied up now, they were being whipped, even cut.

In Scott's case, when the images he found arousing became increasingly violent, he began to question his use of pornography and the effect it was having on his relationship with his wife.

We were interested in whether mainstream films could have the same kind of negative effects on viewers as pornography does. So we designed an experiment in which half of the participants saw excerpts from two popular R-rated movies, *Showgirls* and *9½ Weeks*. The excerpts from these movies did not contain the explicit sexual content found in pornography, but they *did* portray women in a degrading and objectifying way. A second group of participants, the control group, watched cartoons instead of the movie clips.

After the viewing was over, we presented research participants, in the guise of a separate experiment altogether, with a fictional, but convincing-looking, magazine account of an acquaintance rape. Men who had seen the movie excerpts were more likely than those who watched cartoons to claim that the woman in the magazine account "enjoyed" being raped and had "gotten what she wanted."[44]

There is a surprising conclusion to be drawn from this experiment. It is not explicit sexual content per se that encourages belief in rape myths, but, rather, it is the way women are portrayed. This is a very important finding given the endless debate in America about what constitutes pornography. One of the key skills to developing sexual intelligence is to focus less on what people *do* sexually than on what their sexual behaviors *mean* to them. Similarly, it is more important for becoming sexually intelligent to focus not on how much skin the image on the screen reveals, but on the message it conveys. It is not so much what actors *do* on-screen but rather the attitudes the scene conveys about sex and about women that produce a negative effect on viewers.

It's clear from the study we just described that even mainstream films communicate messages that women want or provoke rape. An alarming percentage of the people we surveyed in our Sexual Intelligence Project believe these myths. Fifteen percent of them told us it's true that "although they may deny it, many women really want to be taken sexually by force."

The one best predictor of whether or not people believe in rape myths is their level of sexual intelligence, both their overall level of sexual intelligence and, particularly, their level of intelligence on the scientific knowledge component of sexual intelligence. The more sexually intelligent people are, the less likely they are to believe myths that support sexual violence against women such as "women really enjoy being forced" or "women who are raped get what they asked for." People's level of sexual intelligence predicts their belief in rape myths even more powerfully than social class, gender, or whether or not they have had therapy.

Media images can have a very destructive effect on people's sex lives. Often, they make us feel that we are not attractive enough to have sex and that we are not getting enough sex. These myths can create self-loathing and dissatisfaction, feelings manufactured by the media that we don't have to internalize. It takes courage to disregard these messages, to refuse to let them affect the way we feel about ourselves and rule our sex lives.

The happy irony is this: the great sex life that the media *seems* to promise us is, indeed, obtainable—once we learn to ignore media messages about *how* to obtain it. The fact is, when we stop being self-conscious about our bodies, we are apt to be more relaxed with our partners—and have better sex. When we stop expecting sex to solve old emotional problems, and work on those problems directly, sex becomes more genuinely enjoyable. When we realize that no one's sex life is perfect, we no longer have to feel shame about our own and can enjoy and better our sex lives and find the fulfillment we've always wanted.

How Sexually Intelligent Are You?

Try out your sexual intelligence by considering how you would handle this dilemma:

> Imagine that you are involved in a sexual relationship and your partner suggests watching a pornographic video—just for fun. You watch it, you both become aroused and have more passionate sex than you've had in some time. The next few times you get together with your partner, he or she has a new pornographic video and it seems as if your partner assumes that watching videos together is now a standard prelude to sex. You go along with it several times, but the more you think about it, the more uncomfortable you are—the videos seem artificial and not nearly as arousing as they were the first time, and you're a little uncomfortable with some of the scenes portrayed.

Questions to Consider

1. What if watching videos became something that your partner wanted to do on a regular basis? How would you feel? How would you respond?
2. Would you talk to your partner? How would you bring up the subject?
3. Does having pornographic images in your head help you to connect emotionally with your partner during lovemaking?
4. What do you consider the difference between pornography and erotica? What distinguishes them? Do they have different effects on you?
5. How do you feel about your sex life, your partner, and yourself after watching pornography? After watching mainstream films or television?

Bear in mind these principles:

Scientific Knowledge

Pornography, mainstream films, television, and advertising present exaggerated standards of physical attractiveness that few people can live up to.

People become habituated to sexual content and violence over time, so that they need more extreme images to feel the same arousal.

It's not just pornography, but also mainstream films, that communicate rape myths—the beliefs that women want to be raped or enjoy it.

In real life, sexual violence has terribly negative consequences for people's sex lives.

Awareness of the Secret Sexual Self

Media myths about sex are a powerful source of misinformation that can obscure our genuine sexual desires and condition our secret sexual selves in ways that can be destructive.

When it comes to the effect of the media on our sex lives, it's not so much *what* images the media presents as the *meaning* those images convey that matters—for example, that women want or deserve to be degraded, or that men and women both need to look a certain way in order to have a satisfying sex life.

Connecting with Others

Frequent exposure to pornography can make our real sex lives pale in comparison to what we see on the screen and can make us dissatisfied with our real-life partners.

Very few people have the effortless sex lives portrayed in the media.

PART III

The

Shaping

Of

Individual

Desires:

Becoming Acquainted with

the Secret Sexual

Self

chapter six

The First Time

Do you remember the first time you had sex? Most people carry the memory for the rest of their lives. For some, that first act of sexual intercourse lives on in memory as a magical, wonderful experience, an entrée into a world of sensual and emotional pleasure.

> **The man who has once carried a cat by the tail learns a lesson he can learn in no other way.**[45]
> —Mark Twain

Take Claire, an idealistic twenty-year-old who took a year off before college to participate in the AmeriCorps volunteer program. She quickly developed a crush on a young man she met in the program. As it happened, when the year was over, they ended up attending the same college and became close friends. He was the first person she had sex with, at nineteen:

Todd was the kind of guy I really liked, with a sense of humor, who wasn't so serious, who was clean-cut, and so on. He had approached me not long after I first met him, and I was, "Nah, I'm not really interested." I didn't want to date anybody at the time. But I knew him for about three years before I started dating him, and over that time, he was just fun to be with, and I was actually half in love with him at the time.

We started dating, and it was very romantic, and I liked the way he kissed me. I said, "Okay, this is a guy I could see being in a relationship with." And I made up my mind at that point if he asked me to have sex with him—when the time was right—I would.

And it just so happened, on the third date, he had invited me to his house to watch videos. At that time, I decided it was the perfect time. We were in his room and there were candles . . . we had been watching a movie . . . we had lain down. He fell asleep for a bit while we were watching the movie. When the movie ended, I knew he had woken up, but I pretended to be asleep because I wasn't sure what to do, how to make the move. And then he said, "I know you're awake," and, still, I pretended to be asleep. It was very fun, we laughed, he started kissing me, and then he pulled away, saying, "I shouldn't do this." I kind of flirted with him and said, "Why not?" He came back and we had sex. He actually performed oral sex on me. And at that point I was really excited; I had an orgasm.

Claire's first experience was a positive one largely because she approached it in a sexually intelligent way. She waited to have sex until she was ready, and she had sex with a man that she had come to know and trust. When they did have sex, for Claire, it was a conscious decision rather than something that just happened to her.

Some people's first experience of intercourse is very positive while for others it can be painful, confusing, or destructive. Other people we questioned—nearly 30 percent of our sample—said it was a negative experience.

Trent, for example, a forty-year-old executive in a computer software company, had an older cousin who decided to take charge of Trent's sex life:

One day we were sitting around, just hanging out. It was summer; there wasn't much to do. My cousin Fred was older. I think he was twenty or twenty-one at the time. One thing led to another, and he asked me if I had ever had sex. He couldn't believe that I was still a virgin at the age of fifteen. "We can fix that," he said.

"When are your parents not going to be home?" he asked. Both my mom and dad worked all day, so he said, "Fine, tomorrow, just stay at home around noon time." I stayed there, and right at noon, I saw a car pull up, and this woman showed up at the door, and she said, "Fred sent me." We sat on the couch and chatted for a couple of minutes, and then she asked if she could use the bathroom. She came out and she was buck naked. "Where's the bedroom?" she asked. We went back there, I stripped, and we had sex. It probably took ten minutes, but it seemed like it lasted hours. She was, I figured, thirty to thirty-five, and she was really experienced. She held the reins and I just did what she told me to do.

Previously, with other girls, sexually I felt like I was going a step at a time, and here it felt like I was jumping off a building.

Trent let himself be swayed by pressure from a peer and had a first experience that was anything but positive.

Positive or negative, the echoes of that first time continue to reverberate through people's lives, producing significant consequences in adulthood. People's level of sexual intelligence in adulthood is linked to both the age at which they first had intercourse and their *reasons* for having sex for the first time. People who have sex at an earlier age are less sexually intelligent as adults—particularly when it comes to self-awareness or knowledge of their secret sexual self. Sexual intercourse at an early age is related to both sexual dysfunction and sexual addiction in adulthood. Finally, people whose first sexual experience "just happened"—who had sex for the first time without consciously deciding to do so, are less sexually intelligent in adulthood than those who had sex the first time in a more deliberate way.

When People Have Sex Early

If the main components of sexual intelligence include being able to see through media myths and replacing them with scientific knowledge about sexuality; knowing our secret sexual self; and having the skills to talk to sexual partners about our needs, desires, and fears, it would be a miracle if any of us entered into sex the first time with any great degree of sexual intelligence. Sexual intelligence develops with time, experience, and self-awareness.

It's not surprising that young teens have sex for the first time without having the knowledge of human sexuality or of themselves that would help them to choose an appropriate person, place, and time for their first sexual experience. Given all of the negative effects of messages about sex that people absorb from their families, the church, and the media, plus the immaturity that comes with youth, it shouldn't be surprising that many people's first sexual experiences are a haphazard affair, entered into without talking to their partner ahead of time, without consideration of whether or not sex is right for them at that time, and without much accurate knowledge of human sexuality. We might also expect that people's first sexual experiences would in many cases be motivated by all the wrong reasons: rebellion against overly strict parents, looking for love from a sexual partner when parents are unavailable, succumbing to peer pressure to prove one's masculinity or femininity, and so forth. Many people enter into their first sexual experience with little guidance and end up learning painful lessons in the same way you learn not to pick up a cat by the tail. When one's first sexual experience is negative—as it was for nearly 30 percent of our respondents—it can create painful associations and leave behind a legacy of problems that contribute to sexual dysfunctions in later relationships. When that first experience, on the other hand, is positive, it does so much to set us on the right road to sexual intelligence.

People bring to their first sexual experience whatever understanding about sexuality they've acquired, based on what parents have told them, what they've learned from sex education in school or church, and the messages they've absorbed from the media. We've seen that the sum total of that input is often anything but positive. Given what we know about those influences, we could expect the following:

Because the majority of parents never talk to their kids about sex, teenagers or young adults having sex for the first time are unlikely to talk about it or negotiate it beforehand with their partner.

Worse, people whose parents were strict and punitive—in general, as well as about sex and dating in particular—are apt to feel guilty about sex and, at the same time, to rebel against their parents by becoming promiscuous.

People whose parents paid little attention to them are also more likely to have sex with multiple partners.

Fear about sex inculcated by organized religion creates ambivalence: the very people who disapprove of premarital sex may engage in it without taking precautions against pregnancy or sexually transmitted diseases.

Because media messages create the belief that sex can cure any problem, that everyone is doing it, and that there are no consequences of unprotected sex, young people are likely to see it as the solution to all of their problems.

What's more, the majority of people in our study had sex in their teens, at an age before most people develop a great deal of social experience or maturity. In our study, both men and women first had sex, on average, between sixteen and seventeen. That figure is very similar to the average age of first intercourse reported by other researchers.[46] But in our study there was also a wide range of ages represented: some people had sex as early as eleven. Over a quarter of our sample first had intercourse when they were fifteen or younger.[47]

All of this adds up to a poor preparation for making an informed decision about when to have sex, with whom, and under what circumstances. It's not surprising that many of the people we talked to had painful first sexual experiences.

Debra is one example. She graduated from a large midwestern university five years ago and now works as an account executive at a public relations firm. She appeared for her interview in a teal blue suit that matched her brilliant blue eyes. On the questionnaire that she filled out before we interviewed her, she reported a number of sexual dysfunctions, including lack of sexual desire, being unable to reach orgasm, experiencing pain during intercourse, and not finding sex pleasurable. She also reported that she is not currently involved in a sexual relationship. Debra told us:

I was brought up in a small town in Indiana and I was pretty innocent—I didn't know anything, even about the mechanics of sex. When I was eleven or twelve, Melissa Robichaux told us all these stories in art class, when the teacher wasn't around—Melissa was supposedly this great authority on sex. And I remember we would all gather around, and she would tell us—you know—men have this thing, and, when you're making out with them, it gets really big, and then they push it into you. And how intercourse is really painful. She told us about this one woman who supposedly ended up being taken to the hospital in an ambulance on her wedding night, because she was so ripped apart and had lost quarts of blood.

Later, of course, I realized that Melissa was just making this stuff up. But, by then, I had been through a situation I was not emotionally prepared to deal with and that just reinforced those fears that Melissa planted.

When I was fourteen, I dated this boy who was several years older. . . . My parents liked him, he was polite and all that. But they didn't know what he was really like. We would go parking, and he was just very pushy. We never talked about sex. It was one of those weird dynamics when you're young, it's almost like if you don't talk about it then it's . . . you're not really doing it.

Anyway, he was rough. He would kiss me really hard, so that sometimes the inside of my lips would bleed. And then one night, when we went out parking, he penetrated me digitally—he ended up being very forceful and afterwards I bled. It was really painful—just a bad experience. And I remember I got home and got in the shower, and I was crying; it was a horrible experience. I never told my mom, I could never tell her because I was too embarrassed.

I've had a hard time getting over that.

In college, I had this wonderful boyfriend, but I couldn't tell him how afraid I was of being hurt, physically, and I put off having intercourse. He didn't mind. He said he loved me and wanted to be with me whether we had intercourse or not. I felt so guilty for not having sex with him that I finally tried it. He wasn't rough at all, but I was so paralyzed with fear that I tensed up, and it really hurt. I broke up with him because I just couldn't face the thought of having to go through that pain night after night, and I couldn't tell him—he thought it was because I wasn't attracted to him in that way.

Since then, I've tended to avoid sex.

Although Debra has many opportunities to date, she dates a man once or twice and then finds some reason to reject him. The horror stories she heard in junior high hold her tightly in their grip, and she is fearful of repeating the pain of her first sexual encounter.

It didn't have to be that way for Debra and needn't be that way for our children. They have the chance, through us, to develop the intelligence to choose the circumstances of their first sexual experience wisely, and to avoid the pain that Debra experienced.

Why the Rush?

Why is it that some teens have sex at an age when they simply aren't equipped, emotionally or socially, to handle it? There are a number of reasons. Among our participants, people whose parents had divorced were more likely to have had sex at an early age. We have seen before that lack of attention from parents can lead teens to look for love elsewhere, and that may explain this finding. When parents divorce, they are likely to have less time and emotional resources for their kids. While in some families both parents remain involved with the children, in many others there is suddenly only one parent available—and he or she may be hard-pressed to earn a living, run a household, and still have the energy to monitor teens' activities and provide them with attention and nurturing.

Other researchers also have found that when parents are unavailable or unable to be supportive, teens are likely to have sex at an earlier age. For example, Betty Chewning and Richard Van Koningsveld at the University of Wisconsin-Madison Sonderegger Research Center recently reported a study of 3,419 students in grades 9 through 11 in the Wisconsin school system. They surveyed students from ten schools in 1982, 1984, and 1986. They found that the degree of support kids got from their parents was a significant predictor of age at first intercourse: the more parental support, the older teens were when they first had sex.[48]

There are other factors, too, that influence age at first intercourse. Contrary to some parents' fears that sex education in the schools will encourage teens to experiment and become sexually active at an earlier age, Professor Robin Sawyer at the University of Maryland at College Park and her associate Nancy Gray Smith found just the opposite. They administered a questionnaire to 371 undergraduates and discovered that undergraduates who had had sex education at the middle school or high school level, before they became sexually active, were more likely to have waited to have sex. Among the undergraduates they studied, only 29 percent said that they had had any sort of meaningful conversation with their parents about sex.[49] A number of studies have also found that having sex at any early age is associated with behaviors such as using drugs, breaking rules, and with perceiving oneself as more mature than one's peers—a combination of behaviors and attitudes that seems to represent rebellion against parental strictures.[50]

All these factors—lack of accurate knowledge about human sexuality, unavailable parents, or parents who are excessively restrictive and controlling—increase the chance that teens will have sex early—often for the wrong reasons. Those reasons are tremendously important for their later sexual intelligence.

Reasons for First Intercourse

Our first sexual encounter, in fact, predicts a great deal about our future sexual intelligence. For example, if we have sex for the first time out of negative motives such as peer pressure, an attempt to make someone love us, a need to prove to ourselves that we are desirable or attractive, or a fear of saying no, sexual arousal may become linked to these motives and we may repeat the same negative experiences over and over, heading further away from the path of sexual intelligence and fulfilling sex lives.

On the other hand, if that first sexual encounter is motivated by a desire to show affection or to experience both physical pleasure and emotional closeness with another person, we are off to a sexually intelligent start.

In our study the reason why people decided to have sex the first time predicted how positive the experience was, as well as how the person scored on sexual intelligence in adulthood.

By far the most common reason, given by over half of our sample, for having intercourse the first time was "it just happened," in circumstances ranging from the harrowing to the comical. Consider just a few examples:

- "I was drunk at a party with some girl I had just met. We did it on a tennis court at like 1 A.M. It was not a positive experience."

- "I had sex at fourteen with my first boyfriend. It was just sort of an experiment. I was too young, and I had no feelings for him. I wish I hadn't done it."

- "I was drunk. It was under the boardwalk, with someone I hardly knew. I was twelve at the time."

- "The first time was in my girlfriend's bedroom; I skipped school—she went home sick. One thing led to another. Someone came home; I hid and then was caught half naked in her closet."

These were the people who were most likely to have a negative first experience, compared, for example, with people who had sex the first time to show love or become closer to their partner. On average, they scored only a C on the Sexual Intelligence Test.

The second most common reason people gave for having sex for the first time was to become closer to a partner, a natural step in a process of evolving intimacy. Such was the case for Richard, a thirty-four-year-old stockbroker we talked to who had sex at eighteen with the woman he later married:

> It was with my first serious girlfriend—now my wife—after we had been dating for about six months. We were on a ski trip in Vermont. I always hoped it would happen, but I hadn't wanted to put pressure on her. I felt so strongly about her that it was wonderful. We were both so happy.

The majority of people who first had sex to become closer to their partner (89.6 percent) had a positive experience, as did those whose reason was to show love (83.3 percent). They were the ones who were most sexually intelligent later in life, scoring, on average, a B on the Sexual Intelligence Test.

Then there were people like Rhonda, who were pressured by a partner to have sex for the first time:

> My boyfriend at sixteen pressured me into sex. We were alone kissing and everything else. He was getting very excited and started to go further but I said that I wasn't ready, but he kept begging me until finally I gave in. I definitely needed to wait a couple of years and wished I had.

Not surprisingly, the vast majority (85 percent) of those who were pressured by their partner said it was a negative experience. They, like the people for whom sex "just happened," scored low on sexual intelligence in adulthood—on average a C. The only people who scored lower were those who waited to have sex on their wedding night: their average score was a D.

Differences Between Men's and Women's Experiences

We found some clear differences between women and men when it comes to the circumstances in which they first had intercourse. Equal numbers of men and women said they first had sex on their wedding night, but, other than that, there were differences between the sexes in every other category. Only women reported being raped their first time, and only one man said that his first experience of intercourse was raping a woman. Aside from those differences, we found that four times as many women as men reported being pressured by their partner. Three and a half times as many women as men were pressured by their peer group. Some felt that it was a stigma to be a virgin:

> **I was from a small midwestern town. When I went east to college, the first thing I did was have sex—my virginity was a social stigma I couldn't wait to get rid of.**

Others believed that everyone else was having sex and followed suit to fit in or to live up to others' expectations:

> **I never thought why. . . . All the other kids in school were having sex. I guess I did it to fit in.**

Three times as many women as men said their first experience was negative, reflecting no doubt the fact that so many more women than men had intercourse the first time as a result of pressure from peers or a partner, or were raped. Almost one and a half times as many women as men had sex for the first time to become closer to their partner. More than two and a half times as many women as men had sex the first time to show love.

The single most common response given by men (68 percent of them) for having sex the first time was "it just happened." Interestingly, even though women gave far more varied reasons for having first intercourse than did men, "it just happened" was also the most common response for women (42 percent), closely followed by "to become closer to a partner" (31 percent). Why the differences between men and women? There are a number of possible explanations. It may be simply that men reflect less on the reasons for their behavior. It is also true, though, that the men in our study, on average, scored lower on sexual intelligence than did the women.

How to Move Beyond a Negative First Experience

For so many of our participants, overcoming a negative first sexual experience has taken time and courage and entailed a good deal of pain. For too many people, learning about sex and especially about their own sexuality is a matter of trial and painful error—needlessly so. One of our hopes is that the current generation will be able to spare their children that process by helping them to develop the skills of sexual intelligence before they take that first plunge.

We learned a great deal about how to move beyond a painful sexual initiation from one of our research participants, Gwen, who used her sexual intelligence to turn a bad first encounter into something she could learn from, and thus went on to have a fulfilling sex life.

Gwen is a twenty-three-year-old college student, a petite blond with a sweet smile and a tentative, shy demeanor, who received no information about sex from her parents, and never had a sex education course in school. Gwen first had sex at the age of seventeen.

Gwen had two reasons for having intercourse for the first time. She was angry at her parents and looking for a way to rebel against them, plus she had gotten the message from the first boy she dated that sex is the only way to hold on to a man. On the questionnaire she filled out, Gwen told us she had intercourse for the first time because "I was confused, scared and rebelling, and someone who I trusted and thought cared about me told me to have sex with him to show I cared." In other words, Gwen was pressured, emotionally, into having sex the first time. She continued:

My family are strong Christians, and they definitely believe in not having sex before marriage. They basically didn't talk about sex.

I've lived all over the country—Kansas, Hawaii, California, Virginia, and Massachusetts—and gone to three high schools, all in different states. I can't really say one place that I grew up. My dad got transferred a lot. First he was in sales, then he owned his own business, then he sold that business, and now we're here.

The longest place we ever stayed put was California. There was this boy there I had worked with for a year, and he asked me to the junior prom. We saw each other for three months until he decided he didn't want to see me anymore, because I was a virgin, because I wouldn't sleep with him. I really cared about him a lot: it was devastating.

Then, just at that point, my parents made us move again, to Virginia. Not long after we got there, I met Clay. He got me on the rebound. This was right before I turned seventeen. He was good-looking and popular, and he started saying that he really liked me and wanted to go out. I wasn't completely sure I wanted to. But, on the other hand, it was tempting, especially to a girl who was lonely and didn't know anybody in a brand-new place.

He told me he loved me and all this kind of stuff, and he said that if I really loved him, I would prove it, and I would have sex with him. I didn't really like him; I didn't have strong feelings toward him. But I felt so horrible that my previous boyfriend broke up with me, basically because we hadn't slept together. I think that's why I jumped into it with Clay—I didn't want to have the same experience; I didn't want to lose somebody else because I was a virgin. I think that's why I had sex with him.

Then, too, I was still real mad at my parents about leaving California, because I had been there the longest of any place, and I had all my friends there, and I was a junior in high school, and I hadn't wanted to leave. And then I thought, "Oh, I can get back at my parents for taking me away, by doing something"—which of course, you think that way at the time, and I look back and I think, "How stupid can you be?"

After two or three dates, I did have sex with Clay and regretted it from the moment that it happened.

Gwen had anything but a glorious experience her first time, with Clay.

The first time, I didn't feel anything. I was just numb. I thought, if this is what it's like, what's the big deal? If anything, I just felt empty.

From that point, sex was forced or done under the threat of harm. From then on it was like an obligation, and he would say, "You better, or this will happen." He turned out to be an extremely violent person. He threatened to hurt my sister, and he threatened to hurt me. He did on a couple of occasions—he hit me two or three times. And he would yell and scream. He'd tell me, "You better say you love me or I'm going to do something." So, I just went along with whatever he wanted. No one realized what was going on. I never said anything. I was too afraid to.

That was basically the situation; it lasted for six months. The only reason I got out was because my family moved again. I still wonder if I ever would have gotten out of it if they hadn't.

I was terrified. I was absolutely terrified. I never sat down and talked with anybody. I wish I had; I just didn't want to say anything because I thought it was my fault. And I thought I had done something, because why would someone pretend that they care about you, and then hurt you? That doesn't make sense. I must have said something, I must have done something.

That negative first experience had lasting consequences for Gwen's sex life on many levels. For one thing, she became wary about every new man she met:

I felt like something was taken from me that I could never get back—physical virginity, but it was more than that. It was emotional. That's the hardest part. I've always been a person who wants to see the good in people. And I think that what he took from me was more than just my virginity—it was that innocence. Clay took that away from me, because after that happened, I started looking at guys, any guys that were interested in me, and thinking, "Okay, he's a nice person, but so was Clay at first." And that's always been a kind of lingering doubt.

When she did meet someone kind and trustworthy, Gwen found herself, to her horror, reversing roles. What she had learned from her first experience with Clay was "if you really love me, prove it," and this time she was the one who pressured her partner into having sex. As she describes it:

When I moved here, I met a guy, and the thought immediately in my head was, "The only way to make him happy, the only way to make me happy is to have sex." And, of course, I was wrong, but I hadn't had any relationships since that terrible experience with Clay. And I hadn't been around any guys, I hadn't had any guy friends.

This guy was really, really sweet. I thought that having sex with him was the only thing to do, and that was a mistake. I feel bad for having done that to him—pushed myself on him, making him feel like he had to, you know, have sex. We had been together a month at most, and I didn't really love him. That's the part that made my stomach turn a little, and I realized, "I am going down the wrong path here."

Gwen demonstrated a great deal of sexual intelligence—specifically, insight into her own sexuality—by coming to see how her first sexual experience had left her with the destructive belief that pressuring someone into sex was a way of becoming closer. She quickly recognized the connection between her own behavior and the destructive effect of the relationship with Clay.

Recently, Gwen met and became involved with someone new:

We've been dating for nearly a year, and we were friends before we even started dating. We didn't have sex for several months into the relationship, and he was the first person I actually sat down and told what happened to me. I was scared to death to do it; I thought, "Well, he's gone." And that wasn't what happened. He's extremely supportive of me—never initiated any physical sort of situation until he knew I was comfortable. On top of that, we're like really close friends.

I don't know whether this relationship will go on forever, or whether it will end, but I feel really lucky that I've had this opportunity to meet someone who doesn't hate me for what happened, and is able to look past that.

My sex life now, well, I've enjoyed every time, and not just the physical act of having sex, I've enjoyed the before, I've enjoyed the after—everything has felt good. And it's been like a really good experience, which I never expected. Now, I know what the big fuss is about.

Gwen's recent positive experience, her increasing sexual satisfaction with her current partner, has come about, in part, because she is now able to talk to him about what happened to her as an adolescent and to talk about what she wants and prefers sexually. She told us about the impact that participating in our study had on her relationship, and what has happened now that she has begun talking to her partner about their sex life:

I don't feel like I've ever had the opportunity to think about what I liked and didn't like in bed. Now, with my current partner I've felt, "Well, this is a position I never was comfortable with, but he likes it." I've never really said anything to him. But I don't know that I completely like this.

Since filling out your questionnaire, it's made me think about a lot of things, and I have actually sat down and talked with him about it. And after I talked about it, I felt fine. I told him that sometimes, for a split second, I'm not sure I'm completely comfortable with certain things. And he said, "Well, we don't have to do that anymore. That's fine. I just never knew." And that was lack of communication on my part. And now, since I've talked to him and explained to him, even if we are in that position, I'm fine, I'm comfortable with it. And I don't have that little bit of doubt anymore. So, it was good that I actually sat down and talked with him, thanks to having been in this study.

It's scary to say something—you know, you wonder if he'll just leave, go find some other woman who likes to do that in bed, whatever it is. It's extreme, but that went through my head on several occasions. And I was wrong; he didn't leave.

It's started to feel even better now that I've started thinking, "Well, I'd like it a little different." Then it still feels good for him and it feels good for me, too.

And that's taken a long time. I'm still discovering new things that I don't and do like. I didn't realize that there is actually . . . we always learned there is just one way to do things. You don't realize that that's not true.

For Gwen, as for so many of the people we've talked to, their first sexual experience was entered into with little knowledge, and a lot of misinformation: it was more like stumbling into a train wreck than making an informed decision. For many, many people, that first experience left behind scars that have been slow to heal and false beliefs that still hamper their sexual lives. Gwen is one of the fortunate ones who learned from her experience and has become more sexually intelligent as she has examined her past, become aware of the painful and destructive influence it had on her sexuality, and gathered the courage to talk to her current partner about her genuine preferences and desires.

The combination of being exposed to accurate information about sexuality, being able to look at our past, and taking the courageous step of talking to others—particularly our partners—can be all that it takes to turn our sex lives around, to overcome the aftermath of a bad first experience with sex and go on to a richer, freer sex life.

What You Can Do

Take out your sexual history and read it over. Do you see any pattern in the sexual experiences you have had, beginning with your first experience? Have you had sex frequently in order to cement a relationship in which you felt insecure? Because you began to worry that the other person would think you didn't like him or her or weren't "normal"? Because you were lonely or wanted confirmation of your desirability? Try to identify any lessons—positive or negative—you learned inadvertently from your first sexual experience.

chapter seven

All of the Reasons People Have Sex

People have sex for all sorts of reasons. The key to sexual intelligence is knowing when our reasons for having sex are healthy and authentic, and when they are destructive to ourselves or our partners. Sex can be a pleasurable recreational activity, an expression of emotional closeness with a partner, or a rite of passage—an experience that contributes to defining one's identity as an adult. An important part of sexual intelligence is understanding the reasons people have sex as well as the reasons why you want sex on any one occasion. Is it physical desire? The desire to be close to your partner? A need to be comforted? To boost your self-esteem? To prove your prowess? Some combination of these? On many occasions, we engage in sex for more than one reason. How do we sort out the various factors motivating us? The answer is to look within at the secret sexual self. By examining our own sexuality, including our past hurts, disappointments, desires, and needs as well as our psychological patterns and tendencies, we can tell why

> Sexual activity, we see, is not merely a bald propagative act, nor, when propagation is put aside, is it merely the relief of distended vessels. It . . . is the function by which all the finer activities of the organism, physical and psychic, may be developed and satisfied.
>
> —Havelock Ellis,
> On Life and Sex:
> Essays of Love and Virtue

> Sometimes sex is just sex. You don't want to date him. Or have an intimate relationship. It's just, "Oh, my God, I want him."
>
> —Anonymous research participant

we are having sex on a given occasion and whether or not that sexual activity is healthy for us. Later in this chapter, we provide questions you can ask yourself to explore what your reasons are for having sex on any particular occasion, whether those reasons reflect your genuine desires or whether they are contrary to them.

Sex and a One-Track Mind

When it comes to sex, many people have a one-track mind. They focus on only one or two reasons for having sex, such as procreation. They also have a tendency to make moralistic judgments about "right" and "wrong" reasons for having sex.

Sexually intelligent people have sex for more than one reason, whereas the less sexually intelligent tend to focus on only one reason. Even people who are aware, intellectually, that there are many reasons for having sex may be influenced at times by more restrictive and one-dimensional attitudes. For example, in our study, over a quarter of the participants agreed to some extent with the statement that sex should be restricted to marriage and bearing children. Equating sex solely with marriage leaves out all the other reasons why people have sex—in general and on any one occasion—and can translate into sexually unintelligent behavior. To focus solely on any one reason for having sex and fail to recognize the many reasons why people have sex can lead to disaster.

Take Tim, for example, a fifty-one-year-old Irish Catholic we interviewed, who was brought up in the 1950s to believe that sex meant marriage, that the only permissible reason for having sex was to express love between husband and wife and to have children. Though he was a bright young man who'd seen quite a bit of the world, the messages his parents had taught him about sex and the messages he had absorbed from the church obscured his better judgment. Twenty-eight years ago, as a young man just back from a tour in Vietnam, Tim met and had sex with Betsy, a girl he had already come to dislike. Having done so, Tim believed he had no choice but to marry her, despite the fact that it was absolutely clear to him a relationship between them wouldn't work. Tim was motivated to have sex with Betsy for a number of reasons—physical desire, loneliness, the need to try and find his way back into some sort of normalcy after Vietnam. This is how Tim describes it:

When I came back from Vietnam, I had an awful transition. And during this period in my life, I was hanging out with a girl I met playing in a local rock group. We were buddies, that was all. One night where we happened to be in the same place at the same time, she basically just started stimulating my groin with her foot through my pants. While I was emotionally repelled by that point in our relationship, I responded physically to the stimulation and we ended up having sex. At that point, I basically wanted every woman I saw.

Before it became a sexual relationship, I was really tired of it as a social relationship. I had seen how emotionally dependent she was and it just got more and more. I had an $800 tax refund, and she had to borrow it. I was going away to Florida for a week with my brother, and she had to have my car. I said, "No," and she used it anyway. It was getting like, "This is not a good thing." Believe me, at the point where we had sex, I was completely done with any thoughts about that relationship being workable. At the same time, with my upbringing, after I'd had sex with her, I thought the only thing I could do was marry her. As it turned out, I had four great kids and an awful marriage. The fact that I fathered four kids means I scored a hit 50 percent of the times we actually had sex. I think we had sex about ten times in twenty-five years. It was just terrible.

Because Tim had never been given the psychological tools to separate out in his own mind all the different reasons that motivated him to have sex with Betsy and to question some of the assumptions about sex he had been taught in his youth, he spent twenty-five years in a troubled, sexually unfulfilling marriage.

As an example of a person who took a more sexually intelligent route toward solving the same kind of personal decision, consider Diana, a twenty-six-year-old who has just become involved with a fellow surgical resident. While the sex is great, she is also aware that great sex alone is not necessarily a reason to get married:

I could see us someday moving in together, getting married, having a house and kids. I can see how it's healthy to have these fantasies, but is it healthy to act on these fantasies at this point in my life? I'm already twenty-six, so it's natural I'm going to date someone and think, "Is this someone I could potentially marry?"

But it's not like I'm going to get married anytime in the near future—I have a long road ahead of me before I finish my surgical training. Right now, I would like to relax into a situation where I have a boyfriend, where we go out on dates sometimes, where I see him once or twice a week. Not like, "Oh, I want to take you to meet my mother" already.

In our Sexual Intelligence Project, we were astonished by the number of people who, when it comes to sex, have a one-track mind. When asked why they currently have sex, 57 percent of our sample gave just one reason, 38 percent mentioned two reasons, and only 5 percent listed three or more reasons. The more reasons a person gave for having sex, the higher his or her score on the Sexual Intelligence Test. Those who gave one reason scored, on average, a C, whereas people who listed two reasons scored a B, and those who gave three or more reasons, a B+. The number of reasons people gave for having sex predicted not only their overall score on sexual intelligence, but, specifically, the degree of insight they had into their secret sexual self.

It's not just the *number* of reasons people give for having sex that predicts their sexual intelligence, however, it's *what those reasons are.* The most sexually intelligent people have sex both to express closeness or intimacy in a relationship *and* for physical pleasure. They scored, on average, a B+ on the Sexual Intelligence Test. They are able not only to combine closeness and physical pleasure, but also to tell the difference between when they are feeling pure physical desire and when they are motivated to be close to their partner. In contrast, people who have sex solely to be close to their partner scored lower on sexual intelligence—a C+—while those who have sex for pleasure alone scored lower still—a C.

Then there were people whose reason for having sex seemed to be to assuage their own or their partner's compulsive craving for emotional comfort. For example, one young male student told us:

I have this intense physical craving bordering on real thrill-seeking. Very probably I use sex to try to fill some emotional need for closeness or "love," whatever that is, that I can't seem to figure out how to get otherwise.

Another one of our participants, a woman, told us she has sex as a way of "getting the only kind of love from another person that I know how." A sixty-year-old man told us he has sex "because I am very lonely."

People who said they have sex to assuage cravings of their own or those of their partner scored very low on sexual intelligence, on average a C– or D, lower than any group of participants except those who abstain from sex altogether—they typically scored in the F range.

Reasons People Have Sex

Based on the responses of our research participants, we distinguish three broad types of sex. What we call *visceral sex*—in a word, lust—is driven primarily by physical urges, while *relational sex* is substantially motivated by emotions stemming from an intimate relationship, and *substitute sex* involves using physical pleasure and sometimes the illusion of closeness to compensate for unmet emotional needs. In our view, love has nothing to do with visceral sex. Visceral sex is intense, carnal, and immediate and occurs because of a biological response to an external sexual stimulus. Relational sex, by contrast, involves love, intimacy, and other emotional experiences that are unique to humans. All relational sex, of course, involves biological factors and so should also be seen as visceral. But often people may engage in sex that is far more visceral than relational: in other words, they're having sex primarily to satisfy physical urges and not because their relationship has yielded a strong emotional bond.

Sometimes people have sex for very straightforward reasons: they are aroused or they are attracted to another person. But there are also occasions when people's motives are less clear. Sometimes people expect sex to fulfill needs that are not primarily sexual. Sexual arousal and satisfaction are powerfully rewarding experiences physiologically, and they can be substituted for other needs, such as the need to be loved and appreciated; the need to be emotionally close to someone; the need for self-esteem or needs for reassurance and security when one is frightened or lonely. This is what we call substitute sex.

While sex *may* sometimes fulfill emotional needs, it can also sometimes serve as a quick pleasure fix that bypasses long-standing emotional needs. In that case, the needs for attention, affection, security, self-esteem, power, and so forth, are still there and still unsatisfied. When people have sex expecting it to solve or heal emotional problems, it may do just the opposite. For example, casual sex with multiple partners motivated by a need to feel lovable may actually *worsen* low self-esteem. Part of what it means to be sexually intelligent is to become aware of the reasons why we want sex in general and on specific occasions, so that we can make decisions that are likely to increase our self-esteem rather than erode it. Our reasons become clear only when we are in touch with our secret sexual self. If we can't differentiate among the three types of sex and remain unclear about our reasons for having sex, chances are we are going to suffer in our sexual relationships.

Visceral Sex: The Biology of Lust

Recent research on neurochemicals associated with sexual arousal provides evidence that chemical reactions in the brain play an important role in motivating people to have sex. Or, as one of our research participants put it:

Sometimes sex is just sex. You don't want to date him. Or have an intimate relationship. It's just, "Oh, my God, I want him." That's it. You have sex with him and never see him again.

Sexual behavior is primarily associated with the activity of cells in the hypothalamus, a few square centimeters of brain tissue that play a crucial, complex role in regulating instinctual behaviors such as eating and sex. Located in a part of the brain found among many lower organisms, the hypothalamus evolved much earlier than the brain structures that control higher thought processes in humans, such as memory and language. Among other things, the hypothalamus regulates levels of testosterone, the hormone involved in sexual arousal and performance. Sexual activity among many animal species, and humans as well, is related to hormone levels, in humans chiefly levels of testosterone. Recent research shows that testosterone levels are clearly related to sexual desire and performance, in both men and women.[51] Still, there isn't a perfect correlation between hormone levels and sexual behavior in humans—unlike animals.

More recently, researchers have discovered another class of chemicals that are related to sexual behavior: neurotransmitters, which are messengers that carry information from one cell to another in the brain. One of the first people to study the neurochemistry of love and sex was psychiatrist Michael Liebowitz. He was treating several patients who had a pattern of falling in love and choosing an unsuitable partner too quickly, then ending up rejected, and repeating the pattern. He speculated that these patients might have inadequate levels of a brain chemical similar in structure to amphetamines, phenylethylamine (or PEA), a chemical associated with feelings of euphoria or elation. Chronically low levels of this naturally occurring chemical may have led his patients to seek the "high" associated with romantic and sexual encounters. To treat his patients, Liebowitz administered MAO inhibitors, a class of antidepressant drugs that interfere with the breakdown of PEA as well as various neurotransmitters such as dopamine, serotonin, and norepinephrine. Following treatment, several of his patients stopped "looking for love in all the wrong places," either being comfortable without a partner or choosing a partner more carefully. They appeared not to need the amphetamine-like high associated with falling in love.[52] More recent research has suggested that, in addition to PEA, two hormones, oxytocin and vasopressin, also play a significant role in sex and love. Studies have shown that, in both men and women, blood levels of vasopressin and oxytocin rise during sexual arousal and ejaculation.[53]

The secretion of oxytocin appears to play a role in developing emotional bonds that encourage monogamy. Larry Young and his colleagues at the Emory University Department of Psychiatry and Behavioral Sciences found that oxytocin, among other neurochemicals, is responsible for the regulation of various social behaviors related to monogamy, including pair bonding and the paternal care of young.[54]

Helen Fisher, Research Associate in the Department of Anthropology at Rutgers University and author of the 1994 book *The Anatomy of Love*, argues that these neurochemical systems in the human brain evolved to encourage attraction and mating of individuals, a way of keeping individuals together long enough to bear and raise a child through infancy.[55]

Sometimes people's motivation for having sex is purely visceral, based on a biological response to some stimulus—the pressure of a partner's touch, an image in a magazine or video, the memory of a previous sexual encounter or a fantasized future one. Even in an intimate or committed relationship, there are times when we are motivated to have sex out of pure lust. Take Kyle, for instance, a tall handsome twenty-year-old student we interviewed, with intense dark eyes. He is currently engaged to his girlfriend, and clearly loves her very much, but he told us about a rocky period when they were first dating:

> While I was dating her, I cared about Danielle. I loved her. After we had sex the first time, I just thought about sex, sex, sex. When are we going to do it, I would ask her. Sex became an obsession. That's what I felt like for a while, about six months. I was possessed by my sex drive. At that age, that's all you think about. After we'd had sex, it just got stronger. I had access to it, so I wanted it. I had strong feelings for her, but I still had this strong urge to have sex.
>
> One day, after we had sex, she was very quiet, and then she said, "You are just using me. Every time you call me you just want to have sex." I said, "We hang out." I was lying. We did go out to places but we ended up having sex. She was thinking of going out and not having sex one night. Me, I thought, let's have dinner, maybe a movie, and then sex. That was my expectation.
>
> We had a couple of arguments, but we were able to talk about it and work it out.

Because Kyle's primary motivation for having sex with his girlfriend during those six months was pretty much pure lust, that doesn't mean he didn't care for her. Kyle and Danielle were lucky and sexually intelligent in that they were able to talk about their reasons for wanting sex, and Kyle was able to reassure Danielle that he wasn't using her simply to satisfy physiological urges. Kyle is sexually intelligent in another way, too: he is able to distinguish among the different reasons that motivate him to have sex on different occasions. He was self-aware enough to know that while he cared for Danielle, during the period of their early courtship his motivation for sex was heavily influenced by biological urges. We have found that people who are able to discern whether they are experiencing a purely physical urge for sex, primarily a desire for emotional closeness, or a combination of the two are more sexually intelligent than those who can't tell the difference.

Relational Sex: Is True Love Just Chemistry?

Great sex isn't simply a matter of the secretion of neurochemicals such as PEA, dopamine, and oxytocin. An important component of sexual intelligence is understanding that neurochemical reactions in the brain represent the sum total of *all* of the inputs the brain is processing at any one moment.[56] The hypothalamus has connections with many brain structures: some bring information about sensory stimulation from various parts of the body to the brain, some bring information about what we are thinking and feeling while we are having sex. Our response in a sexual encounter—whether we are aroused, whether we enjoy the encounter—depends on both sets of information. Thoughts and feelings, as well as physical sensations, influence the quality of a sexual encounter. That is the basis of relational sex. Part of the pleasure we experience with a partner in a truly intimate relationship comes from the emotions, memories, and thoughts that accompany sex.

The Myth of Romantic Love: Sex versus Intimacy

The problem is that there is a long history in Western culture of confusing lust with intimacy, a myth that assures us that great sexual passion is a sign that love and intimacy will reliably follow. They don't.

We have found that many people suffer intensely over the distinction between visceral sex and relational sex, or lust versus love and intimacy. For example, 25 percent of the people we surveyed said that having great sex either "means that a couple is meant to be together" or "practically guarantees being in love." The tendency to confuse sex with love and intimacy can lead to repeated disappointments in relationships, to confusion and depression, even to compulsive sexual acting out. The physical sensations of visceral sex are so powerful, it can seem as if such pleasure must be the sign of love. The reality can be very discouraging, when, despite numerous attempts with the same or several partners, sex more reliably delivers physical gratification rather than creating intimacy. That was the experience of one of our research participants, Rolando, a thirty-one-year-old professional photographer:

With my last girlfriend, we had been dating for eleven months before we had sex. That ended the relationship. It was sex to bring us closer; of course, that didn't work. We dated for about a month afterwards. It just didn't work out. It became more evident. That was the only thing we didn't have together, and when we had it together, it wasn't even solving anything. The race to lose the virginity. I think I was pushing it—I think I wanted sex more than she did. But after we had sex, she wanted sex more than I did, for some reason. I felt I wasn't into it. I tried to use sex as a tool to build myself back into the relationship.

People often feel let down when, after experiencing satisfying sex with a partner, one or both discover that there is little or no intimate emotional or intellectual connection to support a relationship that has ongoing depth and meaning. Therefore, it is crucial to be in touch with our secret sexual self so that we don't make the mistake of deceiving ourselves into believing love is involved in a sexual relationship when it isn't.

Couples who have sexual intercourse very early in their relationship typically do so prior to the development of emotional intimacy.[57] This pattern is associated with a more "addictive" style of relationship, characterized by obsessive passion, possessiveness, and a high degree of mental and physical arousal.[58] In a 1994 study, psychologists Eileen Nelson, Debra Hill-Barlow, and James Benedict of James Madison University in Harrisonburg, Virginia, rated the intimacy level of forty couples' relationships. They contrasted couples whose relationships were mature as opposed to addictive. Though addictive couples expressed obsessive longing for each other, they reported less satisfaction in their relationships—including less sexual satisfaction. Put simply, the intensity of their sexual activities did not translate into more emotional closeness. Nor, in the long run, did it deliver genuine sexual satisfaction.[59]

To be sexually intelligent, it's important to distinguish lust from intimacy, which involves sharing central and meaningful aspects of our emotional and intellectual life with another person. Before entering into a sexual encounter, ideally we should be fully aware of what we really want—visceral sex or an intimate connection or both. When we are clear about what we honestly want, it's easier to be at peace with our decisions, and to avoid hurting ourselves or our partners.

Substitute Sex

Sex itself is healthy and life-sustaining, but when we try to use sex to assuage or mask underlying psychological problems or unmet emotional needs, we can damage ourselves and in the process set up a vicious cycle that actually moves us farther away from finding a genuinely fulfilling sex life. The physical pleasure that sex provides is powerfully reinforcing and can substitute for human needs that are not otherwise being satisfied in people's lives.

The substitution works like this: people who are suffering emotional pain—from low self-esteem, loneliness, or a need for love that has gone unmet for years—find that the intense physical pleasure of sex temporarily alleviates the bad feelings. Having sex becomes a learned strategy to avoid pain: whenever the bad feelings arise again, whenever the person feels the onset of loneliness, self-hatred, or neediness, he or she seeks out the momentary pleasure of sex. The problem is that the emotional needs thus bypassed are not addressed; we don't do the psychological work and make real changes in our lives that would lead to better self-esteem, feelings of confidence, security, and so forth.

Perhaps everyone has occasionally used sex to find temporary human comfort, as Gina did:

> **My friend, Susie, died this semester. I met an old friend of mine at the funeral, and the night of the funeral we had sex. We were both very emotional and all this stuff was going on. Susie was one of my best friends and she was someone Mack had dated on and off for ten years, and we both needed to be comforted. We were fooling around and he wanted to have sex and I was like, "I don't want to have sex." I knew we were not in the right frame of mind for this, but we kept on fooling around, and it led to sex.**

While some people, like Gina, may occasionally use sex to cope with the pain of a temporary situation, others do so repetitively, often multiplying painful experiences as they go from one partner to another, trying to assuage the pain of long-standing emotional needs. The irony is that they often end up increasing their pain rather than healing it. Being aware of the circumstances when we want sex and the feelings and thoughts we have at the time—for example, craving sex when we're feeling undesirable or when we're faced with some failure or challenge to our self-esteem—is the skill that will help us know when sex is serving as a temporary salve for old hurts and disappointments.

Pamela's story illustrates the point. She is just one of many people we encountered in our research who have used sex to try to avoid the pain of sorrow, loneliness, self-hatred, or other long-standing problems. She is one of the few we've talked to who came, in time, to understand her pattern of substituting sexual relationships for the need to feel accepted—a need that had gone unmet for a very long time.

The Woman Who Couldn't Say No

Pamela is an attractive twenty-nine-year-old who nonetheless appeared for her interview with her blond hair hanging down lank and dirty, her fingernails bitten, wearing a faded cotton skirt with a jersey in a shade that didn't quite match. She has had a number of relationships, most of them unhappy. She suffers from numerous sexual dysfunctions, including the inability to reach orgasm, pain during intercourse, and lack of arousal. Pamela grew up in California, where her father was stationed in the military. She is the youngest of six children. Like most of the people we spoke to, Pamela was told virtually nothing about sex growing up. Pamela had her first sexual experience at the age of sixteen; like so many others she reports that it "just happened":

> It was the night of my junior prom. It was with my boyfriend, who I loved very much. I knew I wanted him to be my first, but we did not plan it—it just happened that night.

Pamela was devastated when, not long after they had sex, her boyfriend broke up with her and started seeing another girl. But they continued to attend the same school, and, despite what had happened, the next year Pamela agreed to go to the senior prom with him—with the understanding that they were going as friends. Knowing that he had left her for another girl after they had had sex once, and knowing that he didn't care about her in the same way that she cared for him, Pamela had sex with him a second time, the night of the senior prom. It turns out there is a whole list of men Pamela vowed she was not going to sleep with, and did anyway. As she put it:

I've met new guys and said, "I'm not going to kiss them. I'm going to take it really slow." But I would let things happen. I have gone places and decided with certain people, "I'm not going to do it this time." And I'm like, "Why did I do that? I keep doing this." I'm not going to, but I get put in a situation, and I do it anyway.

I would even ditch my girlfriends to have sex a lot of the time, even though my friends cared about me, and treated me well. Somehow I felt closer to the guys than to my female friends. Or, my boyfriends gave me something that they couldn't. I don't know.

I never could control myself, never. It worries me. I think I get too wrapped up in guys. I have trouble saying "No."

Pamela recently had an experience that was so painful it led her to examine her secret sexual self:

This was last year. I basically used sex to try to get an ex-boyfriend back. We had broken up, but we were still friends. I had gone over to his place, and we went in his room to have sex, and he invited his roommate in. I ended up having sex with both of them.

I didn't want to do it—I didn't want to have sex with his friend, I thought it was disgusting—but I thought if maybe I did what he wanted he would like me again, and that completely backfired. That was the worst night of my life. I learned a lot from that experience.

Pamela's attempts to get the love or affirmation that she felt she needed—and needed specifically from men—by having sex with them were unsuccessful over and over again. Rather than getting her emotional needs met in this way, Pamela simply accumulated more and more self-hatred. That is the problem with substitute sex; it really doesn't compensate for emotional needs; it just staves them off temporarily, and then leaves us feeling even worse about ourselves.

Pamela's difficulty saying no, she discovered, stemmed from what she had learned early on, implicitly, from her mother's attitudes and behavior: that other people come first, that making other people happy is the only way to get one's own needs for caring and love met. Pamela believed that it was desperately important to make men happy and that sex was the way to do it, whether a particular sexual encounter was something she wanted or not.

> My mother specifically taught us how to get other people to like us, not how to like ourselves. My mom doesn't have very good self-esteem. She forever has tried to make people feel comfortable; she puts others before herself. She's ingrained that in us in a way. Most of my life I've been trying to make other people happy.
>
> I can see it. My history with men. I wish she had given me more self-confidence to be able to say "No," and mean it. I feel like if I had the strength of character and belief in myself, that sex is not something I had to do and endure, I would have so many times said, "No! I mean it!" And not been afraid that the guy wouldn't like me.

Pamela's mother had a reason for her low self-esteem and desperate attempts to please: her husband was unfaithful to her. He was on the road forty-eight weeks out of fifty-two and rarely available either to his wife or to Pamela and her sister.

> My dad cheated on my mom. It hurt my mom badly. It hurt all of us. It's hard because I'm still figuring it all out, figuring out that my mom didn't give us any esteem at all. She just wants to please people. She just wants to please my dad. Now she's overweight and depressed. I wanted her to divorce him. It's not like I don't love my mom, she's so nice, so caring, but, by putting up with that situation—by not taking action—I feel like she set a terrible example for me. I don't feel I have the strength of character to say "No," so in that respect I think she really failed us. And so did my father. What an awful example that he made to me and my sister.

After the night when Pamela took part in a threesome and was repulsed by it, she had the intelligence to step back and look at her pattern of sexual behavior, her inability to say no. When Pamela examined her sexuality, she discovered that her reason for having sex on many occasions had less to do with satisfying *her* genuine sexual desires and preferences and more to do with pleasing others. Pamela was able to trace that need to please men to her upbringing, some of the unfortunate lessons she had picked up in her family. With that insight into the way her past had influenced her sexuality, Pamela was able to change her behavior, and has good reason now to hope for a more satisfying sex life.

Pamela is not alone in using sex to assuage emotional pain. In our survey, 31 percent of the participants admitted that they have sometimes initiated sex when they were feeling bad about themselves or upset about something in their lives, such as work. What's more, 22 percent said they sometimes deliberately used sex to escape their problems. Nor is Pamela alone in using sex to please another person or to avoid a conflict: 40 percent of the people we surveyed said that they have had sex with their partner instead of talking when there was a conflict that they were afraid might end the relationship. In fact, 7 percent thought sex was a good way to deal with the conflict. Twenty-two percent said they have had sex when they didn't want to, just to please their partner, either often or occasionally.

Substituting sex for unmet emotional needs isn't sexually intelligent because it doesn't meet those needs. In fact, it often exacerbates them, leaving us feeling worse about ourselves. What's more, the sex itself is often not very satisfying physically, or not for long. Among the questions we asked our research participants was how they typically feel after having sex. Eleven percent said they feel depressed. Seventeen percent said they feel either depressed or numb. That is a sign that, once the brief, intense physical pleasure is over, the underlying emotional pain returns, either openly, as depression, or masked as numbness. Consider the man who told us:

If I wasn't feeling good about myself, if some girl wasn't liking me, I'd just go find another girl and think, "Well, at least she wants me, even if the other girl doesn't." It would work, I guess—for a little while.

There may be a biological basis for the substitution of sexual pleasure for unsatisfied emotional needs. As mentioned earlier, in one research study, Dr. Michael Liebowitz speculated that some people repeatedly seek out sexual encounters because they suffer from inadequate brain levels of PEA, a chemical associated with the "high" of falling in love. Even among those who are not suffering from an insufficiency of PEA, however, there is a possible biological basis for substitute sex. Sex is accompanied by the release in the brain of powerful chemicals called endorphins. These are naturally occurring substances similar in chemical structure to opiates such as heroin or morphine. Endorphins are called "endogenous analgesics" because they occur naturally in the brain and they are powerful painkillers; like opiates, they not only kill pain, but also produce powerful feelings of well-being and euphoria. (Endorphins are responsible for the so-called runner's high, for example.) In recent research, Candace B. Pert, a scientist at the National Institute for Mental Health and author of the book *Molecules of Emotion*, showed that, in animals, levels of endorphins increase by 200 percent during copulation.[60] It may be that when people seek out a quick sexual fix to alleviate emotional distress, they are repeatedly dosing themselves with endorphins, those powerful endogenous painkillers, in somewhat the way heroin addicts dose themselves to avoid emotional pain.

A major step to becoming sexually intelligent requires understanding your reasons for having sex. Examining your secret sexual self is the best way to elucidate your reasons for having sex in general and on a particular occasion. Looking within in this way helps us to avoid, for example, fooling ourselves into believing that we are having sex for pleasure when, in truth, we are trying to win over a partner or assuage feelings of insecurity. The secret sexual self can guide us to discover whether we are having sex with someone because of the love we feel for the person or whether, in truth, we are using the person for physical satisfaction, to prove our own prowess, or to avoid loneliness.

An important part of sexual intelligence is being able to communicate with your sexual partner honestly about what you desire from a sexual encounter and your reasons for wanting sex. When we tell a partner, "I love you," either as a way of convincing him or her to have sex or because we fool ourselves into believing that physical passion is always a sign of love, we mislead others as well as ourselves.

The greatest challenge people face in coming to understand their sexuality and achieve a fulfilling sex life is to recognize when they are substituting sex for unmet psychological needs. Some of the questions you can ask yourself to avoid falling into the trap of substitute sex include:

What emotions do I feel immediately before I initiate a sexual encounter—whether it's intercourse or merely flirting?

Are there situations in which I crave sex, such as when things are going wrong at work, when my partner and I have had a fight, when I'm lonely or feeling bad about myself?

How do I feel after having sex in these situations? Contented? Fulfilled? Depressed? Numb?

Is there a pattern in my sexual behavior that is self-destructive, or destructive to others?

Is there some common characteristic among the sexual partners I've had?

Part of sexual intelligence is being honest with yourself about all the reasons you are having sex as well as being honest with the person with whom you are having sex. The people who are the most sexually intelligent and have the most satisfying sexual lives appreciate sex for more than one reason and are able to combine the physical pleasure of sheer lust with an intimate connection with their partner.

How Sexually Intelligent Are You?

Try out your sexual intelligence skills on this dilemma:

> Your partner complains that the minute you wake up in the morning, you roll over and want sex; he or she would sometimes prefer to have sex at other times—after a romantic night out perhaps, or on a lazy Sunday afternoon.

Questions to Consider

1. What would you say?
2. How would you attempt to work this out with your partner?
3. Would you assume that the two of you are sexually incompatible?
4. Do you believe that morning sex is always purely visceral?
5. Would you approach this problem assuming that one of you is wrong or "abnormal"?
6. Do you take it for granted that men and women prefer sex at different times of the day or in different contexts?
7. Do you think that men are more likely than women to have purely visceral sex?
8. How could you tell the difference between sex that is motivated by your physical urges, sex that expresses intimacy, and sex that is compensating for some of your unmet emotional or social needs?

In thinking about this situation, bear in mind the following principles.

Scientific Knowledge

People have sex for a host of different reasons.

On any one occasion, people may desire sex for a combination of reasons—for example, physical desire plus the desire to be close to a partner.

Sex is associated with the release of endorphins, powerful endogenous "painkillers" that also produce feelings of well-being and euphoria.

The pleasurable sensations of sex, and the release of endorphins, may serve as a sort of "drug" that can temporarily assuage the pain of long-standing emotional problems—without solving those problems.

Awareness of the Secret Sexual Self

Try to identify whether your morning arousal feels like a purely visceral response after a good night's sleep or whether it might be related to emotional needs.

Look back at your mood just before you initiate sex in the morning.

Compare it to how you feel after morning sex.

Consider the possibility that your morning desire is linked to an emotional issue such as dread about facing the workplace or uneasiness about being away from your partner for the day.

Connecting with Others

Find out the meaning of morning sex for you and for your partner. Do you see it as an impersonal physical act; a loving, reassuring start to the day; a way to connect?

Avoid simply putting a conflict down to gender differences or personality differences and assuming it's unfixable.

Before initiating sex with a new partner, try to be honest with yourself and your partner about your reasons. Are you motivated by love? Lust? Loneliness?

chapter eight

What's Normal?

Thirty-five-year-old Ellen loved Steve, her husband of eight years, but something was missing in their sex life:

> Love is a canvas furnished by nature and embroidered by imagination.
> —Voltaire,
> *Dictionnaire Philosophique*

It's not that I don't love Steve—I do. But the sex had gotten to be pretty routine. There was no passion, none of that rush you get when you are in that first period when you're still new to each other. It seemed like we were just going through the motions, and I wanted something more.

Ellen blushed bright red and cast her eyes down, but went on, determined, with her story:

I had always had a lot of fantasies where I'm with more than one man: there's my husband, Steve, but also another guy—or even two others. It's this recurring theme in my fantasies. Thinking about this had always been so exciting, but I had never told my husband—I was afraid he'd think it was sick. I thought it was sick. If I was ever faced with this prospect in reality, I would run so quick in the other direction, because I definitely believe in monogamy. I've always been afraid that those intrusive fantasies could destroy what I have.

Ellen never suspected that her fantasies are fairly common, until her *husband* brought up the subject:

It was one of those strange things. One night, after we'd had sex, Steve turned to me and asked me, "Do you ever think about doing it with more than one man?" "Of course not," I said, totally shocked, and, at the same time, knowing that I was lying to him. Then I asked him, "What about you? Would you do it with two women?" I held my breath, thinking, this is where he tells me he's tired of our marriage and he wants out. "Sure," he said. "Three would be better—if they were all you."

"What are you talking about?" I asked him. "You know," he said, "three pairs of your hands touching me, your mouth on me in three different places at once," he said, with a big grin. I thought he was just giving me a diplomatic answer and I pressed him, even though I wasn't so sure I wanted to know. "What about some woman other than me?" I asked him. He got really serious and thought about it for a minute. Finally, he said, "It can be exciting to think about, but in reality it wouldn't appeal to me."

That conversation was such a relief. Now it's amazing to me that we had both had the same fantasies and never said a word to each other. I realized that the fantasies I was so terrified would destroy my marriage weren't sick and weren't so dangerous. I don't know how to explain it exactly, but just having that conversation changed our sex life. There's more passion now and we've spontaneously started trying different things—it's like we're new to each other all over again. Maybe it's just that we were honest with each other, and that somehow freed us up to be more spontaneous and break out of the routine.

If one of the hallmarks of sexual intelligence is knowing our secret sexual self, another key component is knowing how to talk openly about it with our partners. There is a great feeling of self-confidence, safety, and authenticity that comes from being able to be honest about our sexuality. Ellen felt bad about herself, felt indifferent about sex with her husband, even feared that her fantasies would destroy her marriage—until she and Steve finally talked about what they were thinking. Once they were honest with each other, Ellen was able to accept her own sexuality, as well as her husband's, without shame and take advantage of their fantasies to have a more fulfilling sex life together. Of course, feeling comfortable sharing our most personal sexual feelings and fantasies—talking about what excites us sexually— is difficult if we fear, as Ellen did, that our sexuality is somehow deviant or not "normal." Trying to conform to what we perceive as "normal" leads many people, like Ellen, to feel shame and thus to hide or deny their true passions. Our research on sexual intelligence suggests two important truths. First, people don't find sexual fulfillment by trying to conform to so-called normal sexual feelings or behaviors. Second, to find sexual fulfillment, people must first explore and understand their genuine sexual desires and fantasies and be able to be *honest* about them with themselves and their sexual partners.

There is tremendous variation in the sexual behaviors with which people feel comfortable. A surprisingly wide range of behaviors and fantasies are fairly common. How, then, do we begin to say what is normal sexually, and what is not? "Normality" is a relative concept dictated in part by culture, which varies from one historical period to another. We need to take into account the entire context of a sexual activity and the meaning it has for the people involved. The critical question for many people who are having consensual sex with another adult is not so much whether their sexual behavior is normal, but whether it honors what they, and their sexual partner, genuinely desire and are comfortable with. Is it a pleasurable activity that they enjoy together? Does it increase the intimacy between them or function as a way of avoiding intimacy? Is it substitute sex—providing a quick pleasure fix that bypasses underlying emotional needs?[61]

Knowing and Accepting Our Partner's Sexuality

Being sexually intelligent means having the courage to explore our own sexuality and also being open to our partner's. That's not always easy. In our research, one of the questions we asked on the Sexual Intelligence Test was: "If your partner wanted to engage in a sexual behavior that you find uncomfortable, what would you do?" A minority, 9 percent, said they would go ahead and engage in the behavior anyway; 65 percent said they would try to understand why the behavior appealed to their partner, but made them uncomfortable; and 27 percent said they would tell their partner the behavior is off limits—period—or even consider ending the relationship. There was a very significant difference in sexual intelligence between the people who said they would try to understand their discomfort with the behavior—on average they scored a C—and those who said either that they would engage in the behavior despite their discomfort or that they would declare it off limits or even end the relationship, all of whom earned a D on the overall sexual intelligence score. These findings suggest that people who seek to understand their own and their partners' sexual selves—in this case, by exploring their discomfort with a novel sexual behavior—are more sexually intelligent than people who either automatically submit to, or automatically reject, their partners' sexual desires or fantasies. Specifically, the sexually intelligent approach is to focus less on a particular sexual behavior itself, but rather on the feelings, beliefs, and associations the behavior holds for each of us and for our partners. Sexual happiness doesn't depend so much on what we *do* in bed, as what it *means* to us.

Of course, it takes courage to examine our own desires and fantasies and the emotions they stir up. The payoff, however, is greater self-understanding and a richer, more satisfying sex life. Exploring our fantasies, in particular, can enhance arousal, allowing us to enjoy the richness of our sexual imagination without acting self-destructively or making sexual decisions that we may later regret. As we'll see, paying attention to sexual fantasies can also help us to identify subterranean emotional needs that have nothing to do with sex—needs for self-confidence, power, love, nurturing, security, and so forth.

A good way to begin to counter the shame many people feel about their sexuality is to look at how diverse human sexual behavior actually is. Once one realizes that there is little that people *haven't* tried or thought about trying, it helps to reduce our own feelings of shame.

The Vast Landscape of Human Desire: What Americans Do (and Fantasize About Doing) in Bed

People vary widely in their sexual desires and behaviors—whether it comes to the number of sexual partners they have, what they enjoy doing in bed, with whom they do it, or what they fantasize about. Among our pool of generally young research participants (the average age was twenty-three years old), 60 percent told us they were currently in a sexual relationship. On average, our participants reported having sex three times a week, but there was great individual variation: half of the sample reported having sex twice a week, 20 percent said they have sex five times a week or more, and some people reported having sex up to fifteen times a week.

Some people said they skip oral sex, but the vast majority of our participants—70 percent—do engage in it. This, in itself, is an important finding, since, only a few decades ago, researchers like Kinsey and others found that Americans largely abstained from oral sex.[62]

On average our research participants reported having had four sexual partners, but again there were clearly individual differences: 17 percent have had ten to twenty partners and 6 percent said they had had more than twenty partners. There were people who reported having had sex with as many as 50, 75, or even 150 partners.[63] A certain number of our research participants—15 percent—said they had had sex while others watched.

A considerable number of our participants had used pornography. When asked about their consumption over the past year, 39 percent told us they had looked at pornographic magazines, 52 percent had watched at least one X-rated movie, and 19 percent had attended a live pornographic show at a strip club. When asked about their consumption of pornography over their entire lifetime, 84 percent said they had seen at least one X-rated movie, and 33 percent reported they had visited a strip club.

A small number of our participants had paid for sex or been paid. Specifically, 1 percent told us that, in the last year, they had had sex with a prostitute; 6 percent said they had done so at least once in their lifetime; and 2 percent said that they themselves had engaged in prostitution at some point.

Our findings are consistent with other recent studies that have found that people engage in a broad range of sexual behaviors. When it comes to the question of what people are doing sexually, most research currently suggests two general conclusions. On the one hand, there is a wide range of behaviors that people engage in, including voyeurism, exhibitionism, transvestitism, sadism, and masochism; on the other hand, the more unusual or extreme behaviors are practiced by a minority of people.

For instance, Dr. Bing Hsu at the Psychiatry Service of the Veterans Affairs Medical Center in Bakersfield, California, along with his colleagues at UCLA and California State University, recently replicated a study of sexual behavior and fantasies carried out a decade ago by the well-known researcher Dr. Ethel Person. In his study, Dr. Hsu and his associates gave Dr. Person's original questionnaire to 166 university students, all of whom described themselves as heterosexual. The questionnaire asked students whether they had engaged in sixty-seven different sexual practices, ranging from walking hand-in-hand to mate swapping, torturing a sexual partner, and having sex with animals (all of which behaviors were reported by at least some students). Dr. Hsu and his colleagues found (as had Dr. Person ten years earlier) that by far the vast majority of people reported sexual practices that were relatively tame—what Dr. Person had referred to as romantic and conventional behaviors.[64] These included things such as intercourse, kissing, oral sex, and mutual masturbation, which 75 percent or more of the students had engaged in. Less frequent (but still not uncommon) behaviors included anal sex (reported by roughly 25 percent), being tied up (approximately 15 percent), group sex (no more than 13 percent), and torturing a partner (no more than 10 percent). There were very few differences between men and women in sexual practices.

Just as there is great individual variation in our culture in the sexual behaviors with which people feel comfortable, a surprisingly wide range of fantasies are also fairly common. Consider, for example, the most common fantasies previous researchers have found reported by heterosexual men, illustrated by quotations from some of our own research participants:

• Having sex with someone other than one's current partner
It's like, when I'm not with my fiancée, I might think about other women, but when I'm with her, I'm thinking about her. . . . One time I met a girl and I had a crush on her. Her physical appearance made me like her, and I really never got to know her personally. I was so into her physically, that I created a personality for her so she could be that perfect girl for me.

• Forcing a woman to have sex
I saw this video, <u>Faces of Death,</u> and oh, man. The rape scene was particularly terrible for me, because I did feel myself having a physiological reaction, an

erection. I was kind of like, "Why should I be feeling <u>that</u> way toward this scene?" Especially since I knew that the woman died afterwards. . . . It's a movie that some guy put together; it's a series of three or four movies, and it depicts all the ways that people die in various car crashes, suicides, drug overdoses, electric chair. . . . This was an actual rape. The guy videotaped himself doing it. . . . And, the thing is, I used to have these fantasies . . . they would involve more forceful sexual coercion or acts . . .

• Watching other people have sex
I have fantasies about more than one guy with a girl—you know—watching them. My girlfriend knows about it, she just laughs and brushes it off.

• Having sex with another man
I have had homosexual fantasies. I think I've gotten to the point where that part of my life is compartmentalized, so I don't judge it. It's just there, it's something I've needed over the course of time. So I don't walk around like a time bomb during the course of the day. I don't feel particularly good about it, but it is what it is.

• Group sex
I don't fantasize about sex with another man, but I do fantasize about being with a man and a woman together. . . . I wouldn't have anything to do with the guy, just with the woman.

For heterosexual women, the most common fantasies are quite similar:

• Having sex with someone other than your partner
It was mostly with two guys, having sex with two guys at once. My husband doesn't know, I don't tell. We have a monogamous relationship. I don't think I would do it—I would be too embarrassed, so I don't tell him.

• Being forced to have sex
I think I started these fantasies when I was young because of the whole guilt thing, I could be a nice girl and have these fantasies. I'd have fantasies of being tied into a chair, there were no people involved, it was all sort of machinery, and they would make me climax. I think that that was a safe fantasy back then, because there was nobody else involved. "I'm not really doing it, I'm being forced to do it." It took the guilt away.

- Watching others have sex
Watching a woman having sex with another woman . . .

- An idyllic sexual encounter with a male stranger
I was in a barn, in a stall, and there was this really handsome tall man taking care of the horses. I knew in my dream that I had known him, and I had always been attracted to him, and we ended up making love and it was really passionate.

- Having sex with another woman
I don't know if I would really classify myself as bisexual, but I am attracted to both sexes and fantasize about having sex with another woman.

The fantasies of gay men and women are very similar to those of heterosexuals, although the gender of their fantasized partner is reversed. Research shows that for homosexual men, the most common fantasies are (1) images of men's bodies, (2) being forced to have sex with a man, (3) having sex with a woman, (4) an idyllic sexual encounter with a male stranger, and (5) group sex. For homosexual women, the top five are (1) forced sexual encounters, (2) idyllic sex with one's current partner, (3) having sex with a man, (4) memories of past sexual encounters, and (5) sadistic imagery.

Remarkably, while there are some differences between men and women, and between heterosexuals and homosexuals, the "top five" fantasies are, overall, very similar. Indeed, one of the leading fantasies for homosexuals, both male and female, is having heterosexual sex; and, as noted just above, heterosexual men and women frequently fantasize about homosexual sex. The rubric of "normal" sex, then, begins to seem almost absurd in this context.

Looking at One's Own Sexual Desires and Fantasies

Developing the confidence to look at one's own sexual desires and fantasies is not always easy. Consider what Kaitlin, a twenty-four-year-old who is studying for her MBA, told us about her fantasy life:

Often I am disturbed by my own fantasies. I have a lot of fantasies where I'm always the object of desire, and I'm just a sex object. Usually there is another woman or another woman and a guy. I would never share these fantasies with my fiancé. There are so many traditional things that I want, that would be destroyed by acting out any of those fantasies. I want to be in a heterosexual, married relationship. I want my children to have a mother and a father.

Kaitlin is not alone in being disturbed by some of her fantasies. One of the questions we asked our research participants was: "How do you feel about the content of the sexual fantasy you have most often or find most arousing?" Only about 50 percent of our sample said they thought other people have fantasies like their own, and 2 percent were sure that their fantasies are "abnormal"; 12 percent said they might tell a close friend, but not their sexual partner, about their fantasies; 19 percent said they would be embarrassed or even "horrified" if anyone knew the content of their fantasies. These findings are critical, we believe, because they demonstrate just how common it still is for people to feel ashamed of their sexuality.

What's amazing is that, at the same time that people may find some of their fantasies disturbing or embarrassing, the majority—nearly 70 percent—though hesitant to do so, said they would find it exciting to share their most arousing fantasy with their partner. People *want* to share their inner sex lives. They are simply afraid to.

When people can summon the courage to talk to their partners honestly about their inner mental life, the benefits for their sexual life can be enormous. Research shows that there are a number of benefits of exploring and sharing fantasies.

First, fantasies enhance arousal during sex.[65] As one psychologist[66] has put it: " . . . the *mind* is the body's most reliable 'erogenous zone.' "

Second, fantasies may reflect scenarios that, as erotically charged and sexually exciting as they are for people to think about, are not actually behaviors they want to act out. Take the example of one of the most common fantasies among both heterosexual men and women—having homosexual sex. The fantasy of heterosexual sex is equally common among homosexuals. Most people don't act on these fantasies, yet millions of people are routinely fantasizing about having sex outside their usual sexual orientation. Because someone has such fantasies doesn't necessarily mean that he or she is masquerading as a heterosexual or homosexual or is "really" latently harboring a different sexual preference. But most people don't make that distinction between fantasy and reality. Many people are very disturbed by their own such fantasies, and many would jump to the wrong conclusion if they discovered their partner had such fantasies.

In our research, we asked people, "If your partner revealed fantasies about having sex with someone who is the opposite sex to you, what would you conclude?" Twenty-one percent said they would assume that their partner was latently gay (or straight, depending on whether the respondent was heterosexual or homosexual). Fifteen percent said they would take such fantasies as a sign that their partner had psychological problems, and 20 percent would draw the conclusion that their partner no longer found them attractive. Only 44 percent recognized that many people have such fantasies. Those who did were significantly more sexually intelligent than the rest of the sample; they earned, on average, a C, while those who assumed their partner was latently of a different sexual orientation, had psychological problems, or no longer found them attractive all earned, on average, a D. The reality is that for heterosexuals, homosexual fantasies are common, and are nothing to hide. Sharing them with one's sexual partner does not mean they will be acted upon. It's simply a part of many people's real sexual selves. We believe that the sexually intelligent approach is to accept these feelings and talk openly about them with a partner when appropriate; this, in turn, can only enhance one's sex life.

Third, some fantasies offer a safe way to experience sexual desires that would generally be unsafe to act out in real life. The story of Hannah, one of our research participants, helps illustrate how fantasizing about certain behaviors—rather than acting on them—may often be the safest and psychologically healthiest approach. Attractive, bright and witty, sophisticated for her age, but even so, only nineteen years old, Hannah had a persistent fantasy during her first semester at college that she was tempted to act on:

Most of my sexual fantasies I have no trouble sharing with my girlfriends, although I'd be slightly horrified to share some of them. I've had a fantasy about a professor—my adviser at a school I went to in California. He totally hit on me, invited me out, gave me money for Christmas, things that professors probably

**shouldn't be doing. In the sexuality course he taught, I wrote some really per-
verse things. I wrote them partially out of curiosity, but also just to shock. He
was kind of nasty, but in a way his nastiness was attractive in my fantasyland. I
was given the opportunity to go forward but I never did. I once did actually say
something to one of my girlfriends, and she was like, "Eeuww."**

Given her circumstances, Hannah did the sexually intelligent thing:
she neither tried to deny that she was attracted to her professor nor
actually had an affair with him. All too often, when people suppress
their fantasies, they end up putting themselves at greater risk for acting
on their desires in inappropriate or self-destructive ways. Hannah's
fantasies about her teacher seemed to offer a number of psychological
benefits: they gave her a safe way of exploring the possibility of an
affair with a professor without the negative consequences that would
likely have followed, and they taught her something about herself,
namely, that a large part of the allure of this man was based on what
she calls his "nastiness." She learned that there was something about
the forbidden nature of such advances that was exciting to her.

Indeed, our sexual fantasies offer vital clues to our inner sexual landscape, clues to our genuine—and healthy—desires that we can miss
because of fear or shame. When we assume that our fantasies represent
what we really want to act out, the content can frighten us so much that
we fail to understand the meaning of the fantasy.

For example, consider one of the most common fantasies among
women: being forced to submit to sex. In a 1998 study, psychologists
Donald Strassberg and Lisa Lockerd at the University of Utah at Salt
Lake City asked 137 college women, aged eighteen to forty, about their
fantasy life, in particular about a common—and to some people, very
disturbing—fantasy among women: being forced to submit to sex.
Strassberg and Lockerd found that more than half of the women they
studied had in fact had fantasies about forced sex. Having such fantasies was not related to having actually experienced sexual coercion
and did not appear to be a way in which these women dealt with feelings of guilt about sex: in fact, the women who had forced-sex fantasies
scored *lower* on sexual guilt than those who did not report such fantasies. Strassberg and Lockerd concluded that, for these women, the
fantasy of forced sex was an indicator of their "relatively open, unre-
stricted, and varied approach to their sexuality."[67] It would be easy for

a woman to feel disturbed and abnormal for having this fantasy, and equally easy for her partner to be shocked or to doubt her emotional health.

This is where it's important to distinguish between fantasy and action. What could be called "rape" fantasies, of being forced to submit sexually, are independent of any desire to be raped in real life. Other studies examining forced-sex fantasies have shown that women by no means *wish* to be forced to have sex in reality. Our best guess is that fantasies such as these do not express a desire to be hurt or mistreated, but rather a wish to experience intense surrender to an encounter that is passionate and erotically charged, yet physically and emotionally safe. Susan Bond and Donald Mosher, in the Department of Psychology at the University of Connecticut, argued that the typical female erotic rape fantasy involves a sexually attractive male who is overpowered by the *woman's* sexual attractiveness and uses just enough force to overcome her token resistance and who arouses her sexually.[68] Knowing that fantasies such as these are not "sick" or abnormal but actually express a healthy desire to surrender to another person in a safe context can remove the fear, embarrassment, and self-doubt that prevent people from sharing their sexual selves openly with their partners.

Fantasies can help us discover—and share with our partners— our true desires. They are the key we can use to unlock our authentic sexuality. We believe, then, that the sexually intelligent approach is for people to explore their fantasy lives honestly; even when people do not necessarily act out their fantasies, by being aware of them, they enhance their "real life" sexual experiences.

Looking Back to Uncover Our Individual Sexual Selves

Whether we can allow ourselves to feel good about our sexuality—or whether we spend our lives trying to fit the mold of what we think is "normal"—depends, to a great extent, on our earliest sexual experiences. To a large degree, individual sexual response is learned. Biology alone is not enough to explain the *particulars* of what arouses an individual. The meaning of any sexual act is determined by all of the associations a person makes between intense pleasure and the circumstances in which, and the people with whom, it occurs. The meaning an individual person associates with a particular sexual act can, in some cases, be traced back to earlier experiences—ones that can leave long-lasting negative effects on our ability to enjoy sex. For that reason, each of us, in order to uncover our secret sexual self, needs to look back at our past.

Consider, for instance, a 1997 study on sexuality among women done by Professor Nelwyn Moore of Southwest Texas State University and Professor J. Kenneth Davidson of the University of Wisconsin at Eau Claire. They found that the same sexual act—having intercourse for the first time—meant different things to different women. Moore and Davidson looked specifically at whether the women in their study felt guilty about having intercourse for the first time, and whether the guilt they felt had consequences for their later sexual adjustment and satis-faction. Of the 571 college women with whom they spoke, Moore and Davidson found considerable variation in how guilty the women felt about having had intercourse. Compared with the women who said they "never," "seldom," or only "occasionally" felt guilty about having had sex, the women who said they "frequently" felt guilty about it—20 percent of the sample—were significantly less well adjusted sexually and reported significantly less sexual satisfaction.[69] These results are consistent with a 1993 study by David Hurlbert of the Darnall U.S. Army Community Hospital in Ft. Hood, Texas, who found that guilt had a substantial inhibiting effect on sexual development.[70] Both of these studies strongly suggest that the individual meaning sex holds for people—in these studies, the feelings of guilt the research participants associated with sex—was key in determining their sexual happiness.

When it comes to whether you feel good about your sexuality, it doesn't necessarily matter what other people are doing or feeling or whether your sexual behaviors match or deviate from theirs. What matters is what a particular sexual behavior means to *you*. Sexually intelligent people learn how to investigate their sexual history closely and figure out how the messages they were taught and the experiences they have had influence their current sexual feelings and relationships. Getting to the bottom of the associations—both positive and negative—that various sexual behaviors hold for us as individuals can help us to expand our sexual repertoire and have richer, more fulfilling sex lives.

Listen, for instance, to Alexandra, a college senior majoring in art history. Refined, intelligent, and sensitive, with pale blond hair and chestnut-brown eyes, she had been living with her boyfriend for a year when she realized she needed to look more closely at her past and how it had influenced her feelings about oral sex:

> When we first started going out, we had some problems. There were things Ted wanted to do that I wouldn't do. This is sort of embarrassing—it was oral sex. There was no way I would do that to him. I learned about sex early, because it was everywhere in my family. My father had pornography everywhere in the house, spilling out of cupboards, even in the bathroom. He had a whole wardrobe that was full of <u>Hustler</u> magazines and <u>Playboy</u>s, and he ... we were always coming across things when we were opening drawers. So I had seen this stuff—pornography—and you know, these images of women were not great. There would be, I don't know, some woman engaged in oral sex, and she's kneeling in front of the guy with nothing on and the guy is wearing lumber-jacket boots. The images seemed so degrading.
>
> Ted and I argued about it. He thought I didn't care about him, because I wouldn't do it. When I told him I felt like he was degrading me, by wanting me to give him oral sex, he was shocked—he just didn't have the same negative associations with it. It took a long time for me to see that Ted just liked oral sex. He wasn't trying to hurt me or put me down—it just felt good to him. It's still not my favorite thing, but it's become much less problematic.

In our view, Alexandra demonstrated sexual intelligence in how she handled her conflict. At first she was stuck in a seemingly impossible conflict: oral sex simply seemed degrading to her while it appealed to Ted. But by thinking carefully about the deeper meaning and significance she had attached to the act, sharing her feelings with Ted, and then learning from him how he felt about the matter, she was able to better understand this aspect of their sex life and actually feel more comfortable about engaging in oral sex. Alexandra adopted a sexually intelligent approach by looking back at the emotional associations she had to a particular sexual act—the meaning of it to her—rather than dwelling on the act itself. What Ted felt about oral sex—or what society might say is "normal" or not—was not nearly as relevant as what Alexandra learned about *herself*. She was able to look at the messages she had internalized from the media about sex and men and develop a new sense of safety and self-confidence once she saw through the negative messages about sexuality that she had absorbed from pornography.

When we shift our focus from rigid notions of what is "normal" sexually and ask instead what a particular sexual behavior or fantasy means to us, we begin, as Alexandra did, to uncover our secret sexual self and increase our awareness of both our genuine desires and the ways in which our sexuality may have been distorted by negative experiences in the past or by negative messages we encounter in the media and the culture around us. We also become better able to shed feelings of shame and embarrassment surrounding sex and have more honest, richer, and more genuinely exciting relationships.

How Sexually Intelligent Are You?
How would you approach this dilemma?

> There's a particular sex act that you've had fantasies about frequently, one that you would like to try out with your partner, but you hesitate to broach the subject for fear that your partner may consider the act abnormal or shameful.

Questions to Consider
1. What is it, in particular, that excites you about the thought of this particular sexual behavior?
2. Is there a reason or reasons why you fear the behavior is "abnormal"?
3. Is this a sexual act that you and your partner could try out without hurting either of you, physically or emotionally?
4. In this situation, how would you broach the topic with your partner so that you could test out his or her general reaction to the behavior before you suggest trying it yourselves?
5. What if the situation were reversed, and there was a sexual behavior that your partner wanted to try but feared bringing up? Would you want him or her to tell you about it?
6. What if the sexual act that your partner wanted to try was one that you were very uncomfortable with? How would you handle this? Is there a way in which you could explore both of your reactions without blaming each other or immediately assuming the behavior was "sick," "abnormal," and so on?

Bear in mind the following principles of sexual intelligence.

Scientific Knowledge

Many people routinely engage in a broad range of both fantasies and sexual behaviors.

Many fantasies are less compelling in reality than in our minds, and, once acted out, they can lose their power as fantasies.

The ability—and willingness—to examine the secret sexual self is a crucial step toward a better sex life.

One of the "top five" sexual fantasies for many, many people is a sexual encounter with someone of the "wrong" sex (someone opposite in gender to their current or usual partner).

Awareness of the Secret Sexual Self

Try not to blame or condemn yourself or your partner for fantasies: remember that people have many fantasies that they don't necessarily ever want to act upon.

If a particular sexual act makes you uncomfortable, examine your past for any negative associations you may have acquired—through the influence of the media, because of early religious teaching, or your family experiences.

Consider whether it would be more pleasurable to act out the fantasy with your partner or to keep it as a fantasy—perhaps a mutual fantasy.

Connecting with Others

As long as a particular sex act does not cause pain or humiliation to either of you, avoid labeling it "abnormal" or shaming yourself or your partner for wanting to try it.

Talk with your partner about the meaning that your respective fantasies have for you, not just about the behavior.

Ask your partner what aspect of the fantasy makes it exciting to him or her.

Avoid blaming or shaming your partner for fantasies that don't involve harming or humiliating another person.

Allow for the possibility that a fantasy your partner has that you are uncomfortable with may mean something very different from what you assume.

Try to identify the elements of sexual fantasies that excite you and your partner and try coming up with mutual fantasies that you are both comfortable with.

chapter nine

Escaping the Confines of Gender Stereotypes

"It was the worst sexual experience I ever had. It really woke me up," explained Dana, a twenty-year-old college student who participated in our Sexual Intelligence Project:

> Spirits when they please
> Can either sex assume, or both.
> John Milton, *Paradise Lost*

One weekend back in high school, I went to visit friends who had already started college. The first night I spent on the campus, I met Blair. I was attracted, it's true. Blair was good-looking, smart, and really funny. After only a couple hours, Blair invited me to stay at the dorms, and my friends just deserted me, figuring that I was "up for it." We had sex. I didn't intend to at all. I didn't want to. In fact, I was dead set against it. But Blair was very aggressive. The next day I felt disgusted with myself, with the type of person I discovered I might be. I had always prided myself on being independent, thought of myself as a person who wouldn't give in to pressure.

Dana's story, on the surface, is very familiar. But it may come as a surprise that, in this case, Dana is a young man. The sexual aggressor in his story, Blair, was a woman.

Our research suggests that, as "liberated" about gender as our society may think it has become, as open-minded and flexible about gender roles as many of us may wish to be, many of us still feel tremendous pressure to conform to traditional rules about how men and women should behave. But, perhaps even more important, our research shows that people who are able to transcend these rules—those who are able to accept and enjoy *all* aspects of their personalities, whether or not society sees these aspects as being "masculine" or "feminine"— consistently score higher on our Sexual Intelligence Test. There is an important correlation, in other words, between being relaxed about one's gender, on the one hand, and being sexually intelligent, on the other. And our findings support a growing body of research that shows that this same group—people who feel less constrained by gender rules— are also demonstrably happier in their sex lives.

Common stereotypes about male-female differences include, of course, the notion that men are the sexual aggressors, that men have higher levels of sexual desire and are more interested in sex for the physical pleasure involved, while women value and are better at expressing their feelings and cultivating emotional intimacy.

Consider Monique's views. She is a twenty-one-year-old nursing student who has some very definite and negative opinions of men. While she is currently in a relationship, the sex is very unsatisfying: she reported six out of six possible sexual dysfunctions. The only thing Monique's mother told her growing up was "Most of the time guys use you for sex and leave." Her first sexual experience was "painful and scary."

She continues to have sex with her boyfriend—the only sexual partner she's ever had—more for his pleasure than because she has any desire for it:

> **Having sex is more for him than for me. I don't make it a major part of my life. I have other things. If we're together and he wants to have sex, I'll do it, but I don't want to have sex every day.**

She has never told her boyfriend what would give her pleasure, nor how dissatisfied she is with their sex life. She told us: "Mostly, we don't talk about it. I just keep it inside."

Monique distrusts men, believes that they are interested in just one thing—sex—and that they cannot be counted on. She's made up her mind on a life plan based on those assumptions:

> **Mostly I think I don't need a guy in my life to do what I need to do. You can't rely on them. I don't want a father for my baby, I'll just have a baby on my own. And**

my boyfriend will get really mad at that. I don't think the father is needed. The baby would be better off not having a father.

It's a bleak view of the opposite sex. And a highly stereotyped one. Such commonly held stereotypes about differences between men and women obscure the truth about the way individual men and women behave sexually, what they want in bed, how they view sex. Believing these stereotypes can lead to misunderstanding, bitterness, and isolation.

We were astounded by how many in our sample of relatively young people still believe all the old stereotypes about how men and women "should" behave.

The good news is that, despite believing in these stereotypes, when it came to their own behavior, the men and women in our study didn't necessarily conform to "the rules." Even more important, our research shows that people who are able to transcend these rules, those who are able to accept and value both traditionally "masculine" and "feminine" aspects of themselves, are more sexually intelligent and have better sex lives than people who are constrained by gender stereotypes. Sexually intelligent people recognize that there is individual variation, that not all men are "just like a man" and not all women are the same. Further, they recognize that society plays a role in shaping men's and women's attitudes and sexual behaviors, that many of the apparent differences between men and women are learned, and can be unlearned.

Gender Differences: Myth versus Reality

Psychological research about gender shows some differences in how men and women think and behave. Some women may be better than some men at expressing their inner fears and uncertainties. Some men may find it easier than some women to initiate sex. But, when one looks at the research as a whole, the fact is that there are very few documented differences between men and women in sexual attitudes, behaviors, and fantasies; where those differences exist, the size of the difference is for the most part quite small.[71] What's more, the differences that have been found between men and women only apply to *some* men and *some* women; there is a great deal of overlap between the sexes in their behavior and attitudes. In reality, when it comes to the way people behave sexually, what they want in bed, and how they view sex, men and women are more alike than different.

People who know this to be the case, and therefore allow themselves to feel good about both the "feminine" and "masculine" sides of their personalities, are significantly more likely to find sexual fulfillment. A key part of sexual intelligence is becoming aware of and accepting all of the genuine desires and passions that our secret sexual self reveals, whether they seem traditionally "masculine" or "feminine." Men and women who disregard the "rules" and follow their own inclinations— for instance, men who prefer at times to make love tenderly, or women who at times desire to take the lead sexually—are the ones who, much more than their rigidly "sex-typed" counterparts, are sexually intelligent and sexually satisfied.

Rather than making immediate assumptions about gender-based differences, sexually intelligent people learn to recognize the way that expectations about gender taught by our society and culture come into play within their individual relationships. Perhaps most important, the sexually intelligent person tries to understand how his or her partner's behavior and attitudes are influenced by what that person—as an individual—has learned about what it is to be a man or woman. This means exploring what an individual woman confronts in her relationships with men because of what *she* has been taught about gender instead of relying on oversimplified rules about how all women act, or should act. Similarly, this means understanding what a particular man has learned about "masculinity" rather than making easy generalizations about how all men typically behave. Because gender differences are fewer and smaller than most people think, and because individuals vary in the extent to which they conform to behavior typical of their gender, it is critical that we talk openly and with a sense of humor, about when gender differences might be involved in our sexual lives, rather than making simplistic assumptions about how all men, or all women, should or do behave.

Consider, in this regard, what Joyce, a twenty-seven-year-old biologist, told us when we asked her what she believes the differences are between how men and women behave sexually:

For the most part, I think women's desires could be the same and are definitely drifting toward being the same as those of men. Society has told us that if I'm aroused, I'm a slut. Once I let go of that, I no longer have to feel guilty about having sexual desires—and therefore certainly can accept that I do have the same drive as men.

Joyce is sexually intelligent in recognizing that she, as an individual woman, is just as capable as any man of having a strong sex drive. What's more, she is aware of the way stereotypes about female behavior still have the power to make women feel they *shouldn't* have strong sexual desires, or at least certainly should not *admit* to having them. She is listening to her genuine sexual self, as opposed to what society tells her and has told women for centuries. By refusing to be limited by the old-fashioned rule that says women are not supposed to feel sexual pleasure, Joyce frees herself to enjoy her true sexuality.

Along similar lines, listen to Jon, a nineteen-year-old psychology major, who attributes differences in male and female sexual behavior to how men and women are socialized. Jon told us: "I think men and women are different because of society's influence. Men and women would probably have more of the same attitudes and behaviors if we were not treated so differently."

Nina, a twenty-nine-year-old chemist, sees gender differences as exaggerated. She told us:

I think the differences between men and women are overrated, because I think women have a lot of the same sex drives that are attributed to men. People often say that men are driven by appearances, that men are attracted to good-looking bodies. Well, I think that women are too. I know from my own experience that I'm attracted to the very same things. There are definitely differences, but we're all people, and we have similar drives.

Sadly, unlike Joyce, Jon, and Nina, the majority of the people we surveyed in our research still believe all the old myths about the way in which men and women differ in their sexual attitudes and cling to stereotyped notions about how men and women should behave sexually.

Our Research Findings on Gender

One of the questions we asked people in our Sexual Intelligence Project was "Do you think men and women are different in regard to sexual attitudes or sexual behavior? In what ways?" Their answers tended to fall into one of three categories. First, there were people who said there are no differences between men and women. Second were those who said men and women differ in all the ways that cultural stereotypes suggest. The third group of people acknowledged some gender differences, but qualified their response by noting that not all individuals fit the general rule, or by pointing out that many gender differences have their source in social conditioning. They were the most sexually intelligent.

The majority of our research participants still clung to traditional conceptions of two genders widely separated in their attitudes and behaviors. For example, Gail, a thirty-year-old graphics designer, told us, "I just think we are two different species. Men and women differ in so many ways. It's no big deal for a guy to sleep around—I don't think they feel guilt or shame for having casual sex the way women do."

Along similar lines, one of the claims we repeatedly heard from women is that while they want intimacy along with sex, men separate sex and intimacy, preferring sex without "all the emotional stuff." Barbara, a twenty-year-old student in early childhood education, put it this way:

Women are more interested in having a relationship; guys are more interested in having sex and not a relationship. I think that women think that sex actually does mean something—there are feelings behind it. Whereas guys don't have to have the feelings so they don't really think about the whole feelings thing if they can help it—like being cared for, being with someone who loves you or cares for you. That makes me much happier and satisfies me much more—when I know that I'm in a caring situation, a loving situation. It feels good physically, too, but the reason that it does is that I feel like I'm having an emotional connection with somebody. And I think that guys don't feel like that. I'm pretty sure they don't.

Perspectives like Gail's and Barbara's were common among our research participants, over 55 percent of whom, in their responses, asserted stereotypical beliefs about sexual differences between men and women. Only 28 percent of our sample recognized that individuals may vary in the extent to which they resemble the "typical" man or woman, or that gender differences may be influenced by social conditioning. Seventeen percent said there are no differences between men and women at all, which, of course, is also not entirely accurate.

We found a significant correlation between the way people think about gender differences and how they scored on the Sexual Intelligence Test. The 28 percent who recognized that gender differences exist but qualified their answer by noting that individual people vary or that gender differences may be socially influenced were far more sexually intelligent than people who believed the old stereotypes *or* those who denied the existence of any gender differences.

One of our most crucial findings, however, is that if our participants seemed very traditional in their assumptions about how "most" men and women behave, they were much less rigid in how they handled their own sexual activities. Indeed our research, and research done by others, shows that the way men and women actually *behave* sexually may vary radically from the myths they embrace about "typical" men and women. Take, for instance, the question of whether men have a stronger sex drive than women. Nearly 60 percent of our research participants who specifically mentioned sexual desire when asked about male-female differences, claimed that men, in general, have greater sexual desires than women.[72] Eighty-five percent of those who mentioned emotional involvement and physical pleasure when asked about male-female differences told us that men have sex casually, purely for the physical pleasure, while women are more invested emotionally and are more capable of intimacy.

When it came to their own behavior, however, it was a different story.

What Men and Women Believe and How They Behave

Do Men Have a Stronger Sex Drive?

Although nearly 60 percent of our research participants who specifically mentioned sexual desire claimed than men have stronger sexual desires than women do, when we asked our participants how often they themselves had sex, the women in our study reported having sex as frequently as the men. And it was the women in our study, not the men, who told us they were more willing to have sex with someone they didn't know well. One of the questions we asked was "If you had just met someone you liked a lot and with whom you wanted a serious relationship, would you typically have sex very early on in the relationship?" The *men* said they would wait longer before having sex with a prospective long-term partner. This finding, of course, flies in the face of the stereotype that "men only want one thing." And while there were three men in our study who had had far more sexual partners than either the women or the other men we spoke with (one man claimed to have slept with 150 people), on average all the other participants, whether male or female, had had about four partners each.

Twenty-five-year-old Mary understands how misguided it is to assume that men, or women, are necessarily more or less sexually aggressive:

> There are so many clichés. Girls are supposed to be more passive. Men are supposed to be aggressive. But I've been the more sexually aggressive one in almost every relationship I've had. Guys comment on it. They like it.

Janice, a college sophomore, has faced at least one sexually aggressive man, but she defies the stereotype of the submissive woman by knowing what she wants and being assertive about it:

> I dated this guy about four years ago. He was a really nice guy, but I just remember I stayed over at his house a couple of times, and we'd start kissing, and he would move my hand down on his crotch, and I would move my hand away because I wasn't ready to be sexual with him in that way. And he would move my hand back down again, and it was this whole thing, you know, girls are supposed to be nice, boys are the aggressors. I just finally had to say, "I know where your penis is, and if I wanted to touch it, I would touch it."

Though surveys have found varying figures for the number of partners men and women claim to have had, how often they have intercourse, and how strong their sex drive tends to be, researchers recognize that, in cases where men seem to be more sexually active than women, the apparent discrepancy may be due to the pressure many men feel to exaggerate their prowess, and women their virtue.[73] Professors Mary Beth Oliver at Virginia Polytechnic Institute in Blacksburg, Virginia, and Janet Shibley Hyde at the University of Wisconsin in Madison, in what psychologists call a "meta-analysis," analyzed the overall results from 177 research studies looking at gender differences in sexuality, from the 1960s to the present. These researchers found little difference between men and women in frequency of intercourse. What's more, they found that the difference, small as it is, has decreased over time.[74]

Are Women More Capable of Intimacy?

Another example of the way our participants' behavior didn't match their beliefs about gender differences was in the area of intimacy. We've already heard from one participant, Barbara, the stereotyped view that men have sex casually, purely for physical pleasure, while women are more invested emotionally and are more capable of intimacy. She's not alone in her belief.

What we found, though, in our research, is not that men aren't *capable* of combining the physical pleasure of sex with emotional intimacy, but rather that they can't tell the difference between the two. Specifically, when they are aroused, they are less aware than women are of whether they are feeling purely physical urges, the desire for emotional closeness, or both.

Other researchers also have found evidence that specifically debunks the pervasive stereotype that women have a greater capacity for emotional intimacy than do men. An important aspect of intimacy is the ability to disclose one's feelings to another person. In a number of studies, psychologists have compared men and women's degree of self-disclosure. While some studies have found that women seem to be better at self-disclosure than men, longitudinal research in which dating couples are observed over time indicates that, in reality, the degree of self-disclosure by men and by women is generally the same.[75] One study, done by psychologists Susan and Clyde Hendrick at Texas Tech University, in Lubbock, Texas, surveyed undergraduates at three different times, in 1988, 1992, and 1993. They collected data from over 1,000 students. Their results showed that men and women don't differ in the extent to which they value sex as an emotional experience.[76]

Researcher Jerry Barba, in a 1998 study, using psychological tests that measure a person's capacity for intimacy, also found no difference between men and women's capacity for intimacy.[77]

George, an attractive, successful thirty-year-old lawyer, told us how uncomfortable he is having sex with a woman with whom he has no emotional connection:

> **I don't want to go to a club and pick someone up, bring her home, and then wake up the next morning only to drop her off and never call her again. What I don't want to happen to me, I don't want to do to other people.**

Gender Differences in Sexual Intelligence

The one striking difference that we did find between men and women is a significant difference between the sexes when it comes to sexual intelligence: in general, women were more sexually intelligent than men, both overall, and particularly on the Scientific Knowledge component of sexual intelligence. That means that the women we studied are more knowledgeable about human sexuality and better able to put that knowledge into practice. It also means that the women were better able to see through the myths about sex all around us in the culture. Men, on the other hand, were more likely to fall prey to misinformation about sex—such as rape myths, for example. It's important to emphasize, however, that even though the women in our sample, as a group, were more sexually intelligent, there were individual men who were highly sexually intelligent.

Learning to Be Ourselves: Communicating Honestly

Stereotypes about men and women are harmful in two ways: they are unfair and misleading when applied to individuals, and they create the belief that men and women are from two different planets, and that it is impossible to understand the opposite sex, at least without a guidebook. One of the questions we asked people was "How much do you feel you understand the behavior of the opposite sex?" The most sexually intelligent people acknowledged that there are times when they don't completely understand the behavior of the opposite sex, while those participants who said that the behavior of the opposite sex was a complete mystery to them were far less sexually intelligent.

The key to overcoming stereotypes about gender differences is communication. It's only through talking with each other that partners can discover what their individual experiences with gender-role socialization have been, what masculinity means to a particular man or femininity to a particular woman. That knowledge can then be used to further their understanding of each other. When we asked our research participants what they thought is the most likely cause of sexual problems between men and women, we found that the more sexually intelligent people believed that sexual problems might be due to a lack of communication about each other's needs and desires. Less sexually intelligent people said sexual problems are due to the fact that the two people involved aren't right for each other, that men and women just want different things in bed, or that men and women are polar opposites in their psychology.

Unfortunately, there is still very little support in our culture for people to be honest with themselves and their partners about their real sexual desires. Karen, a twenty-year-old student with whom we talked, understood that men still receive more social encouragement than women to speak openly about their sexual behavior while women still have little support for admitting their desires or talking about their behavior:

> It's definitely true that if you ask a guy if he masturbates, he'll gleefully tell you how often, and what he thinks about. But ask a girl, and she'll deny, deny, deny, while looking horrified that it was even thought she might masturbate.

Isaac, a thirty-six-year-old accountant also articulated the way in which men are encouraged—even expected—to brag about sexual exploits:

> I've always had a hard time finding women. When I'm around other men, sometimes I've felt pressured to make up stories. I think a lot of guys do. It's not that we are oversexed or something. We just feel like people will see us as wimps if we can't say we've "scored" recently.

On the assumption that many of our study participants might not feel comfortable reporting their true sexual feelings (or might distort what those were), in certain cases we asked indirect questions designed to gauge their attitudes toward various sexual activities, rather than asking them directly about their sexual behavior. For example, instead of asking people how often they masturbate, we inquired whether or not they thought masturbation is wrong or a "normal" outlet for sexual desires. We found that there were no differences between how men and women answered this question. We also asked people, in an indirect way, about the strength of their sexual drive. Again, we found that there was no appreciable difference between the sexes. While society may goad men to brag about their sexual activities, and women to remain silent, neither men nor women are given consistent encouragement simply to be completely honest, with themselves and others, about their desires.

To be sexually intelligent and enjoy a better sex life, it's crucial that people not fall prey to easy generalizations about what all men are like, or what's true of all women. It's also important that they talk to each other about what masculinity and femininity mean to them *as individuals.* But there is an even more powerful way in which people can increase their sexual satisfaction—by transcending gender-role limitations altogether.

How to Have a Satisfying Sex Life: Freedom from Gender-Role Stereotypes

What our research, and that of our colleagues, all seems to show is that there are two sorts of worlds we can create for ourselves. One is a "gendered" or "sex-typed" world in which men and women feel that they have to abide by traditional notions about what makes a man "masculine" and a woman "feminine." In such a world, when men and women discover that their true feelings and tendencies don't necessarily fit these standardized expectations about gender, they tend to feel shame about not being "masculine" or "feminine" enough and they have little choice but to bury some part of themselves. In the other sort of world, one in which men and women feel free to accept and be honest about *all* of their feelings and behaviors, whether or not they conform to gender rules, shame and embarrassment are no longer necessary. People can be themselves, can enjoy and value all of their inclinations, both traditionally "masculine" and traditionally "feminine" ones. Not only is this approach freeing, it actually leads to healthier, more satisfying relationships—and better sex.

In the past two decades, psychologists have become interested in the concept of "androgyny." A person who is "androgynous," in the sense in which psychologists use the term, is high in *both* masculine and feminine characteristics. Androgynous men and women are at times assertive—in the boardroom, for example—and at other times sensitive and nurturing—for example, with a frightened child. They adapt their behavior to the situation, whereas people who are "sex-typed"—"macho" men and ultrafeminine women—are more limited in their behaviors. Androgynous people are neither abnormal nor asexual (nor transsexual). They are healthy, normal people who simply are more open and flexible in their behavior, combining useful elements of masculinity and femininity.

Research studies have shown that androgynous males are more likely than sex-typed men to give warm compliments, and androgynous women are better at refusing unreasonable requests than are sex-typed women.[78] But people who are able to express both a masculine and a feminine side also enjoy a whole range of other advantages. Chief among them is that they are more sexually intelligent than people who adhere to traditional gender roles. Since sexually intelligent people have more satisfying sex lives and fewer sexual dysfunctions, we believe that it's important to cultivate and incorporate both masculine and feminine traits into our personality.

The results of our research consistently showed that sexually intelligent people are less constrained by traditional sex roles: they said that men should not be limited to traditionally "masculine" behavior on a date. They told us they possess and value *both* masculine and feminine traits, and they don't feel shame about living up to cultural expectations about what is masculine or feminine.

Years of research by our colleagues show that there are many psychological benefits of being free of gender-role stereotypes, that is, cultivating both masculine and feminine aspects of one's personality. Investigators have found that androgynous people have higher self-esteem and confidence and, in particular, that androgynous men are more comfortable and confident on dates and in sexual encounters.[79] Men and women who are androgynous have more positive attitudes, as well as more liberal attitudes, toward sex than do sex-typed individuals.[80]

Research has also found that androgynous men and women are more sexually satisfied.[81] Highly sex-typed individuals—macho men and ultrafeminine women—tend to have rigid, conventional views about gender-appropriate behavior that may actually get in the way of sexual enjoyment. To cite just one example, traditional rules about gender assume that men have higher levels of sexual desire and dictate that they should be the ones to initiate sex, while women should be passive. For sex-typed men, these stereotypes, and the expectations they raise, may lead to the inability to perform with a woman who takes a more active role.[82] Likewise, highly traditional women may, as a consequence of role demands, fail to communicate what they want and need from a partner. Androgynous men and women, by contrast, tend to be more accepting of whatever feelings and behaviors come naturally to them and their partners. They tend to feel more comfortable being honest and forthright about expressing these natural proclivities. Thus they tend to feel more like "themselves" in sexual situations, more relaxed, and happier.

Women who are androgynous may actually find it easier to achieve orgasm. In one study comparing androgynous and sex-typed women, researcher Shirley Radlove at Miami University recruited married women through advertisements in Cincinnati newspapers. The women completed a series of questionnaires, including the Bem Sex Role Inventory, which measures the degree to which people are androgynous or sex-typed. Radlove also asked the women to rate the percentage of times they typically reached orgasm during intercourse. After controlling for factors that might affect a woman's likelihood of achieving orgasm, such as her knowledge of sexual techniques or premature ejaculation by her husband, Radlove found that, compared with sex-typed women, androgynous women more consistently had orgasms. What's more, the androgynous women were much more likely to take the responsibility for their own stimulation.[83]

Androgynous couples tend to experience far less violent conflict in their relationships. In a 1996 study, psychologists Amy Ray and Steven Gold at Northern Illinois University in DeKalb, Illinois, measured the degree to which dating couples adhered to gender roles and the impact this had on their relationships. Ray and Gold found that aggression was higher in couples where either the woman was hyperfeminine or the man was hypermasculine. Couples in which at least one of the partners adhered to traditional gender roles engaged in more verbal abuse, including swearing, yelling, name calling, and stomping out of the room. Hypermasculine men perceived themselves as being more abused in their relationships, which appeared to lead them, in turn, to assault their female partners. Likewise hyperfeminine women perceived their self-esteem as being attacked in their dating relationship, which seemed to provoke them to retaliate with verbal abuse.[84] Other studies have supported the conclusion that sex-typed men are more likely to abuse their female partners.[85]

Finally, research has also established that androgynous people are more *loving* than sex-typed men or women and that two androgynous people are likely to have a happier marriage than a couple in which the man and woman both adhere to traditional gender roles, or one in which one partner is androgynous and the other is more traditional.[86]

As an example of a person who has transcended gender-role stereotypes, consider Craig, a thirty-four-year-old computer programmer we interviewed who clearly has both a traditionally masculine side and the capacity for sensitivity, caring, and intimacy—traits traditionally considered "feminine." Craig's story makes it clear that he and his girlfriend enjoy all the benefits that researchers have found of incorporating both masculine and feminine traits in their personalities.

Craig earned a master's in fine art and is a sculptor, although he quickly discovered he couldn't make a living at his art. So he went back to school to learn computer programming. He is also a sergeant in the Army Reserves. Craig is tough enough to command soldiers, but sensitive enough to be an accomplished artist. He is also able to function in a highly competitive field—computer software design—and is able to make a conscious decision about how he wants to behave and what his values are. He told us, for example:

The field I've been in is very competitive, but I don't feel like I'm ultra-competitive anymore like I used to be when I was younger. Winning really meant a lot. Now, discovering means more to me than winning.

Craig, perhaps because he does not conform to any simple stereotype about what it is to be a man, for a while had a tough time connecting with women. He told us about some of his frustrations in trying to find a sexual partner who was right for him:

I must have dated every woman in town before I met my current girlfriend, Alissa. What an exercise in frustration. A lot of these women were very attractive, some of them were intelligent and well educated. It never lasted more than a few months with any of them; I went out with most of them only two or three times. Maybe it was me. I felt like I couldn't "read" them, almost like there was some secret code of behavior that they knew and I didn't.

There was certainly something about me that turned some women off. They'd smile and say they had a good time and then when I called them it was always "My mother just died," or "I'm really busy with work right now." I don't know what it was. I always felt I wasn't masculine enough for them, or masculine in the right kind of way. Like, one woman was telling me all about her problems with her car, and when I told her I don't really know much about cars, she just looked at me like I was an alien. It wasn't too good for the ego, let me tell you.

Everybody had advice for me about how to find a woman. My brother told me, "Act cool; women can never resist that." At the same time, my female friends at work were telling me, "Do this, don't do that." Some women I went out with would offer to pay for their own dinner, and I would never argue with them. I didn't want to come off like some male chauvinist. Then these women friends at work would say, "Are you crazy? I'd never go out a second time with a guy who didn't pay for dinner."

When I did get as far as the third or fourth date, there was the whole question of sex. Do I make a move? How do I know whether she wants me to or not? How is she going to react? It was so nerve-racking that half the time it didn't turn out too well.

Then I met Alissa at a New Year's party, and right away I was interested. She's very attractive, but not in a movie-star sort of way. She has an interesting face. Plus she's tall—6'1", two inches taller than me, and I found that a turn-on. Right from the beginning, it felt totally natural to talk to her about anything and everything. I never wondered, "What is she thinking of me?" or "How am I coming off?" I never felt I had to avoid certain topics—car repair or whatever—because she might not think I was man enough. It's funny, with my friends there's a lot of boasting and anxiety over masculinity, performance, even penis size. When it comes to conversation with my male friends, of course, I'm going to be more macho—start talking a bunch of nonsense. I know and they know, but we still do it, because it is a part of it. With Alissa, I express how I really feel. I can be myself.

We enjoy each other. We just hang out in the same room, and we're happy to be together.

Craig told us how well his sex life is going these days. He rated his sex life with his girlfriend, Alissa, a "6" on a scale of sexual satisfaction where "7" is the maximum. He reported that they have sex two to four times a week, despite the fact that they are both computer programmers who often have to work eighteen-hour days and even Saturdays and Sundays when a particular project heats up. Craig told us:

When Alissa and I first met, we were right on the same page sexually. We both had strong desires that equaled each other.

Part of their ability to maintain a satisfying sex life is due to Craig's freedom from traditional gender-role stereotypes that dictate that work is a man's highest priority and that it is women who take the responsibility for monitoring the health of a relationship and, when there are problems, initiating dialogue about the relationship:

Sometimes, she will be thinking about sex a lot more than I will. The last couple of weeks, I've been more interested in sex than she has, but she has been working eighteen hours a day. They're trying to meet a client deadline. I understand during a time like that, things are going to be different between the two of us.

We haven't seen each other much in the last couple of weeks, because of the job, so we haven't really been communicating much about such things. So last night I didn't go to work. I took the night off and we went out for dinner and had a long talk. Just about where we both are, what we're thinking about, what's going on, what my concerns are, what my thoughts on the situation are. And she told me what she's thinking about and what she's going through. It was good to talk. We both felt much better about it afterwards.

Craig also values intimacy as much as physical pleasure, defying the stereotype that men value sex for the physical sensation, while women are the ones who want an emotional connection:

Our episodes are right now usually of the shorter nature, because she's working so much, and there are times when we're both comfortable enough with that. But we also try to put a block of time aside, when we'll have time to really enjoy each other a little more. There are times when I don't want a "wham-bam-thank-you-ma'am," because you know you're not going to have the time to lie there with each other afterwards. It feels almost incomplete without that.

Craig and Alissa clearly have their moments of conflict, but they also know how to resolve conflicts without violence:

We're both very strong-willed people, and we're both very vocal people, and we wind up clashing about things. For example, if she really sees things one way and I really see things a different way, we'll get into a huge argument about it. But by the end of the night, we've dealt with it. We're able to talk to each other. It's kind of like we've set a rule for ourselves whenever we fight; no matter what, at the end of the night, when we go to bed, the argument's over until the morning. It usually works. A lot of times when you sleep on it, you wake up, you feel a lot differently about the situation.

Above all, one senses from the way he describes the relationship that Craig and Alissa have something precious: a durable relationship that makes them happy, sustains them through hard times, and includes great sex:

I never, ever want to feel beneath her; nor do I want to be above her. But everything I want in a woman, she's got it, and she's taught me a great deal.

We're both there for each other. When you are in a long-term relationship, there's someone you can depend upon, someone who's there for you, someone you can talk to, someone you can confide in. And being there for someone else, is something you get a lot out of yourself.

Craig's story says it all. By allowing himself to be androgynous—by not having to worry about whether his mate will see him as being "masculine" enough—Craig adopts what we believe is the sexually intelligent approach to gender. He allows himself to be who he is, no matter what society's rules of gender may be.

Remembering the Secret Sexual Self

A key component of sexual intelligence is acknowledging that some aspects of our secret sexual selves are influenced by gender. We have all been conditioned to some degree to conform to gender stereotypes. Within our relationships, we are sexually intelligent when we explore the differences that can arise—or that simply appear to arise—because of gender. Rather than making broad assumptions about what all men or all women are like, sexually intelligent people focus on how gender, and expectations about gender, come into play within their individual relationships. Sexually intelligent people are aware that, contrary to cultural stereotypes, there are few differences between men and women in sexual attitudes and behaviors, and individual men and women vary in the extent to which they are typically male or female.

Where there is solid evidence for differences between men and women that influence sexual desire and behavior, knowing about such differences and being able to use that knowledge to one's advantage is an important aspect of sexual intelligence. But knowing the truth about false stereotypes is critical for people to break free of the restrictive—and often negative—effects those stereotypes have on relationships. Finally, knowing the truth about gender differences can free us to incorporate both masculine and feminine traits into our personalities, to develop our sexuality in more complex and interesting ways. Stereotyped beliefs about how we "should" behave in bed, as men or women, or how our partner should or will behave prevent us from having the most fulfilling sex and the happiest relationships. Transcending old rules about how men and women should behave sexually frees us to be ourselves and actually leads to a better sex life.

How Sexually Intelligent Are You?

What would you do in the following situation?

> Your partner begins to behave in bed in a way that you associate with someone of the opposite gender—that is, your female partner becomes more aggressive sexually—initiating sex, for example—or your male partner becomes passive.

Questions to Consider

1. Would you be uncomfortable and disturbed by this, or find it exciting?
2. Which behaviors in bed do you associate with masculinity and femininity?
3. In this situation, would you worry that your partner's different behavior in bed signaled a change in his or her overall personality? A change in the nature of your relationship?
4. In general, how do you tend to react emotionally when someone deviates from what you consider the way a man (or woman) *should* act? Are you uncomfortable?
5. Do such deviations have a broader meaning for you? For example, if you are a woman and you are uncomfortable when men are passive, do you fear that your rock of Gibraltar might crumble? If you are a man, do you tend to feel insubstantial or incompetent around assertive women?

Bear in mind the following principles.

Scientific Knowledge

Not all men are alike, nor are all women alike.

Consider the possibility that differences between men and women in their sexual attitudes and behaviors are socially conditioned—and can be unlearned.

Try not to fall into the trap of assuming either that men and women are exactly the same in the way they think and feel, or that men and women are so different that it is impossible to understand the opposite sex.

Research evidence suggests many of the old stereotypes about male/female differences in attitudes toward sex simply aren't true; avoid making one sex or the other "the bad guy."

People who are not constrained by traditional gender roles have the best sex lives and the best relationships.

Awareness of the Secret Sexual Self

Don't let yourself be limited by traditional ideas of how men and women "should" behave.

Experiment, in bed and out, with behaviors you associate with the opposite sex.

Cultivate in yourself some of the traits of the opposite sex.

Expand your sense of your own identity to incorporate a range of sexual behaviors, both those you associate with masculinity and those you associate with femininity.

Connecting with Others

Don't assume that men are not interested in intimacy or able to combine it with sex, but remember that some men are not as skilled as women are at recognizing and articulating their needs for intimacy, as opposed to their purely physical desires.

Try not to condemn or reject a potential sexual partner who doesn't fit your ideas of how a *real* man (or woman) should behave.

When sexual problems arise, consider the possibility that they may be due to a lack of communication, rather than to differences between men and women in what they want in bed.

Talk to your partner about his or her expectations about the way men and women should or do behave in bed.

chapter ten

Abandoning the Secret Sexual Self:

The Legacy of Sexual Violence

Knowing and accepting the secret sexual self is a hallmark of sexual intelligence; losing touch with it can lead to tremendous pain, confusion, and even self-destructive behavior. The secret sexual self, as

> **If someone hit you over the head with a frying pan, would you call that cooking?**
> —Mike Lew, *Victims No Longer*

we've seen, represents the truth of who we are as sexual beings. It is the sum total of all our feelings and lifetime experiences with sexuality. It represents our genuine sexual desires as well as the learned associations, sometimes unhealthy, that we develop based on our sexual history. As we've stated earlier, a significant number of the participants in our Sexual Intelligence Project scored low on the questions in our study relating to the self-awareness component of sexual intelligence, namely, the extent to which they knew, understood, and accepted their true sexual selves.

The single best predictor of low self-awareness in adulthood was having been sexually abused as a child. Childhood sexual abuse specifically impairs people's awareness of their secret sexual self, as opposed to their cognitive or social skills. People who have been abused often split off from everyday awareness feelings and experiences connected with the past that could help them to understand their sexuality in the present. Not surprisingly, people with a history of childhood abuse are loath to examine closely their own sexuality because it is too emotionally painful. Society, too, still encourages people to bury early sexual experiences, to suppress the truth of their sexual history, to hide their shame in silence.

While childhood abuse survivors' lack of self-awareness is understandable, it carries a heavy price: they are unaware of some of the complex associations between sex and violence or humiliation that have distorted their genuine desires and preferences. People who were sexually abused as children are more likely to suffer sexual dysfunctions in adulthood, to report lack of sexual satisfaction, and to have a significantly greater number of sex partners, potentially putting them at risk for being infected with—and spreading—sexually transmitted diseases such as AIDS. What's more, they may be at risk for developing sexual addictions. People who have been sexually abused in childhood may become at risk for being repeatedly victimized sexually in adulthood or—in a small percentage of cases—for victimizing others.

The hopeful news from our research is that having been sexually abused doesn't have to condemn a person to a lifetime of such problems: reclaiming the secret sexual self holds the key to overcoming the legacy of sexual violence and going on to have a fulfilling sex life. Our research suggests that people who seek to understand their secret sexual selves are far more likely to overcome past sexual experiences that were frightening or uncomfortable or confusing, grasp how such experiences have shaped their sexuality, and build sexual relationships that are intimate, meaningful, and fulfilling. As challenging as it may be, it is possible, with the help of friends, trustworthy partners, and professional help when necessary, to go back, reexamine the past, discover the truth of our sexual experiences, and find a way, perhaps for the very first time, to connect with others in relationships that are healthy and sexually fulfilling.

The Legacy of Sexual Violence

Sometimes people assume that forms of childhood sexual abuse that don't involve penetration—things like fondling or an adult exposing himself or herself to a child—are less serious and leave little trace on a person's adult sexuality. Although the more severe and chronic the abuse, the worse the long-term consequences, "lesser" forms of child molestation still leave terrible scars.

Consider, for example, Krystal's experiences with early sexual trauma.

Krystal is twenty-two years old, a slight blond with pale blue eyes who is majoring in criminology. In response to one of the items on our initial questionnaire asking, "What do you think your parents could have done differently to prepare you for a healthy sexual life in adulthood?" Krystal wrote: "I wish my mom didn't date a lot of perverted jerks. It makes me hate sex sometimes."

Krystal was born and raised in the affluent suburb of Scarsdale, New York, by a divorced mother who dated a number of different men while Krystal was growing up. One of those men, Ira, eventually moved into the household, fathered Krystal's half-sister and brother, and sexually molested Krystal:

When I was about three, my mother dated Ira, who is my brother's and sister's father, and he lived with us until I was about thirteen, for ten years. Then, he moved to Queens to his own place, but he would come back every once and again to see the kids, watch TV, mooch off of us. He was disgusting. I remember him just being smelly, like a slob, always walking around with his underwear on, nothing else. There was something grimy about him, like he was doing it purposely. Just really nasty. And I also remember times when he would look at me funny. At that time, I didn't know it was in a sexual way, but it felt really uncomfortable.

At night he would come into my room a lot. He never touched me, but it would be dark and he would walk into my room and he would stare at me. That made me really uncomfortable. I remember . . . I really knew it was wrong, because I remember him coming to sit on my bed and me screaming for my mother, like, "MOM!" and he would rush out of my room really quickly. He was afraid of my mother finding out.

I remember watching pornography with him, I was probably six or seven. When I would come home from school, he would be in his underwear on the couch, watching porn. I would just walk by, and he would say, "You want to sit on the couch with me?" And I'm like, "What are you watching?" I'd say, "No," and go into my room, but then I would come out and I would kind of look to see what was happening. He knew I was there and he would say, "Do you want to come and watch?"

I was intrigued because I knew this was something only adults did. Not so much that it was "sex," but that it was "adult movies," something only adults got to see. I saw him masturbate a couple of times. I was like, "I guess that's what happens when guys watch these movies."

It made me not want to have sex for a very long time. And I didn't have sex until I was eighteen. He was disgusting . . . a T-shirt full of spaghetti sauce . . . a pot belly. I think that's a big reason that I have a lot of distrust of men. When I'm about to start a relationship with a guy, I wonder: "Is there something hidden, is this just an act you're putting on for me now? If I get you home, if I've been with you a long time, will this side of you show up, really nasty and grimy?"

Krystal's story illustrates the deep and lasting damage that even "subtle" forms of childhood sexual abuse can do. By being exposed to sex in such an inappropriate way at such a young age, Krystal internalized feelings and developed assumptions about sex that haunted her into adulthood. Because she could not trust her mother's boyfriend to respect the boundaries that children need to feel with the adults who take care of them, Krystal has had to travel a long, difficult road to reclaim her sexuality. Krystal, like most victims of child sexual abuse, ended up disconnected from her secret sexual self.

Reclaiming One's Secret Sexual Self: The Path Back from Sexual Violence

Because they are disconnected from their secret sexual selves, people who have been sexually violated may unwittingly repeat the trauma of the past. Many behave in ways that are self-destructive or destructive to others. In what amounts to a vicious cycle of sexual violence, people who score low on sexual intelligence, especially those who score low on the "self-awareness" component, find themselves at increased risk of becoming either victims or perpetrators of sexual violence. They are more likely to be promiscuous, to become sexually addicted, and to believe in rape myths that women want or enjoy rape, beliefs that may put some people at risk for hurting others. They may lose all desire for sex. Finally, we believe they are much more likely to become physically ill since they may lack the self-knowledge, self-respect, and judgment to steer clear of sexually transmitted diseases.

The first step in overcoming the past and reclaiming one's secret sexual self is to stop reenacting the past. This can be accomplished by spotting destructive behavioral patterns and becoming aware of the pain they cause to oneself or others. The next step is to recognize the connection between the present and the past: the way in which compulsive sexual behavior in the present is an outcome of sexual violation in the past. Finally, it's necessary to stop the compulsive behavior and to choose trustworthy sexual partners with whom one can talk about the past, overcome the stigma and low self-esteem that many abuse survivors carry, and learn to trust again.

In this chapter, we examine four ways that people who have experienced sexual abuse unwittingly reenact the trauma: by pursuing sex with multiple partners, by becoming addicted to sex, by victimizing others due to their misguided belief in the myth that women want or enjoy rape, or by becoming "sexually anorexic," losing desire for sex.

Krystal and Promiscuity with Abusive Men

Krystal, like many abuse survivors, behaved promiscuously for a time. In the past, she repeatedly had sex with men who mistreated her.

> **In my late teens I went through a promiscuous stage. I definitely did things that were really stupid and that hurt me, such as sleeping with a boy that I really liked right away. I didn't stop to think that you probably shouldn't sleep with someone if you don't know them, if you just met them at a party. You don't feel really good about yourself after doing something like that. I've had a lot of not so great relationships with men. They were always the same kind—users, not very nice. They mainly wanted sex. I knew I picked those people on purpose.**

In our research, people who were sexually abused as children had a significantly greater number of sexual partners in adulthood than those without a history of abuse. We are not alone in finding a relationship between child sexual abuse and adult promiscuity.

For example, in a study published in 1996, psychologists Robyn Walser and Jeffrey Kern of the University of Nevada in Las Vegas recruited a sample of 116 women currently in psychotherapy from Las Vegas mental health agencies and clients of private practitioners. Of the total, 71 women reported having been sexually abused. The women who reported sexual abuse showed significantly higher levels of sexual guilt. Despite the fact that sexual guilt is usually associated with *fewer* sexual partners and a less active sexual life, the women with childhood sexual abuse experiences were significantly *more* promiscuous. This included having intercourse at an earlier age (excluding the abuse experience), being more likely to have sex on a first date, having a greater number of sexual partners, and being more likely to have had extramarital affairs. The greater the severity of the sexual abuse, the more promiscuous the women were.[87]

Victims of childhood sexual abuse are often at risk for being victimized again in adolescence or adulthood. Studies have shown that women with a history of childhood sexual abuse not only have a tendency to be more promiscuous but are also more likely to be raped in adulthood.[88]

It can be very difficult to believe, or accept, that someone who has suffered a sexual trauma would later become promiscuous. We've already seen one reason why a person might do so: Julia, the woman we met in chapter 2 who inexplicably found herself sobbing during sex with her boyfriend, was raped in college, and thought of herself as a "weirdo" because she subsequently sought out sex. As she told us, her promiscuity was a way of trying to master the trauma of the rape, a way of trying to convince herself that sex wasn't a problem for her. There are other reasons, too. One of the most devastating effects of sexual violence, whether it happens in childhood or adulthood, is the damage it does to the victim's self-esteem and self-image. Survivors typically carry a sense of stigma, of being "marked," contaminated, or evil, even "whores,"[89] as well as suffering from feelings of guilt and shame.[90] In our own study, we have found that childhood sexual abuse contributes significantly to sexual guilt. A third reason is that people can become conditioned by experiences that occur early in life and later, in adulthood, exert the pull of familiarity, no matter how unpleasant they may have been at the time. For all these reasons, abuse survivors often reenact their trauma in adulthood, entering into sexual encounters with the very people who are apt to treat them badly and even abuse them.

An important step in overcoming the past is not simply recognizing a destructive behavior pattern, but also making the connection between past and present—understanding the link between one's present behavior and the abuse. Krystal, in retrospect, saw that during her period of adolescent promiscuity, she not only picked abusive men "on purpose," but that they were all too familiar, that she had been conditioned early on to associate sex with a particular type of man:

I noticed that there were certain guys that I always wanted to be with, that I was really attracted to. They were always the ones like that messy, nasty guy, Ira, that my mother was with. . . . but these guys were always abusers.

Krystal also came to see another reason why she slept with abusive men: she had been taught early on that it was "normal" to be mistreated and developed her sense of identity accordingly. Sadly, she was incapable of allowing herself to be treated kindly and with respect by men:

That was the only way I knew men, as being not nice. So I guess when someone was nice, I thought, what is wrong with them? That wasn't how I was used to being treated. That's what I was most comfortable with or all that I could relate to.

People who have been sexually abused in childhood typically have great difficulty trusting other people and forming intimate relationships in which they feel they can be themselves. Their relationships with friends and lovers are often seriously impaired by their difficulties in trusting others, their need to be in control and to guard the secret of what happened to them in childhood. Many continue in adulthood to feel isolated from other people.[91]

Intimacy plays a crucial role in people's mental health, and even in their physical well-being, just as a satisfying sex life does.[92] Lack of intimacy in one's relationships is even more damaging than having few relationships. It is the warmth and affection, the closeness and mutual interdependence, and the ability to disclose one's thoughts, feelings, and experiences that seem crucial for mental health.[93]

Krystal is working on sustaining intimacy and being able to trust a man who has given her every indication of being loving and trustworthy. She is also learning to embrace her own perception that her boyfriend, Sean, is really safe:

I think it comes from my past. He notices and gets really angry, but I don't trust him not to hurt me. He says, "I want to be with you forever, I want to marry you." He's done everything positive for me. He's given me no reason to doubt him. We just recently came back from Miami, and the women down there were gorgeous.

Not once did I notice him looking at another girl. But I don't trust his feelings for me. So I'm thinking this has to go back to my distrust of men.

Although Krystal still struggles with trust, she is aware that her distrust of Sean stems from her past. Talking about one's feelings about past abuse requires, not only having close relationships with friends, family, or a romantic partner in which self-disclosure is possible, but also being willing and able to reveal what happened. Many abuse survivors are not able to talk to their partners, even though they have continuing evidence that it's safe to do so. You can hear, for example, in Krystal's voice, the anguish of knowing that, even though all the evidence suggests she can trust her boyfriend, Sean, she still is not able to be completely honest with him:

> **I can't trust him completely; I don't feel that I can tell him everything. And in looking at it, I don't see any reason why I couldn't, because he's done everything.**
>
> **For example, take when I'm flipping the channels and come across pornography, I have to turn it off really quickly because I feel really uncomfortable. I definitely can't watch it with him, and he doesn't understand, and I can't tell him why. I've told him about my mother's boyfriend. I told him the guy used to come into my room, and Sean got really upset about that. But I can't tell him that my mother's boyfriend also made me sit down and watch porno with him, because I don't want Sean to think, "Well, why'd you do it?"**
>
> **And then maybe he'd think, "Well, you have traces."**

If as individuals we are disconnected from the truth of our experience, it is obviously very difficult to share that truth, with any sort of honesty or intimacy, with friends or loved ones. Survivors have such difficulty disclosing what happened to them in part because they are often so disconnected from their own experience and in part because of the long-term damage sexual abuse does to one's sense of self. As a result, it is easier for many survivors to be promiscuous and disconnected with multiple partners than face the truth of their experience with an accepting partner.

The most difficult thing for Krystal, as for many abuse survivors, is that memories of her abuse in childhood periodically intrude when she and Sean are having sex:

Actually, I remember thinking about it when we were having sex, and I remember having to stop because of it. It felt gross. I just didn't want to do it. I'm afraid this whole thing is going to make it weird forever. That's sad for me; that's not what sex is about. It's not supposed to be a bad thing.

Krystal's challenge is to share her discomfort and pain with Sean when they are having sex. By not doing so, she runs the risk of fleeing this healthy relationship and losing this opportunity to reclaim her sexuality.

A 1999 study confirms how damaging sexual abuse is for a person's ability to function sexually in adulthood. Dr. Jillian Fleming and her colleagues at the National Centre for Epidemiology and Population Health at the Australian National University in Canberra, Australia, and Dr. Paul Mullen at Monash University in Victoria, Australia, conducted a large epidemiological study of the effects of sexual abuse on women. Using a mail questionnaire, they contacted 710 women. The women who reported having been sexually abused before the age of sixteen reported significantly more sexual problems than did those with no history of abuse, including problems with lubrication, inability to achieve an orgasm, pain during intercourse, lack of interest in sex, and lack of sexual arousal.[94]

While studies like these suggest that childhood sexual abuse may directly cause adult sexual dysfunction, our own research shows that the picture is more complicated. We found that childhood sexual abuse does not necessarily *directly* cause sexual dysfunctions in adulthood. Rather, we found that such abuse specifically impairs people's awareness of their secret sexual self, and that it is this lack of sexual intelligence that is responsible for sexual dysfunctions in adulthood, not the childhood abuse per se. This conclusion is based on a statistical technique that allows researchers to look at the relative contribution of two different factors—in this case childhood sexual abuse and awareness of the secret sexual self—to an outcome such as sexual dysfunctions. In this case, the analysis showed that childhood sexual abuse lowers awareness of the secret sexual self, which in turn is associated with sexual dysfunctions.

The hopeful news from this finding is that having been abused in childhood does not necessarily mean that sexual dysfunctions are forever. Since the direct cause of dysfunction is lack of sexual intelligence, becoming aware of one's secret sexual self, untangling the learned associations created by the abuse from genuine, healthy desires offers the promise of overcoming sexual dysfunctions and having a more satisfying sex life.

Krystal reported experiencing all of the sexual dysfunctions we inquired about, including lack of desire, difficulty achieving orgasm, and pain during intercourse. She worries about the effect her difficulties with sex could have on her relationship with Sean:

> **Sean's a great guy and the sex is okay. . . . Well, I lie to him a lot. . . . I don't want to say, "Well, no, it didn't happen for me."**
>
> **I'm just really worried about how sex is going to play a role in the relationship. He's asked me to do certain things, like he's asked me to do oral sex, but I won't do it. I feel very uncomfortable with him touching parts of my body. There are things that I should tell him, things I should say like, "This isn't pleasing me, I want you to do this more," but I can't. I think we have a really good relationship now other than sex, and I don't want to ruin that relationship by how our sex life is, but I know that in a realistic world you can't have a good relationship without having a really good sex life.**

For all the progress she has made, Krystal still needs to work on one key aspect of sexual intelligence: she needs to talk openly with her boyfriend about what she needs and wants in bed and what she doesn't want. The chances are that Krystal would discover that being more honest with her boyfriend would actually make sex easier for her and improve their sex life.

Krystal has come a long way toward understanding her secret sexual self and reclaiming her sexuality. She sees how her early experiences with her mother's boyfriend conditioned her to become attracted to a certain type of man who would only use her and mistreat her. That insight into how her sexual desire was conditioned in childhood is the first and critical step in reestablishing contact with her secret sexual self. Krystal has also taken a second step toward reclaiming her genuine sexual self: today she is able to tolerate being involved with a "nice guy," rather than pursuing relationships with abusive men in which she would end up simply reenacting her childhood trauma again and again. That is a very good sign that Krystal is no longer comfortable with being mistreated. Although Krystal has come a long way, she still needs to talk openly with Sean, in order to challenge her own assumption that she is permanently stigmatized by her past—that Sean would blame her for what was done to her as a child—and to improve their sex life.

Ryan and Belief in Rape Myths

At twenty-nine, Ryan tops six feet and is built like a linebacker. He grew up in a suburb of Chicago and spent four years in the military as an M.P. He is currently finishing his B.A. and planning to become a social worker. Ryan is unsure whether he was sexually abused as a child by an older girl in the neighborhood. He has no clear memories of the abuse, only suspicions. Regardless, his first sexual experience at the age of fourteen itself bordered on abuse, as it involved a woman four years older who orchestrated the sex.[95] As Ryan told us:

> She was eighteen, a friend of my sister's. I was in the debate club at the time, and she was, too.
>
> I was drunk at a party. We went for a walk and then got in the back of a car and had sex. She was the more experienced one. As for me, I was drunk. I don't remember most of what happened.
>
> Before that . . . I can't say I remember, but I do sometimes have these thoughts that I had these sexual experiences with an older girl that lived next door to us. Sometimes I think I just imagined it. Most of the time I'm just wondering whether it actually happened or if it's just in my mind.

Like Krystal, and other abuse survivors, Ryan has had multiple partners. So many that, when we asked him how many sexual partners he's had, he told us, "I honestly don't know."

Ryan has frequently ended up having sex with women he doesn't want to, seemingly despite himself:

> I've had girls I'm friends with interested in me. And I've ended up sleeping with them, even though I really don't like them on that level. I don't know why I do it, and then, afterwards, I feel like chasing the person out of the room. I'm like, "I don't want to see you again."

It was only at the end of our interview that Ryan revealed more about why he has ended up sleeping with women he's not attracted to. We ended the interview as usual, by asking "Do you have any questions?" Ryan referred back to several items on the initial questionnaire, specifically, items from the Rape Myth scale:

> **The questions that really stood out for me was girls setting themselves up to be raped. I think it was something like, "Do you think some girls actually set themselves up to be raped?" or something to that effect. Well, I thought it was kind of true, even though everybody resents the thought of a girl setting herself up to be raped, because everybody thinks, "Oh, it is so traumatic, how could somebody set themselves up?" But I thought there was a grain of truth to it.**
>
> **Because I think I've come across girls that actually created the situation where I would have no choice but to have sex with them. Made me feel like I had the power, I was in control, when they were running the whole show. They had everything set up, they were going to be alone at the house, and get me in the room, or send me up to their room and then come up in the room, and do certain things. Not directly, but things that ... make me start thinking, things that rape my mind, so I end up, you know. ...**

Ryan feels victimized by women, feels that they hold all the power in sexual situations and that they deliberately "do certain things" to "rape" his mind. And he continues to sleep with women he doesn't like, without any insight into why he does so. He is only vaguely aware of a pattern in his behavior and has not yet begun to wonder about why he continues it. He attributes his own feelings of being helpless in sexual situations to the actual sexual machinations of women, rather than connecting those feelings to his dimly remembered past experience of being abused by a neighborhood girl. Ryan's perception of his experiences with women seems to go beyond a description of seductive behavior; it sounds like the experience of a young boy who has been exploited by someone older, with more power, perhaps the neighborhood girl that he vaguely remembers. Not surprisingly, after having sex, Ryan is angry, feels like chasing the woman out of the room. His belief that women control sexual situations has led him to conclude that it is possible women actually set themselves up to be raped. This perception—that women really want to be raped—could leave someone more violent than Ryan at risk of actually becoming an aggressor, completing a vicious cycle of abuse by becoming the abuser instead of the abused.

The way that childhood abuse confuses an individual's sexual self and pushes that person to enact violence may be subtle, but it is real. Psychologists David Lisak, at the University of Massachusetts at Boston, and his colleague Susan Roth, in a 1988 study, found that when they didn't actually use the word *rape* in their questions, 15 percent percent of their sample of college men admitted to having done things that legally constitute rape, such as using force to subdue a woman. Lisak and Roth showed that underlying anger and power, not pent-up sexual need, were important motivating factors of the men's behavior. They speculated, "Perhaps men who are highly sensitive to feeling put down and dominated by women are more likely to find themselves in interactions with women that lead to angry feelings and reactions and are more likely to be hypersensitive to feelings of being betrayed, deceived, and manipulated."[96]

Ryan certainly seems to feel manipulated by women and to find himself repeatedly in situations where he feels "raped" and angry after having sex with a woman. That is not to say that Ryan will ever rape a woman; the vast majority of people who are sexually abused in childhood do not go on to hurt others. But his lack of insight into his secret sexual self leaves him potentially at risk of ending up in a situation in which he assumes, mistakenly, that some woman is setting up a situation where he "has no choice" but to have sex with her. What's more, Ryan's lack of insight into his own sexuality and the way it has been shaped by past experiences leaves him powerless to alter a very unsatisfying sex life.

Nick and Sexual Addiction

We've seen in both Krystal's case and Ryan's that the pain of childhood abuse, and the need to try to master that experience, can lead some people to become promiscuous; it can also lead some people to become "sex addicts," compulsively pursuing sex that brings them little joy and often damages them.

Nick, a tall, dark-haired, twenty-five-year-old student with chiseled features and green eyes, is one of them. Nick told us about being violated by a friend of the family when he was a child:

I was sexually abused a couple of times by a male friend of the family when I was seven or eight. He was staying with us after just having come to America.

I don't remember any feelings about it; I was confused. No one ever found out. I put it aside; never really thought about it.

Nick fell into a pattern of behavior in his early twenties that went beyond promiscuity and became an addiction. Nick first had voluntary sex at the age of fourteen; between then and the age of twenty-three he had sex with forty to fifty partners. He even made his living for a time as a male prostitute. Nick suffered during that time from both alcohol and drug addiction. In describing his sexual desires in those days, Nick used the language of a drug addict:

I had urges; it's the strongest thing. It's like being an addict. A good metaphor is that I kind of got my fix, and then I could focus on the world and things.

Sexual addiction is a way that people unwittingly avoid emotional pain and thwart access to their own emotions in general. It is a way of cutting themselves off from the secret sexual self. Numbed and out of touch with their genuine feelings, they may find it impossible to be emotionally open or honest with others, whether they are friends, co-workers, or intimate partners. And because sexual addiction often begins in the teenage years, it may lay an unfortunate groundwork for highly complex, often troubled adult relationships.[97]

A substantial number of people in our sample shared some of the characteristics of sex addicts. For example, 19 percent said that they frequently promise themselves to stop certain sexual behaviors, while 14 percent said that they fail to keep that promise and do it anyway. Eighteen percent said they have sometimes felt degraded by their sexual behavior. A quarter of our sample said they worry about other people finding out about their sexual activities and feel they have to hide those activities from others. Fifteen percent admitted that they use sex as a way to escape their problems.

What's more, in our study, childhood sexual abuse was a highly significant predictor of later sexual addiction: those who reported a history of abuse scored much higher on a scale measuring sexual addiction than those who were not abused. But by far the most significant predictor of sexual addiction was a lack of sexual intelligence, and not just sexual intelligence in general but, specifically, lack of awareness of the secret sexual self.

Despite public ridicule of the concept of sexual addiction, there is a growing awareness in the clinical community that individuals can be "addicted" to sex, just as they can be addicted to drugs or alcohol. Sexual addicts include both men and women, and people from all walks of life. What leads someone to become a sex addict is still a matter of research and debate among the scientific community. Some researchers argue that there is a genetic predisposition to addiction, while others observe that there are neurochemical changes associated with the development of an addiction. There is also good evidence that sexual addiction is one outcome of childhood trauma. A history of other forms of abuse, physical and emotional, is also common among sexual addicts. Psychologist Patrick Carnes, Clinical Director of Sexual Disorder Services at The Meadows in Wickenburg, Arizona, found in a national survey of recovering sexual addicts that they had a background of extensive sexual, physical, and emotional abuse.[98]

There may be a biological explanation for why compulsive sex—just like drug or alcohol addiction—drives people to seek out their "drug" more and more frequently, while deriving less pleasure from it over time. As we saw earlier, recent evidence shows that sex is accompanied by the release of endorphins, powerful endogenous chemicals whose structure is similar to that of opiates such as heroin and morphine. Other recent research suggests that people can suffer withdrawal from endogenous opiates, just as they suffer heroin or morphine withdrawal. An initial surge in endorphins, released during sex, produces powerful feelings of well-being, including relief from pain and anxiety, even a "high" or state of euphoria. When endorphin levels then drop, people may experience irritability, anxiety, and other painful emotional states. Over time, people may seek out sex more frequently, not so much to get the original rush of an endorphin high, but simply to escape the painful effects of endorphin withdrawal.[99] Or, as Nick put it, sex is like a "fix" that people need before they can focus on other things.

Nick began his recovery from sexual addiction after he had spent six months in inpatient treatment for drug and alcohol dependency. The hospital where he was treated had strict rules against engaging in sexual encounters during the rehabilitation process, which forced him to stop his pattern of compulsive sexual encounters for six months and confront the truth of his secret sexual self. Once Nick faced the pain of his past and completed treatment for his drug and alcohol problems, he was more aware of his sexual self and of the difference between purely physical pleasure and his need for an emotional connection with a sexual partner:

> They had strict rules against sexual activity or having relationships. When I got out, you're not allowed to have an intimate relationship until you've been clean for two years. I was young and I had needs, so my counselor said I could go to a prostitute, that that would be the best thing to do. I did it about six times. I didn't really like it. I hated it. It was just physical, there was nothing there. I tried to talk with them and be friendly, and they didn't like that. They were being really technical and they had to move on, it was their job. It was just something for pleasure; it reminded me of drug use. I felt kind of dirty. It's not legal. The first time I had to get my friend to call up the pimp, and the guy would wait outside, and I'd pay him money. It was kind of scary. It wasn't relaxing; it was too crazy. And it wasn't emotionally satisfying.

Nick is currently in a stable monogamous relationship with a woman and is continuing, with her help, to recognize what he feels and to reclaim his genuine sexual preferences:

> I believe I am in love now, although it was kind of scary at the beginning. My girlfriend is teaching me ways the sex and emotions are going together. Intertwined. She tells me that I'm not very much in touch with my emotions, not as much as she is. She hugs me and that's all she wants, and I think that she wants to sleep with me. I'm kind of confused sometimes. Lately I'm trying to be really honest with her.

All of Nick's efforts to free himself from compulsive, repetitive sex that ultimately left him unsatisfied, to rediscover his secret sexual self, and to risk sharing it with another person have paid off for him. For perhaps the first time in his life, he has a genuinely satisfying sex life:

> My current relationship with her is sexually satisfying, so much more satisfying than the things I used to do. For example, pornography doesn't really talk to me anymore. I haven't watched porno in a long time. I feel empty when I watch it now. I'd rather spend time with my girlfriend, not even have sex, but just doing things. When we have sex, it's so nice and real and satisfying. My relationship with my girlfriend now is so deep.

When is a sexual behavior compulsive, and what is the difference between sex addiction and a healthy appetite? We suspect that the behavior has crossed over into addiction when it consumes large amounts of time, energy, perhaps money, and threatens one's health without producing much pleasure; when it diminishes rather than enriches one's life; when it crosses over from passion, however all-consuming, into obsession. Other signs that sex has become addictive is when it has to be carried out in secrecy and cannot be integrated in any way into our sense of who we are, or when it has a negative impact on a primary sexual relationship that one values and wants to maintain. Finally, we suspect that someone's sexual behavior has become addictive when being prevented from carrying out the behavior produces a great deal of unmanageable emotional pain, pain that the sexual behavior may be covering up. Sexually addictive behavior, in many ways, is the opposite of behavior that is sexually intelligent.

Avoiding Sex Altogether

Not all survivors of childhood sexual abuse have multiple sex partners in adulthood or develop sexual addiction. Some avoid sex. Some, in fact, have an extreme aversion to sex, a disorder called sexual anorexia or Sexual Aversion Disorder. Patrick Carnes, a clinical psychologist and Clinical Director of Sexual Disorder Services at The Meadows in Wickenburg, Arizona, published findings in 1998 of a study of patients, many of whom had been abused in childhood, at The Meadows who were diagnosed with Sexual Aversion Disorder. Those with an extreme aversion to sex had high levels of shame and self-loathing and avoided forming relationships in order to avoid sex. Over a quarter of them engaged in self-mutilation. Plus, they were rigidly judgmental about other people's sexual behavior. Beyond the obvious consequences to their physical health of self-mutilation, and the physical benefits they miss from not having sex, these people are also likely to suffer the negative psychological effects of isolation from loving human relationships.

In some cases, abuse survivors alternate between promiscuity and abstinence or, after a period of promiscuity when they are young, develop an aversion to sex.[100]

It is not surprising that survivors of sexual violence would score low on awareness of their own sexuality. There is so much pain buried under the surface and such a frightening, tangled web of associations between sexual arousal and violence, fear and degradation, that they could hardly be blamed for sealing off the past and all of those connections. But the key to healing the effects of sexual violence is to develop awareness of the secret sexual self. Without delving into and exploring the connections between sexual arousal and anger, fear, or feelings of inadequacy, people can be at risk for repeated sexual victimization or for hurting others. For many people, this undertaking is not something to do alone. There are qualified therapists who can make it easier to face the aftermath of experiencing sexual violence.

It *is* possible, with the help of friends, one's partner, and, in some cases, a therapist, to heal the damage caused by sexual violence and to enter a whole new world in which sex is a source of joy.

How Sexually Intelligent Are You?

Think about the following situation:

You meet someone new who is attractive, intelligent, nice, someone with whom you have a lot in common and would like to pursue a relationship with. Everything is going fine until the first time you have sex. The sex isn't disastrous, but it isn't that good either, and it doesn't improve over the next few times. You have a funny feeling that something's wrong, but you can't quite figure out what. Then your partner reveals that he or she was sexually abused as a child.

Questions to Consider

1. How would you respond to this disclosure?
2. What would you say to your partner initially?
3. Would you question whether the abuse really happened?
4. Would you wonder whether your partner might be mistaken, perhaps misled by a therapist or influenced by all the media coverage of child abuse?
5. What do you think your own emotional reaction would be to your partner's childhood experiences?
6. Assuming you believe him or her, would you find it difficult to hear about the abuse?
7. What about hearing the details?
8. Would you feel that your partner should have told you about his or her past earlier on?

9. Would you continue the relationship?
10. What if your partner needed to take a break from sex for a while, or needed to avoid certain sexual behaviors? How would you feel about that?
11. How would you feel if your partner sometimes confused you with his or her abuser?
12. How would you handle this situation if you yourself had also been abused?
13. What elements in your own personality attracted you to someone who was abused?

Bear in mind the following principles.

Scientific Knowledge

Try to remember, and help your partner remember, that sex itself isn't toxic, shameful, or destructive.

In your partner's experience, sex has been used as a weapon to assault him or her.

Resist authoritative pronouncements in the media that claim memories of sexual abuse are mainly the product of suggestion by therapists, or a way to get back at one's parents, or a bid for attention, and so on. The research evidence suggests that childhood abuse is far more common than most people think.

Before you decide to end the relationship and find a partner who hasn't been sexually abused, consider that as many as one out of three people you will meet may have been abused.

Awareness of the Secret Sexual Self

Be compassionate toward yourself when you find either the fact of the abuse or the details difficult to hear.

Think about your own sexual history and how it may have influenced the kind of person you are attracted to.

Connecting with Others

Check out with your partner how he or she experiences your sexual behaviors, including even the most harmless or ordinary ones.

Talk to your partner about what sexual behaviors each of you is comfortable or uncomfortable with.

Encourage your partner to get professional help and to build a network of friends and confidantes to talk to when you're not able to hear some of his or her past experiences.

Experiment with all the myriad ways of being physically intimate, aside from intercourse.

Be aware that your partner may have been conditioned to be aroused by degrading or hurtful sexual practices. Don't shame him or her for these involuntary conditioned associations.

PART IV

Sexual

Intelligence

In

Action

chapter eleven

The Mysteries of Sexual Attraction

Why is it that we are attracted to one person while another leaves us cold? Isn't this the question to which everybody wants an answer?

Attraction often takes place in mysterious ways. We have certainly heard stories from our research participants of love at first sight. Take Connie, for example:

> ... it was a very elevated, intellectual sort of thing. I wanted to undress him with my teeth.
> Ruth, in Tom Stoppard's *Night and Day*

When I met Bruce, it was really weird. I just knew. I drove into a parking lot, and I saw him standing by his car, and I thought there was something about him. The second I started talking with him, it was different than any other person I had met in my life, and I think before we had our first date, I knew we were going to get married. It just felt like we were, and we did. We've been married for six years.

Falling in love with him was so consuming. He lived far away when we met. We didn't even know each other, and he was coming here every weekend, or I was going there. It was just so exciting. It was so much fun. I loved it. That was such a great time. It passed so fast; I felt like I had known him my whole life. We met in April and we got married the next December. But we knew in June that we were going to get married, that was the first time we talked about it. We decided we would, but we weren't going to tell anyone—not when it had only been two months since we met. They would all be saying, "Oh, they'll be divorced in a year." (laughing) So we didn't say anything, and then we got officially engaged in October, and we got married the next December. It's worked out pretty well—a few little bumps in the road.

On the other hand, we have also heard of experiences where one person feels hopelessly ambivalent toward a potential sexual partner due to a lack of "spark" or passion. Claudia, at thirty-nine, has been through the gamut of ways to meet Mr. Right: personal ads, singles' dances, fix-ups, Internet chat rooms. She's been looking for a long time. The man she's currently dating, Jack, has a number of good qualities, but Claudia can't get past the fact that he just isn't her "type":

> I'm involved with a man now, but I'm not really passionate about him. I hate to admit it, especially since men do this to women all the time, but it's his appearance. He's so different from my type. I love the clean-cut look—guys who are tall and really lean, and look great in a business suit—a white dress shirt, pressed within an inch of its life, turns me on every time.
>
> Jack, well, he's a bit overweight—not obese, but definitely chubby and sort of rumpled looking. And his taste is awful. He'll show up in a red and purple rugby jersey with olive corduroys that are bagging in the seat, with the knees almost worn through.
>
> That makes me sound terrible. I'd hate to think that I was that superficial, to judge a person by his body or his clothes. Because, otherwise, Jack's a great guy. And there are other things—the intimacy, the fact that we can really talk, and that we love to be together. I consider him a good friend. I could see myself marrying this guy, having kids with him, if it weren't for the fact that I'm just not attracted to him.

That quickening of the pulse and heightening of the senses when someone who is physically your "type" walks into a room can be one of life's best moments, but that visceral reaction to one particular physical type—blonds, brunettes, men in a well-pressed white shirt—doesn't necessarily guarantee a satisfying sex life. As a matter of fact, it might be a sign of danger ahead. When people limit themselves to dating a particular type, they may not only be losing out on a truly happy sex life, but be continuously hooking up with partners who are unhealthy for them. Being sexually intelligent means understanding all the different influences that make one person seem more attractive to us than another.

Sexual attraction works on many levels and is different for each person. The type of person we are attracted to has a lot to do with our personal history, the positive and negative associations we have formed over time to different personal characteristics—whether an athletic physique, a particular hair color, or personality traits such as intelligence or warmth. In other words, our immediate attraction to a particular type reveals a great deal about the secret sexual self.

We have found that sexually intelligent people—the people who have the most satisfying sex lives—are aware of their visceral attraction to certain physical types, but are not limited by that in forming relationships, having the ability to appreciate and be attracted to a wide range of people with different physical appearances. They are not addicted to their type. In other words, because they are aware of their secret sexual self, they know that, due to their unique history and learned associations, they might be conditioned to find a certain type of individual attractive. They also know that this type might not be healthy for them, that this type might represent an association with a negative past experience, and that they no longer have to give in to that kind of attraction. What's more, highly sexually intelligent people notice and are attracted to personal characteristics, such as someone's intellect or sense of humor, rather than focusing immediately on a person's physical appearance. As a result, they create for themselves a larger pool of potential sexual partners to choose from and increase their chances of a satisfying sex life.

Derek is a good example. When we asked him what he finds attractive in a woman, he told us:

> **I'd say it's something more inner than outer. You look at my last girlfriend and my current girlfriend, and they're polar opposites. My current girlfriend is 6'1", blond and blue-eyed; my last girlfriend was 5'5", dark hair, brown eyes. I've never been attracted to just one kind of person; all different shapes and sizes appeal to me.**

Across a Crowded Room: Immediate Attraction

One of the questions we asked the people we surveyed was whether they are aware of the physical characteristics that constitute their type. The people who told us, "I'm immediately drawn to people who look a certain way" scored lowest in sexual intelligence. In contrast, people who chose to exert some control over the way in which physical attractiveness influenced their behavior, those who answered, "I'm attracted to individuals who look a certain way, but I don't always choose to be in a relationship with them," were significantly higher in sexual intelligence. Highest in sexual intelligence were those who answered, "I'm attracted to many different physical types."

Many of us do, indeed, have a type to whom we are immediately attracted and onto whom we project all of our hopes and fantasies. Many people who are looking for a sexual relationship automatically rule out anyone who isn't their type. In doing so, some people set themselves up to be disappointed, or even hurt repeatedly because they are unwittingly drawn to people who frustrate their unmet needs (we discuss this problem later in the chapter). Even those whose type doesn't represent a fatal attraction are still limiting their chances for a satisfying sexual life by waiting for someone who is their type to come along. It's far wiser to open ourselves to a wider range of people and, in the process, increase our chances for a good sex life.

The most sexually intelligent people, it turns out, aren't attracted so much to a person's physical appearance as they are to his or her personality. When we asked people to tell us what makes a person sexually attractive, the responses fell into several different categories: facial characteristics such as a nice smile; a person's body; whether or not the person is emotionally supportive; and personality characteristics such as intelligence or a sense of humor.

In terms of their sexual intelligence, what was particularly revealing was the *first* thing people mentioned when asked what makes a person attractive to them. Both men and women who mentioned facial or physical characteristics first were significantly lower in sexual intelligence than those who first mentioned personality, emotional supportiveness, or who said, "I'm attracted to all kinds of people," or "It depends on the person." Finally, the greater the number of personality characteristics people listed as appealing to them, the more sexually intelligent they turned out to be.

Why Do Looks Matter?

People prefer a partner who is physically attractive, at least as defined by a particular cultural stereotype, for a number of reasons. For example, many people want a partner who is attractive because of the social status it confers on *them*. One of our interview participants told us how his girlfriend, an aerobics instructor, raised his sense of self-esteem and status:

A lot of people feel that my girlfriend is physically attractive, and I do, too. So it makes me feel good that I have someone who looks so good, who is wanted by other people.

When people associate a certain physical type with rewards such as increased social status or even the powerful reward of sexual gratification, they may come to be conditioned to prefer one physical type—blonds, brunettes, and so on—over another. This is a matter of *conditioned arousal*, when we associate sexual pleasure with a particular appearance or particular circumstances. In the same way, using pornography repeatedly can condition people to experience sexual arousal to particular physical types or stereotypical scenarios that constitute typical themes in pornography.

There is another reason, though, why people value physical attractiveness in our culture. Researchers have found that there is a clear stereotype about physically attractive people: we assume that those who are good-looking are "more sociable, dominant, sexually warm, mentally healthy, intelligent, and socially skilled" than physically unattractive people.[101] It turns out, however, that these stereotypes aren't true. Beautiful people aren't necessarily any smarter, saner, or sexier than people who don't conform to a stereotyped look.

As we discussed earlier, people who are constrained by traditional sex-role stereotypes about how men and women should behave have less satisfying sex lives. People constrained by such rigid gender roles are also more likely to fall prey to the assumption that physically attractive people have more desirable personality characteristics than do those who are less attractive. Psychologists Susan Anderson of New York University in New York City and Sandra Bem of Cornell University in Ithaca, New York, conducted an experiment in which they asked men and women to talk by phone with a person in a different room. The research participants were given a photograph, supposedly of the person they were speaking to. As Anderson and Bem suspected, people who were constrained by rigid gender roles were more responsive in conversation with a stranger when they had been led to believe that the person was attractive. Androgynous people—those who have and value both masculine and feminine traits—were equally responsive to the individuals they were talking to, regardless of whether they believed the person to be attractive or unattractive.[102]

Why Are We Physically Attracted to Some People and Not Others?

Many people assume that sexual attraction is a mysterious affair, the last unanswered and unanswerable question about sex. There may be an ineffable quality to sexual attraction, but we know some things about how sexual attraction works that can help us to make intelligent choices about our sexual liaisons.

The Influence of Biology

One biological explanation for attraction is based on smell. Biologists have found a class of chemicals called pheromones that, in many species, are released to signal sexual readiness and attract potential mates. From insect species to mammals, the role of smell in attractiveness has been established, and humans—women, in particular—certainly spend a great deal of money trying to smell right in order to attract members of the opposite sex. It's only recently, however, that researchers have found evidence for the role of smell in human attraction.

In a 1999 study, Winnifred Cutler had one group of male college students wear a pheromone she has identified and another control group dab on an inert substance. She then asked them to keep track of their sexual behaviors over a two-month period, including formal and informal dates, sleeping next to a romantic partner, and having sexual intercourse. The males using the pheromone had more sex, compared with the control group. Her results need to be replicated, but they support the argument that humans, like other species, can be attracted by pheromones.[103]

The Role of Evolution

Novelist W. Somerset Maugham once wrote, "Love is only a dirty trick played on us to achieve a continuation of the species."[104] Or, to put it in scientific terms, evolution has led us to be attracted to the people we can mate with successfully, for example those whose appearance signals health or fertility. There is some evidence for that argument. For example, psychologist Leslie Zebrowitz of Brandeis University and her colleagues have found that in the United States the faces that people judge attractive tend to be very youthful in their features. Additionally, psychologist Judith Langlois and her colleagues have found that faces judged to be more attractive are "average," reflecting genetic heterogeneity and presumably better health. Psychologist David Buss collected data in thirty-seven different countries and found that men prefer female characteristics that indicate the capacity for producing children.[105] But there is also reason to doubt this evolutionary hypothesis. In a 1998 study, University of Massachusetts, Boston, professor Don Kalick and his colleagues examined a sample of hundreds of individuals born between 1920 and 1929 for whom there were photographs rated for physical attractiveness and also yearly doctors' health ratings. While the evolutionary hypothesis would predict that the individuals judged to be more attractive would be healthier over their lifetimes, there was, in fact, no relationship between appearance and physical health.[106]

To the extent that biological and evolutionary factors such as pheromones influence attraction, they are probably only a small part of the story.

Researchers have found that, within a specific culture, there is considerable agreement among people about what constitutes physical attractiveness. But standards of physical attractiveness vary from culture to culture and within a given culture over time. For example, the female body type considered most attractive in nineteenth-century Europe and America would today be considered unattractively overweight. Culture obviously plays an important role in determining how we judge attractiveness.

The Influence of the Media

The mass media is one aspect of culture that plays a significant role in influencing standards of physical attractiveness. Television and film actors, models, even newscasters all tend to conform to a particular appearance considered attractive: these days, women actors tend to be very thin and have large breasts, while male actors and models tend to be tall and muscular, with angular features. Media images bombard us daily with the same stereotyped vision of what constitutes physical attractiveness.

Just as media images have a very negative effect on people's self-esteem, an effect that influences their sex lives, those images also create discontent with one's *partner's* appearance. Some years ago, psychologists Douglas Kenrick and Sara Gutierres demonstrated the power of the media to influence how we judge other people's appearance. They went to dorm rooms at Montana State University during the hour when the television show *Charlie's Angels* aired. Kenrick and Gutierres asked male students in the dorms to rate the attractiveness of a woman in a photograph, explaining, "We have a friend coming to town this week and we want to fix him up with a date, but we can't decide whether to fix him up with her or not, so we decided to conduct a survey. We want you to give us your vote on how attractive you think she is, on a scale of 1 to 7."

The students were then shown a picture of a woman of average attractiveness. Some of the men questioned had just been watching an episode of *Charlie's Angels* and they rated the woman in the photograph significantly lower on physical attractiveness than did men who had not been watching the show. Media images not only define the look that is considered attractive, but also lead people to judge those who don't conform to "the look" more negatively.[107]

And it is not just television and advertising that hold up an image of physical perfection that few prospective partners can match. Pornography, not surprisingly, showcases actors selected specifically for their physical attractiveness—as well as exaggerated sexual endowments. It wouldn't be surprising if, by comparison, one's real-life sexual partners began to pale. Dolf Zillmann and Jennings Bryant, the University of Alabama researchers whose research we discussed earlier, found that a diet of X-rated videos caused, not just disillusionment with one's partner's sexual performance, but also dissatisfaction with his or her physical appearance.[108]

What Makes Us Attractive to Others?
It's not just *other* people's looks that matter to us; most people are equally concerned about their own attractiveness. A national survey

done by Louis Harris Associates found that over 70 percent of individuals polled said it is important to them that they feel attractive to the opposite sex. This is not particularly surprising. What may come as a shock are the results of a poll conducted in March 1996 by ABC News/ *Washington Post.* They asked respondents: if there was a pill that they could take that would make them 10 percent happier, but would also make them 10 percent less attractive, would they take it? Of the 1,512 adults questioned, 67 percent said absolutely not: they would rather give up happiness than be less attractive.[109]

Freeing ourselves from society's influence in defining physical attractiveness is important not only because it can determine how we view other people's appearance, but also because it influences how we feel about ourselves. How people feel about their appearance has important consequences for their sex life. We asked our respondents how their appearance affected their feelings toward having sex. Those who said either that they were "not attractive enough to have a good sex life" or that their appearance affected their chances for a good sex life "somewhat" were significantly lower in sexual intelligence than those who responded, "No effect, I'm quite happy with my appearance." Freeing ourselves from exaggerated, arbitrary standards of physical attractiveness that surround us in the media is an important step toward sexual intelligence not only because it expands our ability to appreciate and be attracted to a wider range of people but also because it can free us from self-consciousness, even self-loathing, about our own appearance.

So if you are concerned about your physical appearance, whom might you talk to? We asked our respondents this question, and the answers were revealing. Those who said that they wouldn't talk to anyone about it, or who would just talk to a professional about it, were significantly lower in sexual intelligence than those who said they would talk to a friend or to their sexual partner. Very often people are preoccupied and self-conscious about some perceived physical flaw of theirs that their partner doesn't notice or care about. As we have said before, talking with your sexual partner is a key aspect of sexual intelligence, and it applies in the realm of physical appearance as well.

Early Learning

In a number of cases, the physical type our research participants found most attractive was that of his or her opposite-sex parent. Unlike Freud, we would not necessarily see that as evidence that young children experience sexual desire for their opposite-sex parent. Rather, children may come to find their parent's appearance preferable to other physical types because they associate it with positive feelings they have for their parent, or simply because it is familiar.

Consider, for example, one dark-skinned, dark-eyed young man we interviewed who is from Iran. When we asked him if there was a particular type of woman he finds attractive, he told us: ". . . always, the blond-haired, blue-eyed California chick." We initially supposed this preference was due to the influence of American media images, but later in the interview we got a surprise when he described his mother to us:

My mom has Turkish descent in her, she's light-skinned, she has green eyes, and dirty blond hair.

There is actually recent scientific evidence that, even among animals, familiarity breeds attraction. Imagine you were a male sheep and, as an infant, had the bad luck to lose your mother. If it weren't for the female goat in the barnyard who adopted you along with her own young, you wouldn't have had a chance for survival. But what happens when you hit adolescence: do you look for a girl just like dear old Mom? It sounds like a bad joke, but it is actually a study done recently by Professor Keith Kendrick, a neurobiologist at the Babraham Institute in Britain. Professor Kendrick took some baby goats and baby sheep and switched their mothers—the goats were raised by sheep mothers and the sheep were raised by goat mothers. Come mating time, he found that male animals raised by a surrogate mother preferred, *100 percent of the time*, to mate with a female of her species, rather than their own: male goats raised by sheep mothers tried to mate with female sheep, while male sheep raised by a goat were attracted to female goats. Female animals raised by a foster mother behaved differently—they eventually mated with their own species—but the males were quite single-minded in their pursuit of a female who resembled their surrogate mother.[110]

Early Learning and Fatal Attractions

Attraction operates on two levels. There is the initial attraction that
may lead a person to ask someone out on a date, and the attraction
that leads a person to want to spend the rest of his or her life with
another person. What about long-term relationships? Why do people
choose the partners that they do? In our research, we found not only
that sexually intelligent people focus on a potential partner's personality rather than physical appearance, but also that the most sexually
intelligent people are attracted to people with a range of personalities.
What's more, they tended to value personal characteristics that were
intrinsic to the other person and made him or her unique—the person's
sense of humor, and so forth—more than they focused on personality
characteristics such as compassion or sensitivity, characteristics that
promised a partner would meet *their* emotional needs in a unilateral
way. These two findings are important because people who are attracted
to one personality type may end up zeroing in, again and again, on people who frustrate their needs in much the same way that their parents
did. Similarly, those who are attracted primarily to compassion, sensitivity, and other signs of emotional supportiveness, regardless of the
potential partner's unique personality, may be trying to heal old wounds
rather than form a mutually sustaining partnership.

We heard a number of stories from people who either married or
became involved, over and over again, with someone who was like their
opposite-sex parent, not so much in looks, but in personality. That can
be a very positive thing in the case of people whose parents were capable of giving them love, nurturing, and a positive sense of identity. For
example, when we asked our respondents what makes someone sexually attractive to them, one woman said:

**If he is intelligent, wise, smart, committed to me, he loves me and I love him, and
if I have known him for a long time—building from a friendship based on personality—if he's like my dad. [our emphasis]**

But for others, choosing a partner who interacts with them in the
same way that their parents did can be an exercise in frustration.
Sexual attraction toward someone who arouses unmet emotional needs
in us can be very powerful, but the sex often fails to satisfy those emo-

tional needs. In many cases, at best, the sex serves as a pleasurable "fix" that bypasses the person's emotional needs altogether; at worst, the sexual involvement may repeat earlier negative experiences and add to the emotional pain. That was certainly the case with Glen. He came to understand his history of "fatal" attractions to the wrong women in this way:

> I had a period in my twenties and early thirties when I pursued a particular type of woman—what I thought of as women who were sharp, bright, ambitious, and independent. I always picked the driven types—the lawyers, the doctors, the ones who were climbing the corporate ladder. I wanted a woman who was intelligent. In fact, I'd look at the personal ads in the paper and turn immediately to the ones that began with: "Extremely intelligent." But it was more than that—there was always an edge to the women I dated, a bitchy streak. They weren't nice people. But those were the women I went after, never the ones who were both intelligent and nice. To me, "nice" meant boring.
>
> I'd fall hard for one of these women, right off the bat, and do everything for her—send flowers, take her out to fancy places I couldn't afford. In the beginning, with every one of these women, things were great—the sex was great, the relationship was exciting. But then there'd come a point when they'd either start to back off or turn nasty and demanding, almost like they were trying to see how much I'd take from them, how far they could push me.
>
> It's embarrassing now admitting this—I made a fool of myself more than once chasing after a woman who treated me like dirt. Once a woman started to turn cool, I'd go crazy. I felt like I <u>had</u> to have her. I'd do anything to be with her. It wasn't good for me, not only because I was crazy half the time, and concentrating on some woman instead of on my job, but also a lot of those women were users—I think they liked having a guy around that they knew was a sure thing—a backup guy.
>
> At some point, I got it that every relationship I was in turned out the same way. I knew I must in some way be picking those women, and I didn't want to do it anymore. I decided to change my life, so I did it—I went into therapy.
>
> And I definitely began to see a pattern. With every woman I went out with, within months, I'd be in a state—just waiting for her to either leave me or blow up at me. In some ways, they were like my mom in that regard. Not that she was a driven career type. She stayed home with us. This was in the fifties so it was kind of expected. She was actually very loving and affectionate, funny, almost too attentive, I mean to the point where she picked up after me and my

brother all the time, made our beds in the morning, picked our socks off the floor—everything. But she was also "high-strung"—that's what my father called it. Every once in a while, she'd blow up. Out of nowhere. I'd come home from school and walk in the door to this tirade, "I'm not your maid,"—that kind of thing. I think when I was a kid, I always imagined that she was on the verge of leaving us for some other family, where the kids were more considerate.

There came a point in therapy when I could pinpoint to the day, almost to the hour, with each woman I'd gone out with, the moment I first felt this kind of sick, scared feeling in the pit of my stomach. And then I realized it was the same feeling I used to get as a kid when my mother went into one of her rants.

I was in therapy for about a year before I met my wife. Probably, if I hadn't done it, I wouldn't have liked her, because she was too nice. Not that she puts up with stuff from me. I have a bad habit of leaving socks around and she'll just say, right out, "Honey, would you put those in the hamper? They smell." But with her, it's not personal. It's no big deal. I know she's not going to leave me over my dirty socks.

Glen spent a long time suffering in one unsatisfying relationship after another before he saw that he was repeatedly attracted to women who aroused in him the fear of abandonment. Only when he saw the connection between his sexual desire for unavailable women and his own unmet emotional needs was he able to find a sexual partner with whom he could have a fulfilling relationship. He accomplished this by facing his secret sexual self, as opposed to running from it.

Experiences in relationships during childhood, with parents and siblings, play a significant role in contributing to people's emotional needs and to their assumptions about the kind of person they expect will meet those needs. The primary psychological theory concerning the development of love is called "attachment theory," primarily associated with the work of psychologists John Bowlby and his collaborator, Mary Ainsworth. Research in attachment theory has established that a child's attachment to his or her mother (or other primary caretaker), reflected in the child's "attachment style," tends to be fairly stable. Researchers using this theory classify a child's attachment as secure, anxious, or avoidant, depending on how responsive the caretaker is to his or her child during the first seven years of life.[111]

Of interest to our discussion of sexual intelligence, psychologists Cindy Hazan and Phillip Shaver at the University of Denver in Colorado have shown that the attachment style developed in childhood is significantly related to the type of romantic relationships one has as an adult.[112] This suggests that people choose partners who interact with them in the same way that their parents did. It makes sense that people would gravitate to relationships that feel familiar, "normal," according to what they experienced earlier in life.

Hazan and Shaver conducted a survey in which they asked people to characterize their most important romantic relationship along a series of dimensions. They also asked people to describe the parenting they had received from their mothers. Fifty-six percent of the sample of 620 respondents were classified as "secure" in their romantic attachment, meaning that they were able to establish trust and friendship with their romantic partner. In addition, their relationships tended to be long-lasting: on an average, ten years or more. People who were in secure relationships, interestingly, described their mothers as having been responsible and caring, just the behaviors that foster trust and a sense of security. People who had experienced this type of parenting were able to bring that sense of security and trust into their adult relationships. We can speculate that people who are capable of secure attachments have the skills to develop intimacy, an exchange of feelings and thoughts as well as positive emotions for their partners. For them, sex is likely to serve as an expression of emotional closeness as well as a source of physical pleasure.

In contrast, 25 percent of the people in Hazan and Shaver's sample were classified as "avoidant" in their adult romantic relationships, meaning that they were distrustful of their partners and had a fear of intimacy. Their relationships didn't last as long—six years, on average, as compared with ten years for people with secure attachment styles. As predicted, these people described their mothers as having been cold and rejecting in childhood. We would expect that people in avoidant relationships, because of their distrust and fear, would have difficulty negotiating satisfying sexual lives, even avoid it or engage in it in a perfunctory way, without the emotional closeness of people with secure relationships.

Finally, 19 percent of the respondents were in adult romantic relationships characterized by extreme sexual attraction toward and preoccupation with their partner. People in such "anxious/ambivalent" relationships remembered their mothers as having alternated between treating them lovingly and then seemingly withdrawing that love. These relationships lasted on the average less than four years. The extreme sexual attraction and preoccupation typical of anxious relationships makes sense if one has learned in childhood always to anticipate that love can be withdrawn suddenly, without warning. It may be that the partner you feel you stand to lose at any time becomes the one you feel you need to have at all costs. That certainly was the case with Glen. The divorce rate among people in secure relationships (6 percent) was about half that of people in avoidant (12 percent) or anxious (10 percent) relationships.

It is important for sexually intelligent people to be aware of the influence that childhood experiences may have on their sexual and romantic inclinations. Coming from a family with parents who were not responsive and caring can predispose someone toward romantic and sexual relationships characterized by obsession and lack of trust. Knowing one's secret sexual self helps a person to break these destructive patterns and relationships.

How often do unattached people lament that "there just isn't anybody out there" to date? The good news is, that simply isn't true. Many people overlook the many potential sexual partners available to them because they set their sights narrowly on a particular type. We miss out when we assume, for example, that the person who likes computer games is a "geek" or the ballet enthusiast is pretentious. By widening our horizon beyond a particular physical type so that we can appreciate different looks, and by focusing on personality as well as physical appearance, we automatically increase our number of potential sexual partners and our chances of finding sexual fulfillment.

By examining our secret sexual selves, we can begin to see how we may have become conditioned—through our own past experiences or by media images—to gravitate toward people with a certain physical appearance or personality. For those people with a history of "fatal" attractions to relationships that always seem to turn out badly, identifying the type that arouses unmet emotional needs in us can be the beginning of true freedom to find a genuinely satisfying sexual and romantic life.

How Sexually Intelligent Are You?

Try out your sexual intelligence by considering how you would handle this dilemma:

> Imagine that you met a person who is smart, interesting, kind, caring, who makes you laugh, who is the one person you feel you can talk to about anything. There's just one hitch—he or she is anything but your type physically. In fact, the person is somewhat nondescript—not someone who makes heads turn, though not unattractive either.

Questions to Consider

1. Would you consider becoming involved sexually with the person? Would you consider a committed relationship with him or her?
2. If you became involved with the person, do you think that over time you might become aroused by his or her appearance—by brown hair if you're generally attracted to blonds, plumpness if you go for slender bodies, and so on?
3. What if you then met someone else who was your type?
4. Would you end the committed relationship with the person who wasn't your type?
5. What if the reverse were true—you meet and fall in love with someone who tells you that, although he or she loves you, you're not his or her physical type? Would you become involved with this person?
6. What if you became attracted to someone who is your type physically, but with whom you had nothing in common? Would you have sex with him/her?
7. Do you have a particular type? Do you know what it is—slender, tall blonds; short, intellectual types who wear glasses? Is your type based on physical appearance, on personality factors such as intelligence, a good sense of humor, or on other characteristics such as ethnic background, race, occupation?

Bear in mind the following principles.

Scientific Knowledge

Weigh the intoxication of visceral sex against the pleasures of relational sex.

Consider the role of the media in conditioning us to prefer certain types, such as thin blonds, square-jawed men, and so forth.

The physical characteristics that most appeal to us in many instances represent *conditioned arousal.*

Awareness of the Secret Sexual Self

Ask yourself what past relationships or experiences may have conditioned you to find a particular type attractive.

Cast your mind back over the past sexual relationships you've had with people who were physically your type. How good was the sex over the long term with those people? How good was the relationship?

Have you found yourself repeatedly drawn to the same personality type, only to find yourself confronting very similar kinds of emotional conflicts?

You may always be viscerally attracted to a certain physical or personality type, but you may find a better sex life if you decide not to become involved with someone simply on the basis of first attraction.

Ask yourself if you have repeatedly been disappointed in sexual relationships with people who treated you the way one or both of your parents did, or whose personality resembled that of one of your parents. Could it be that you gravitate toward or find familiar people who treat you the way your parents did?

Try developing an appreciation for many different physical characteristics—rich, deep brown eyes as well as blue eyes, slender bodies as well as big muscular ones, and so forth.

How do you feel about your own appearance? Do you let concerns about your appearance affect your chances for a successful relationship? Talk to a friend or your partner about it.

Connecting with Others

When you meet someone new, try focusing on their personality traits rather than their physical appearance, and try finding out more about their personality and interests before you decide whether they are your type.

If you are dating, try not to instantly type someone, based on very little information. Instead of looking for reasons to pass over someone and go to the next "candidate," try seeing how many things you can appreciate about the person before making your decision.

chapter twelve

Your Daytime Sexual Self

Madeline, a twenty-five-year-old who is studying accounting, married her high school sweetheart the day after graduation. Growing up, she learned little from her parents about sex— other than that it was sacred and reserved for marriage. As Madeline put it:

> **A lover without indiscretion is no lover at all.**
> —Thomas Hardy,
> *The Hand of Ethelberta*

Sex was absolutely not even to be part of our life before marriage. Even on TV the station would be switched when sexy scenes came on.

The first time Madeline had sex was with her husband, on their wedding night. The marriage has been a happy one, and everything seemed to go well for Madeline—until she became attracted to a man at work. It was a mutual attraction:

It came about from the interest he showed in me—as a person—and the friendship we developed. We were peers in the organization but he was older and wiser.

When Madeline realized how serious the attraction was, she quit her job. She explained to us her reasons:

I think that I found other justifications, but my attraction to my coworker, Tom, had a lot to do with it. It wasn't the reason I gave my husband for why I quit, and it wasn't the reason I gave them at work. I said I was pursuing my goal to go back to school full-time and get my degree. And that was a very legitimate reason as well. But I think the guilt that I felt . . . and constantly being tempted, thinking all the time, "Here is this guy I'm attracted to, and I know that he is attracted to me, and it could very easily turn into something more."

I still haven't told my husband. I still wonder, "Should I have told him about that?" The situation at that particular job is not an isolated event. It happens all the time and it bothers me. Like, I'll find, that even though I am married, I still am attracted to other guys, and especially guys that have put time in, getting to know me, and that I've spent time around. It's easy to form attractions. I think because I'm young, and because I got married young, it's still something that I'm sifting through . . . it's something I'm still learning about myself.

It definitely bothers me. I think, "Why can't I just not be attracted to other people?" But, at the same time, that would take away the enjoyment that you have being with other people, men and women. You're attracted to people because they are nice or friendly, or maybe they look nice. And so, whether that is a man or woman, there's some reason you're attracted to them, and that itself is not a problem. But when it goes beyond simply "Wow, he's really cute," then I feel, "I shouldn't have these thoughts, because I'm married, and I don't want to be attracted to other men," but I find that it happens. So, how do I avoid letting that become more . . . you know?

It's not just work related. It comes up in other situations—school, social situations. I can't quit all of my life and not be attracted to other people. I need to find a new way to deal with this, to be able to have friends and get to know people and still safeguard myself so I don't fall into a relationship with someone and hurt the relationship that I want the most, with my husband. Temptations are always there.

Madeline recognizes what less sexually intelligent people have trouble admitting to themselves—that we can't simply turn off all sexual feelings when we leave the bedroom. Our sexuality is a part of our personality—twenty-four hours a day. One of the hallmarks of sexually intelligent people is their ability to integrate their sexuality into their overall identity, rather than attempting to compartmentalize it and deny the sexual feelings they have throughout the day. The most important context in which we're called upon to deal with sexual feelings during daylight hours is at the workplace.

Romance in the Workplace

Workplace romance is very common and becoming more common: studies have found as many as 75 to 80 percent of employees say they've been involved in either a social or sexual relationship in the workplace.[113] Of the people we surveyed, 31 percent had had a sexual relationship with a coworker.

People today spend more time in the workplace than ever before, and less time in social settings outside work, such as church activities or clubs. In fact, after college, work may be the one way—aside from the Internet and newspaper personal ads—that adults can meet potential romantic partners. Although the workplace is an obvious setting in which to find a mate, actually pursuing a sexual relationship in this context can mean risking a charge of harassment, finding oneself in an awkward, painful situation if the romance sours, even losing one's job. Many people are unwilling to risk a workplace romance because they are unclear where the line falls between workplace romance and sexual harassment, as standards for behavior in the workplace—and for sexual behavior in general—continue to evolve. Some scholars, for example Catherine MacKinnon, have raised the question of whether *all* workplace romances are really just sexual harassment in one form or another.[114] We disagree. We don't have to live in the modern conception of a politically correct, sexless workplace where we have to be on our guard about everything we say or do, where we can never be ourselves. Sexual feelings that arise on the job needn't be bad or wrong. They may express our vitality and creativity and may add something to our working relationships. Nor are all sexual relationships between coworkers necessarily a matter of harassment: workplace romance, in contrast to sexual harassment, involves mutual passion and a genuine desire to be together.[115]

At the same time, because people spend so much time in the workplace, we have to be very well acquainted with our sexual selves, in order to make decisions based on our real desires and ones that won't jeopardize either our own or other people's careers and outside relationships. If you don't know your secret sexual self, you can easily find yourself in very uncomfortable situations at work.

The sexually intelligent person knows how to choose the level and type of sexual expression appropriate to various settings and is aware of when sexual desire for a coworker masks unacknowledged emotional needs—for acceptance and approval, or for power and revenge. The sexually intelligent person also can determine when acting on sexual desires would likely jeopardize one's work relationships, one's career, and one's life at home. But don't fear—the workplace does not have to be a sexual minefield full of confusing decisions to make. As you will see in this chapter, it is when people deny their sexuality and don't take a good hard look at their behavior that they get in the most trouble at work. The sexually intelligent approach, which includes knowing your sexual self, and being honest with yourself about your actions, can help banish the confusion surrounding workplace romances.

Old Taboos

Although workplace romances have always happened, traditionally, we have pretended that they don't—or shouldn't. Generally, people attempt to separate their sexual selves from their "work selves." Adopting an asexual demeanor at work is even considered a hallmark of professional integrity, as well as the only way to avoid being accused of, or becoming the victim of, unwanted sexual behavior.

Regardless of traditional wisdom, we have found that adopting a sexless façade at work is neither necessary nor sexually intelligent. It can even be dangerous. Remember Natalie, the graduate student who was powerfully attracted to one of her students, Mark? On the one hand, she was appearing in class dressed in dowdy clothes and telling herself that getting involved with Mark wasn't an option; on the other hand, she was going out at night to jazz clubs where Mark would be—just to hear him play, of course. Someone less sexually intelligent than Natalie could easily have found herself in bed with her student at the end of one of those evenings.

Natalie's experience is a good illustration of how illusory it is to think that we can just jettison our sexual selves for all of the hours in the week when we're not with an intimate partner. The danger with compartmentalizing the sexual part of ourselves is that it can lead us to act out in a variety of ways—being jealous, being overly sensitive to criticism, taking minor comments the wrong way, becoming excruciatingly self-conscious—as Natalie did. It can even paradoxically increase the likelihood that we'll fall into an inappropriate sexual relationship. We are not suggesting that people be sexual in every arena of their lives, but that they accept their sexuality as part of who they are, and not compartmentalize their sexual feelings apart from the personality they show to the world. Compartmentalizing feelings leads people to be blindsided by their sexual feelings and can ultimately get them in trouble.

Sexually intelligent people recognize that neither they, nor their colleagues, are likely to be able to turn off their sexuality for the better part of every workday, and that they must proactively manage the sexual feelings that arise at work. In many work settings, sex becomes a dangerous and disruptive force precisely because people attempt to simply deny their sexuality and interact with coworkers from the stance of an outwardly sexless self. As a result, these feelings are often acted out secretly and dishonestly in ways that disrupt work and leave people in vulnerable positions, professionally and personally. We believe it is much better to break down the barriers between the sexes at work, address sexual tensions head-on, and come up with a way of expressing sexuality that is not secretive or disruptive, and will not lead to unhealthy consequences.

Our study bears out this position. One of the questions we asked people was whether it is necessary to adopt a completely sexless demeanor at work in order to safeguard themselves against inappropriate behavior. Over a fifth of our research participants said it was—and they were significantly less sexually intelligent than those who recognized that it is neither necessary nor a good idea to try to maintain a sexless façade at work.

What's more, the most sexually intelligent people *weren't* the ones who had avoided getting involved in a workplace romance. The most sexually intelligent people reported having relationships with peers, bosses, even subordinates: the difference between them and less sexually intelligent people was the outcome of those relationships. The more sexually intelligent people reported that their relationships at work were a positive experience, while the less sexually intelligent had either never attempted a romance at work, or they had been involved in one that ended badly. Sexually intelligent people have the skills to know when, with whom, and how to have a workplace romance without suffering negative consequences.

How Does It Happen?

The fact is, sexual feelings inevitably come up in the workplace. Work is where we interact repeatedly and, in some cases, over long periods with people who share our interests and values. Work is also a place where powerful emotions are apt to come up, ones that people often seek to manage through sexual behavior. At work, we confront challenges to our self-esteem; questions about our adequacy; needs for approval, recognition, and belonging. Having sex with a coworker can be a way of proving to ourselves that we are desirable to that person when what we really want is to feel valued for our skills, to be recognized, or to feel that we belong. Having sex with someone at the office may also represent an unconscious attempt to gain power, or to equalize power in a relationship. It is important, and sexually intelligent, to recognize when sexual attraction to a coworker may be substituting for these kinds of unmet needs. For almost everyone, issues of love, romance, and sexuality come up sooner or later in the workplace: that is why it is important to learn to manage sexual feelings at work. It is critical, too, that we understand and anticipate the impact of workplace sexual decisions on our relationships not only at the office but also at home.

Various warning signs can indicate that you may be acting inappropriately with a coworker. Assuming that you are *not* interested in getting involved with a coworker—because you are already in a committed relationship or because of the possible consequences for your job security—one warning signal to watch out for is frequent highly charged conversations with your coworker. A little innocent flirting may not be serious, but repeated flirtation that becomes explicitly sexual or more and more daring is playing with fire. So is spending a great deal of time with a coworker you're attracted to, finding excuses to be near him or her, dressing differently on days when you expect to see the person, and so forth. You should be especially cautious if you realize that you are sharing—or are tempted to share—intimate secrets with a coworker about your current relationship, or you are discussing your partner's faults with someone with whom you could become sexually involved. An important warning sign is if you start to lie or to keep secrets from your partner about the things you talk about with a coworker. A lack of openness or honesty indicates some guilt about the nature of one's work relationship. What is important is to analyze your own actions and behaviors and try to be honest about what your real motivations are.

Take Cheryl's experience. She is twenty-one and works as a software developer in a start-up company. She inhabits a workplace that, in some ways, resembles a social club more than a corporate setting: employees work in one big open room that has a basketball hoop mounted on one wall. When tensions rise before a big deadline, basketballs fly, the squirt guns come out, and, in general, there's a great deal of horsing around that would raise eyebrows at a more conservative workplace. Plus, employees often work such long hours that they end up eating breakfast, lunch, and dinner together—take-out food at the company's expense. The company also rewards employees for all those long hours with ice cream parties, and outings to amusement parks or the beach. It wouldn't be an exaggeration to say that, for many of the employees, their coworkers *are* their whole social circle.

In this context, Cheryl became friends with her project manager:

He was like a really good friend, rather than a boss. We had a lot in common. He's a little bit older, not that much older. Like, five years. We used to go out all the time, on trips together, all of us in a group. And it just formed with him. He and I could understand each other. Listening, talking—we just bonded. One thing led to another . . . there was always attraction, but I didn't want to pursue anything with him because he was my boss. I just put the wall up, and I am actually transferring jobs.

Cheryl's story illustrates the specific factors that predict a romantic relationship between coworkers. Simply being near each other physically or working together can lead to attraction.[116] One study, in fact, found that 63 percent of workplace romances could be predicted simply by the location of employees' work stations![117] People who spend time together—even as little as five hours a week—are also more likely to form a relationship.[118] What's more, a great deal of research in social psychology suggests that, in general, people who have similar attitudes will be attracted to each other. A political conservative who is a staunch opponent of abortion is unlikely to match up with a liberal abortion rights activist, for example. Lisa Mainiero, in her 1989 book *Office Romance: Love, Power, and Sex in the Workplace*, points out that corporations and other organizations tend to hire people who fit the organizational culture and, therefore, have attitudes similar to those of the organization they're joining.[119] In a way, then, workplaces are like a club of highly compatible and, in some cases, eligible dating partners.

Organizational culture plays another role in workplace romances, too. Whether or not coworkers form relationships depends in part on whether the organization frowns on workplace romance or tolerates it. In general, workplace romances are less common in staid, traditional settings such as conservative law firms and more common in high-pressure fast-paced organizations, such as computer companies.[120] It's not surprising that Cheryl and her boss became attracted to each other, given their proximity, their constant exposure to each other, the similar attitudes they shared, and the informality of their workplace.

Consequences of Romance in the Workplace

What consequences can you expect if you get involved in a workplace romance—assuming it is a relationship desired by both parties and not sexual harassment? Tough to say. Few workplaces have either written or unwritten policies on romance between coworkers, and most organizations tend to respond on a case-by-case basis.[121] Different companies respond to workplace romances in very different ways, ranging from, for example, IBM, which bans romantic relationships between supervisors and subordinates, to Ben and Jerry's, which makes no attempt to interfere with workplace romances.[122] Some organizations ban adulterous or gay romances—the U.S. military being the best example. Several studies found that the most frequent managerial response to a romance between coworkers was to simply ignore it and take no action at all.[123] Still, there are virtually no legal restrictions on an employer's power to forbid and punish romance between coworkers—on the job and even off.[124] While it may not be the most common outcome, employees *are* frequently fired for on-the-job dalliances. Employees can also be forced to transfer to a different department within the company or a different location, and they can be passed over for raises or promotions—particularly the partner who has lower status.[125] Given the potential seriousness of the consequences, and the lack of guidelines in many companies, how do you know when to act on romantic feelings for a coworker and when not to?

Let's *Not* Give Them Something to Talk About

There are a number of situations in which the sexually intelligent course is to avoid getting involved in a workplace romance. For one thing, certain occupations have a very clear historical taboo against workplace romance, and those prohibitions have become stronger, rather than weaker, over time.[126] Medicine is one such occupation; psychotherapy and academia are others. In all three occupations, it is considered highly unethical for a physician or psychotherapist to become involved with a patient, or a teacher to become involved with a student. The difference between a boss/employee relationship and a teacher/student or physician/patient relationship may seem subtle, but it's an important difference: for a teacher or physician to have sex with a student or patient is not only an abuse of power but also a betrayal of trust.

There are other situations in which a workplace romance may not be strictly forbidden by company policy or tradition, but nonetheless is less than sexually intelligent. Employers naturally have an interest in maintaining productivity and avoiding disruptions in the workplace; they are likely to fire or transfer employees involved in a workplace romance when they fear that it will have negative consequences for the organization. From management's point of view then, a key question is what consequences a romance will have for workers' productivity, for harmony in the workplace, workers' motivation, and so forth. The research suggests that whether workers involved in a romance will be more or less productive, motivated, and satisfied with their jobs— and what ultimate consequences they will experience as a result of the romance—depends in large part on their motives for becoming involved in a workplace relationship.

People have varying motives for becoming involved with a coworker: sometimes two people are genuinely in love, sometimes one or both are seeking an ego boost, sometimes a worker uses sex as a means of job advancement. In general, the workplace romances that turn out worst—for the company, as well as the people involved—are ones in which one or both partners are motivated by factors *other* than genuine love for each other.[127]

Take Sonja's experience, for example. She is twenty-eight and works as a paralegal for a large law firm. She made the mistake of becoming involved with her boss, a lawyer who had something of a reputation for coming on to female employees—particularly attractive, young ones. At first, their sexual relationship resulted in a number of perks for Sonja, but that didn't last long:

> There was a lot going on in my life at that time, and we were always together. We talked. He was someone there who listened to me, and it just developed from there. There were comments, flattering comments, flirting, wanting to go out. He knows a lot about me; I've known him for four years. Probably in the last year and a half, things got heavy. About eight months ago, we started having sex.
>
> Suddenly there were all these advantages I had that none of the other paralegals did, like parking privileges. It actually became very noticeable to everyone around us. It sounds petty, but at the firm you are not allowed to park certain hours in the garage, and he has power over that. I was able to park there for free. He did things like that for me. He would let me leave early . . . things like that. And still log on that I was working.
>
> Then when things got rough, he took it away from me. He sent me e-mails that were, well, unpleasant. . . . It took a toll on me. He did abuse his authority, and that's why I'm leaving. I think it was all about his own ego, big-time. I requested a transfer. Never again.

Sonja's boss apparently initiates romances with subordinates to boost his ego. He uses his power to reward women subordinates involved with him. Sonja's experience is typical of boss-subordinate relationships in that they often result in special privileges and favoritism for the subordinate.[128] The problem is, when the romance sours, those privileges disappear and the boss may use his or her power—as Sonja's did—to make it very uncomfortable for a subordinate to continue on the job. Those special privileges may not be worth it in the long run and may actually be dangerous for one particular reason—they visibly set an employee apart from his or her peers.

As it turns out, often it's not so much management's reaction to a workplace romance that one has to fear, but rather the reaction of one's coworkers. Many people go into a workplace romance thinking they can keep it a secret and, in that way, avoid negative consequences. When it comes to workplace romances, however, there is no such thing as a secret: trying to keep a relationship hidden typically doesn't work. And when coworkers disapprove of a workplace romance, they can make things very uncomfortable for the lovers, even going so far as to ostracize or blackmail them. Not surprisingly, the disruption in the workplace created by disgruntled employees can be the impetus for management to take action, transferring or firing one or both employees involved in a romance.[129]

Coworkers are most apt to engage in disgruntled gossip about a romance that they perceive as involving a motive other than genuine love—job advancement, gaining power in the organization—about a highly visible romance, or when a romance, in their view, leads to exploitation or disruption in the workplace. They disapprove more of romances between a boss and subordinate than one between peers.[130] Indeed, romances between boss and subordinate can be very damaging, because of *coworkers'* responses—jealousy, perceived favoritism, and suspicion.[131] Those parking privileges and early departures that Sonja enjoyed, as she herself recognized, made it obvious to her coworkers that she was involved with the boss—and could easily have gotten her fired. Sonja's involvement with a boss motivated to boost his ego with office affairs ended as such relationships often do—badly for the woman, who is typically the lower-status employee and hence the one to suffer the fallout—whether it is being fired, transferred, or voluntarily quitting—of a workplace romance gone sour.

Sonja's story illustrates one of the most important principles to keep in mind before becoming involved with a coworker: know what your motives are and, as best you can, try to gain some insight into your partner's motives. Sonja's boss, for example, had a history of womanizing that was widely known and should have served as a red flag to her. The fact is, many office affairs involve substitute sex—sex motivated by an attempt to assuage some unmet, often unrecognized emotional need, for power, approval, status, or even excitement to compensate for a job that isn't challenging or fulfilling. Such unmet needs can go even deeper—as we've seen, sex can be used almost like a drug to try to deaden serious emotional pain. And the key thing to remember is that substitute sex doesn't work. It ultimately does not meet those long-standing emotional needs.

That was the case with the woman Eugene got involved with. She was his supervisor in the clothing store where he's employed:

> She had more power than I did, but in a different department—she was a buyer
> in lingerie, and I worked in men's casual. She was always finding some excuse to
> walk by my counter, and one day, she suggested we go out for drinks after work.
> My mistake was to say yes. We slept together a couple of times, but then she
> became overbearing—within five weeks, she had moved to be closer to where I
> lived, she was calling me constantly and stopped by my apartment all the time
> without even calling—it gave me claustrophobia. It was some weird addiction. I
> couldn't stand it. To tell you the truth, it scared me a little. Luckily, she had a bet-
> ter job offer from one of our competitors and took it.

It is important, and sexually intelligent, to recognize when sexual attraction to a coworker may be substituting for other needs. It is also sexually intelligent to be able to separate fantasy from action and to understand and anticipate the impact of sexual decisions on our relationships at work and at home. In situations where a workplace romance may have catastrophic consequences for one's career or an outside relationship, the sexually intelligent person may decide to leave sexual feelings toward a coworker in the realm of fantasy rather than acting on them.

While management's response in any one case is hard to predict, the general conclusion that has come out of twenty years of research suggests that the people most at risk of being fired for an on-the-job romance are (1) women, (2) the lower-ranked, and hence presumably less valuable, member of the couple—typically a woman, and (3) employees involved in extramarital affairs. Women, because they are more often in the lower-level position, are twice as likely as men to be fired.[132]

That doesn't necessarily mean, however, that workplace romances never work out. When coworkers genuinely fall in love, the consequences—for the company and the lovers—can be quite positive. But it takes a certain amount of sexual intelligence to conduct such a romance.

True Love Conquers All—Or at Least Has the Best Shot

Caroline's case is a good example of a workplace romance that prospered—largely because of the fact that she had the sexual intelligence to make smart decisions about the person she became involved with, the way she behaves in the workplace, and the way she balances work and romance. Caroline is twenty-five years old, an assistant manager at one of a chain of coffee shops. She works the late shift, from 2 P.M. to 10, under a female manager, and her boyfriend, Ned, is the manager on the morning shift, from 6 A.M. to 2 P.M. This is Caroline's story:

> We met last July at my job. Ned's the manager on the morning shift, so, technically, he's my superior, but he's not my supervisor. We've been dating for three months, but I've known him for about eight months. We were really good friends before we started dating. He's a great guy. I really like him as a person, a really, really good guy.

Caroline was sexually intelligent about her workplace romance in several ways. For one thing, although she got involved with someone superior to her in the organization, it was a man who isn't her direct supervisor and, in fact, works a different shift, so that, for the most part, they aren't even in the workplace at the same time. For another thing, Caroline and Ned genuinely love each other. They had the basis for an intimate relationship in a good friendship before they became involved sexually.

For another thing, Caroline was smart enough to be wary of how her coworkers might react and has been careful to keep a low profile when she and Ned are in the store at the same time, lest their relationship lead to gossip:

> I don't really work with him too much. When I'm coming in, he's leaving. Still, when we first started dating, I told him I felt really uncomfortable with him working at the same job as me, because I felt that other people would see. . . . I'm very conscious, of how people might look at me and what they might say about me. He's like, "I should be able to kiss you when I leave, I should be able to pull you aside and talk to you." And I'm like, "No, really, I don't feel comfortable with it." But when we first started dating he still would do it to the point where I said, "Listen, this is not working," and he was, "Okay, okay, okay." I told him "it's not appropriate." I kind of had to check him on that at the beginning of the relationship.

Caroline is also careful not to create hard feelings with her coworkers—jealousy or suspicion or the perception of favoritism—by strictly doing her job at work and letting Ned do his:

Ned's a great supervisor, but he makes decisions that people aren't always happy with . . . just like any supervisor. Sometimes, I agree with the decisions he makes, and sometimes I disagree with him. But I feel like I can't question him in front of other people, because that wouldn't be right for me to do. And, in the same way, if someone is saying something against him, I really have to struggle not to say anything—to keep my mouth shut—because I don't want it to appear as if I'm biased, even if I agree with something he did.

Even though Caroline and Ned love each other and the relationship is going well, the fact that she fell in love with a coworker has produced complications: for one thing, because of her relationship with Ned, Caroline is privy to information that someone else in her position wouldn't have. She is both uncomfortable with that information and has to be consciously discreet, again to avoid alienating her coworkers:

Ned will talk to me about things that are going on at work. He's a manager, and he tells me a lot about my manager, a lot about his supervisor—personal things about their lives, their problems, that they wouldn't necessarily tell me. And so that makes me feel uncomfortable, even though I still want to know [laughs]— I'm a nosy person, and I like gossip. But it still makes me feel . . . like I can look at my manager and think, "I know things about you that you don't know that I know." And so it kind of makes me feel uncomfortable when I'm talking to my manager.

Also, I know about things that are going down at work, like, "This person on your shift is about to be fired." And so, I feel like I can look at that person and know they are about to be fired or be moved to another site, and I'm like, "God, I wish I didn't know that." That's not my place to know that.

For another thing, their work relation has produced certain complications in their private relationship. Caroline has had to make it clear that, at home, Ned is *not* the boss:

Not only is he a supervisor, but he can be very controlling in our relationship. A lot of times I have to check him. For example, he likes to cook, so he does all the

cooking. But when he cooks, he insists on preparing the meals <u>he</u> likes, what he decides to eat.

Perhaps the chief reason for Caroline and Ned's ability to have a relationship and still keep their jobs, aside from Caroline's savvy about not alienating coworkers or creating the perception of favoritism, is the fact that they genuinely love each other.

Despite employers' worries that workplace romances will lead to lost productivity, long lunches, distractions, and general disruption in the workplace, studies have found that couples involved in a workplace romance are actually more productive, more involved in their jobs, and more satisfied with their jobs—when they are truly in love, as opposed to seeking excitement, ego enhancement, or job advancement.[133] One author suggests that workers who are truly in love may be more productive and devoted to their jobs to try to avoid negative consequences from their superiors.[134] Plus, a happy romance—unlike one that sours, leaving both people uncomfortable and unhappy with their jobs—can increase job satisfaction and, important from management's view, worker retention.[135]

Sexual Harassment

As we discussed earlier in the chapter, we do not want to live in a sexless workplace where we have to constantly monitor everything we say or do for fear of crossing some invisible line. That line, however, does exist. Being sexually intelligent in the workplace is not just about how to conduct a healthy and successful relationship with someone you are attracted to, but also how to manage sexual overtures from coworkers. Are these approaches healthy or do they cross the line and turn into behavior that is uncomfortable, if not harassing? The issue of sexual harassment has plagued the military, government figures, even the President of the United States and a justice nominated to the Supreme Court. It is also an issue that men and women potentially face every day in the workplace. Since the widely publicized hearings over sexual harassment charges against Clarence Thomas, federal complaints of sexual harassment have increased nearly twofold, from 6,892 in 1991 to 12,537 in 1993.[136] The numbers of employees reporting having been sexually harassed are alarmingly high. In two surveys in the 1980s, 42 percent of female federal workers and 15 percent of male federal workers complained of harassment.[137] More recent estimates range from 42 percent to 88 percent of working women reporting having been sexually harassed.[138]

Sexual harassment is a serious problem when it harms individuals and disrupts the workplace. It is also a problem that has caused a great deal of misunderstanding, uneasiness, and mistrust between men and women in the workplace. Many men worry that any joke, no matter how benign, could be taken as sexual harassment, as could an innocent compliment on a woman's appearance. Many women, on the other hand, find it frustrating that some men in the workplace seem so oblivious to the reality of sexual harassment and the damage it causes.

Where do you draw the line between romance and harassment? Professor Christine Williams has pointed out that sexualized interactions in the workplace cover a wide range of behaviors, from bantering and joking around, to compliments, and flirtatious comments, to intercourse.[139] As a matter of law, sexual harassment is defined very narrowly: it must result in discrimination against the victim on the basis of gender in order to be actionable. Courts, for example, have allowed companies to fire the lower-ranked partner in a romance—usually a woman—as long as the policy is uniformly enforced; that is, when the same company fires men, too, if they are the subordinate partner.[140]

Here, as elsewhere, we would argue that the sexually intelligent course is to focus on the meaning of the behavior at issue, rather than the behavior itself, and to make a distinction between coercion—in its many forms, some of them subtle—and behavior that is consensual. Behavior that in some situations employees consider unobjectionable— enjoyable bantering and flirtation that lightens the work atmosphere— may in other instances be experienced as unwanted and even threatening sexual attention, whether it is legally actionable or not.[141]

Consider Lauren's experience. She's head nurse in the emergency room of a busy city hospital that receives a large number of trauma cases—car accidents, stabbings, shootings. She regularly has male doctors flirt and banter with her:

I'm not ugly, so I get my share of flirting and comments. There is a fine line between advances that might be welcomed and those that aren't. Sometimes, slight flirting doesn't make you feel uncomfortable. . . . But coming from a guy

that's really sleazy or a jerk, you feel like saying, "Why are you being so friendly?" or "Why are you really laying the compliments on? I don't need that." But someone who says, "Oh you look nice." Or "Did you do something with your hair?" Those can be welcome compliments, where sometimes that same compliment coming from someone else would be, like, "Eww, don't notice me, because I know what you are noticing me for."

One of the difficulties in drawing a clear line between consensual and coercive behaviors on the job is that men and women differ in the way they perceive—and the meanings they assign to—verbal and nonverbal behavior.

Take Joanie, for example, a twenty-four-year-old student who has been working her way through college in a succession of jobs—waitressing, secretarial work, and so forth. She expressed the confusion that many women—and men—have about what is appropriate behavior on the job:

Men at work seem to feel free to touch me, to put their arm around me . . . is it because I'm short or friendly or because I've been nice to them? I'll think, "Have I led them on?," to let them feel that they are free to touch me or come around and pat me on the shoulder? Well, that's sort of unwanted, that's definitely unwanted. I can't figure out why they do that stuff. Maybe if I were taller, or wore a suit jacket that made me look more reserved, more dignified, maybe I wouldn't be seen as "cute" and they wouldn't be touching me. Then, too, I haven't finished school, so I'm not in a position of authority; I'm usually in a subordinate position whether it's a secretary job or waitressing. I don't think men would behave the same way to someone they thought was in more of an authority position. You know, they wouldn't treat you as if you were a toy or a pet.

Joanie's male bosses might well be shocked to discover that, to her, being clapped on the back or clasped around the shoulders feels like being treated as a toy or a pet. Social psychologists have repeatedly found that women are more likely than men to distinguish between touch that is intended to be friendly and touch that has sexual overtones. Perhaps because men don't make this distinction, or perhaps because *they* respond positively to casual touch from a superior, they are twice as likely to touch a woman casually as women are to touch men. Social psychologists have also found that men are more likely than women to misperceive a woman's friendliness as sexual interest.[142] It's easy to see how these gender differences can potentially lead to misunderstanding—and discomfort—in the workplace.

Our research shows that sexually intelligent people are aware of these gender differences and are less likely to misconstrue the actions of the opposite sex. For example, the more sexually intelligent people in our sample did *not* interpret a woman's friendliness as a sexual overture. However, a fair number of people in our sample thought because a woman is friendly toward a man, she is seductive or wants to have sex with him. Being aware of gender differences in verbal and nonverbal behavior can help people to avoid misconstruing their coworkers' intentions or unintentionally behaving in ways that may be unwelcome. Simply knowing that men experience a clap on the shoulder from their boss positively, while women experience the same behavior as a potential come-on can make it easier for men and women at work to talk about and clarify their intentions.

Many attempts to address the issue of sexual harassment are based on the assumption that harassment is nothing *but* a misunderstanding or a lack of knowledge on the part of the harasser, or simply oversensitivity on the part of women due to "political correctness." No doubt in some cases, such as Joanie's, unwelcome touch may indeed be based simply on a misunderstanding stemming from differences in the way men and women interpret verbal and nonverbal behavior. In other cases, however, the offender's behavior is much more extreme.

Take Vicky's experience:

I cocktail waitressed for years, and you never knew what's behind those eyes. They give you a look that goes right through you. And you get these unwanted advances all the time. Oh, all the time. They touch you all over. They put their hands all over you, they constantly grab your butt. They make comments all the time, like "Oh, can I see your breasts?" or "Come with me. You're beautiful. I want to marry you." They're always giving you their phone numbers. And then they come back and they're, "You didn't call, you didn't do this." Half the time these guys are married.

You try to just ignore it, shrug it off, but then you hear the stories of what happens to women—about women being followed—and you don't know what's behind the comments, what's behind the eyes. What they're capable of. I lived

alone, and I was coming home at 3:30 in the morning by myself. It just got too scary; I stopped doing it last December.

Such behavior may not legally constitute harassment, but it's definitely threatening to many women and unwelcome. While there may be a fine line between bantering and badgering, it's a line that's clear to most people. Sexual harassment is not simply something in the imagination of oversensitive women: research shows that both men and women agree on what constitutes sexual harassment in commonsense terms. It is the seriousness of the behavior that determines whether a particular incident will be labeled sexual harassment—by both sexes.[143]

What motivates sexual harassment and how can it be prevented? Researchers in social psychology recently have taken a largely cognitive approach to sexual harassment, arguing that men who harass women hold a set of sexist beliefs and attitudes, in some cases attitudes that—at least, as far as the men are concerned—are positive toward and protective of women.[144] This set of attitudes has been referred to as *benevolent sexism* (that is, benevolent in the eyes of the man).[145]

In his research, Michael Milburn has found that harassment in many instances is not the outcome of benevolently paternalistic attitudes; rather, it has its roots in rage, fear, hostility, and denial. When men deny these negative feelings, they are more likely to act on them.[146] Milburn's research came out of our previous finding that authoritarians—people raised by harsh, punitive parents—in adulthood tend to take their anger out on substitute targets.[147] Authoritarians harbor a great deal of rage about the way they were treated as children. When they are small, their parents are so forbidding that they cannot afford to recognize—let alone express—how angry they are at their parents. Plus, they are raised to glorify and submit uncritically to authority figures, such as parents and bosses.[148] For these reasons, in adulthood, they take their anger out on less-threatening targets such as subordinates and—in the case of male authoritarians—women in general.

Authoritarian men also adhere rigidly to traditional gender roles and tend to be hypermasculine.[149] In addition, they are more likely to batter women and be sexually aggressive.[150] What has never been established is whether that same rage stemming from childhood leads some men to sexually harass women at work.

With his student Joe Begany, Milburn recently conducted a study of 104 men enrolled at the University of Massachusetts at Boston.[151] The men were presented with a number of scenarios concerning sexual harassment. For example, in one, they were asked to imagine that they were high-level executives in a large corporation, interviewing replacements for a secretarial job. One of the interviewees is a young woman, very attractive, and clearly desperate for the job—though no more qualified than the other applicants. Respondents were asked (a) would you give her the job over other applicants, (b) would you offer her the job in exchange for sexual favors, (c) would you ask her out to dinner to discuss the job?

After controlling for a number of factors such as occupation, income, and people's tendency to give socially acceptable responses, Begany and Milburn found that authoritarian men are more likely to report a willingness to engage in sexual harassment than nonauthoritarians. Interestingly, the reason why authoritarian men are more likely to harass women at work is because they, unlike nonauthoritarians, believe in rape myths—that women are "asking to be" or really want to be raped. Begany and Milburn found no evidence that benevolent sexism—protective paternalistic attitudes toward women—predicts sexual harassment. Their research suggests that emotion—specifically unrecognized rage from childhood mistreatment—fuels sexual harassment. Men who carry that anger around with them typically create what seems to them an acceptable target for their anger. Previous research has shown that authoritarians vilify people or groups that they feel less threatened by: minorities, women, their subordinates at work. First they come to believe that the vilified group is blameworthy in some way, and then they feel justified in taking out their anger against members of the group. Men who convince themselves that women "are asking for it" clearly will feel more justified in engaging in sexual harassment.

As an example, take Kaylee's experience. She is just beginning her undergraduate education at the age of twenty-four, having worked since high school to save up tuition money. She started out working at the counter at a fast-food restaurant, taking orders, and quickly became the assistant manager. Shortly after she was promoted, she began to have trouble with her manager:

He was making all these lewd comments to me. He was like, "You need to go take a bubble bath with candles and touch yourself," and saying all these things to me. He was somewhat of a promiscuous person. I think he liked to "conquer" as many women as he could. One day, he was doing this massaging thing to me, and I was, "Get off." And he was like, "No, no, no, you'll like it." I just kind of let it go—I had to work with him—but it got worse over time. Finally, he made it clear that, unless I cooperated—had sex with him—I could expect to go back to working the counter. Definitely a power issue. When I said no, he told the district manager that I had said all this stuff to him—come on to him. And he threatened a lawsuit against both the company and me—for sexual harassment. So I had to go through this whole thing with the company.

The district manager immediately told me, "We're not taking a side on this. The organization wants nothing to do with this. If we hear any more complaints about you from your manager, you're going to be fired." So I did some checking on my own—it's a small town; people talk—and I found out that this guy—my manager—had a reputation for this crap. It had also happened at his last job, so I told that to the district manager. And I was like, "How can you take his side when I'm the victim, and you should be protecting my interests." I had to go through all this stuff to clear my name.

Finally, the district manager agreed to look into it, and the company found out that things like this had happened at previous jobs of his. They fired him, and they told him that if he went ahead with the lawsuit, they would take my side.

Kaylee's boss showed several signs of an authoritarian personality: he had a pattern of victimizing subordinates, his approach to sex had overtones of hostility—more a matter of "conquering" women than of liking them, and he assumed his victims "really wanted it"—the typical rape belief. It's very likely that Kaylee's boss was trying to assuage anger from his own past by taking it out on the women who worked under his supervision, a pattern that had already cost him one job. Learning to recognize when sexual desire is substituting for anger from the past can help people to avoid behaving in ways that constitute sexual harassment and can put them at serious legal risk.

Sex, in one form or another, is something we all inevitably face at the workplace. There is a modern conception of a politically correct, sexless workplace where we have to be on our guard about everything we say or do, where we can never fully be ourselves. We've found that there is an alternative, more intelligent way to manage sexual feelings in the workplace. Those who know their sexual selves, who can discern whether they are genuinely attracted to someone at work—as opposed to experiencing desire that masks emotional needs for acceptance, approval, or power—can act intelligently on their feelings without necessarily jeopardizing their jobs.

How Sexually Intelligent Are You?

Consider what you would do in the following situation:

> There is a very attractive person at work who seems interested in you—who is very friendly, often seems to be "just passing by" your desk and always stops to chat, always lights up in a smile when you pass each other in the hall, and lately has once or twice suggested getting together over coffee to talk about a work-related issue. You're not sure whether your coworker is interested in you sexually, but it seems likely.

Questions to Consider

1. Would you consider getting involved with your coworker sexually?
2. What if he or she were your boss?
3. What if he or she were one of your subordinates?
4. Under what conditions would it be safe to get involved with a coworker? Under what conditions would the risks be too high?
5. How would you know or how could you try to establish whether the person is interested in you out of genuine affection, or whether his or her motives have more to do with boosting his or her ego or with job advancement?
6. What if the person interested in you were someone you admire and you want praise and approval from? What if the person were someone who admired you, looked up to you, and made you feel you could do no wrong? How would this influence your likelihood of becoming involved?
7. How would you go about trying to get to know the person better without committing yourself to a sexual relationship right away—and without causing gossip?
8. What if you got involved and later the relationship ended badly? What options would you have?
9. What if someone at work were interested in you and you didn't feel the same way? How would you handle this?

10. If you're not interested in someone, and the person pursues you, at what point is it sexual harrassment?

Bear in mind the following principles.

Scientific Knowledge

When trying to decide if a coworker is signaling sexual interest in you, bear in mind that men are more likely than women to perceive friendliness as a sign of sexual interest.

Be aware that men and women interpret casual touch differently.

Even if you don't choose to date or get involved with people at work, that doesn't necessarily mean you have to adopt a rigid, sexless demeanor.

If you are a woman and you are tempted to become involved with a superior at work, be particularly careful to think through the possible consequences, since you are more likely to bear the brunt of negative fallout than is your superior.

Sexual harassment is often motivated more by anger than by sexual desires.

Awareness of the Secret Sexual Self

Before becoming involved with a coworker who has a great deal more—or less—power than you do, ask yourself whether you have unmet emotional needs—for approval, for power, and so on—that might be playing a part in your attraction to this person.

Try to be clear on how you feel about your job in general—the workplace, relationships within it, your feelings about your own competence, career progress, and so forth. Could your attraction to a coworker be serving as a bright spot in otherwise miserable days on a job you don't like?

Connecting with Others

Become aware of any existing policies or traditional ethics at your job or in your profession concerning workplace romances.

Consider talking with coworkers with whom you have a good relationship about the general subject of sexual issues in the workplace to get a better sense of how workplace romances are viewed in your organization.

If you are interested in becoming involved with a coworker, look at the possible long-term effects of a sexual relationship on each of you—on your careers and on your other relationships, at work and at home.

Consider what the other person's motives might be for wanting a sexual relationship before you get involved.

Imagine how your fellow coworkers would react to an affair and try to avoid antagonizing them or creating envy or suspicion.

chapter thirteen

Infidelity:

Using Sexual Intelligence to Stay Faithful

Of all the areas in which a healthy understanding of sexual intelligence is beneficial, perhaps the most important is fidelity—remaining in a monogamous relationship without succumbing to the temptation to stray sexually.

> **The course of true love never did run smooth.**
> —William Shakespeare,
> *A Midsummer Night's Dream*

Few situations can wreak greater emotional havoc on a person in a committed relationship. Most people know or can imagine the trauma of finding out that their significant other has been intimate with someone else. Yet surprisingly, cheating occurs with alarming regularity, even by those who have always considered infidelity morally reprehensible, and who could never even imagine being unfaithful. Consider the following statistics:

- In our Sexual Intelligence Project, the vast majority of people (93 percent) said that infidelity has very destructive effects on a marriage, yet 28 percent had cheated and 24 percent said that they might in the future.
- In a recent national survey, 81 percent of Americans said sex outside of marriage is always wrong.[152]
- One-fifth of Americans actually think adultery should be punishable by law.[153]
- National survey data suggest that approximately 25 percent of Americans have cheated on their spouses, and about the same number imagine that they will cheat in the future.[154]

As these statistics reflect, we are not alone in finding a discrepancy between what people believe and what they do. Despite believing that cheating is wrong, many Americans have sex outside of a committed relationship. Why is it that, in so many cases, people's behavior doesn't live up to their own moral standards?

The overarching reason is a lack of sexual intelligence. People who have been unfaithful score very low on awareness of their secret sexual self, far lower than those who have never cheated. Whether or not a person is unfaithful is better predicted by sexual intelligence than any other factor we looked at, including gender, age, and the person's degree of sexual satisfaction. More specifically, people behave in ways that belie their own values because they are unaware of their own sexuality—both their genuine sexual desires and the experiences and messages that have distorted their true sexual self. Also, our research suggests that people who cheat have not developed a sense of *sexual empathy*, the ability to imagine how their partner is likely to feel when betrayed, and the subsequent consequences for their relationship. Finally, the largest number of people who cheat in a committed relationship do so spontaneously, without consciously desiring or intending to. They may be led down a path they don't want to follow by situational factors they're not aware of—situations that, by taking some time to work on their sexual intelligence, they can come to recognize and avoid.

When Do People Stray?

Our research revealed that there are several common situations in which a lack of sexual intelligence can lead someone to infidelity.

When the Romance Is Over

Hailey, a thirty-two-year-old architect, was raised by her Roman Catholic family to believe in the sanctity of marriage, and to take the promise of being faithful "till death do you part" very seriously. Hailey held this belief quite deeply; she still does. Yet in spite of her deep commitment to her religious values, she cheated on her husband of five years by sleeping with another man. For a long time, Hailey's marriage seemed to be a happy one. She had a good job and a nice house. Then her husband received the job offer of his dreams—hundreds of miles away. That's when the trouble began:

My husband and I were living in Boston. I had a good job, we had a house. Then Josh got this job offer, the job he'd always wanted—in Washington, D.C. We were having trouble with the distance thing. A man I worked with, we went to lunch together one day as friends, and had a great time. I had fun with him. It was such a contrast—to laugh again—because my husband and I were having trouble and things with him had been so tense. I guess I was supplementing a need with Arnie—the guy I was having an affair with. A need to have fun. With your partner you want to laugh and have a good time. It was a supplement for what I was missing from my marriage.

Arnie was just sort of taken with me, more so than someone you've been with for five years. They're not so captivated by you as they were initially. And when you're with someone new, they're not used to you. They respond to what you do—you know, every little gesture, the way you laugh. I think that was part of it.

It's hard to say when an affair starts. Is it the initial lunch, or the first time you kiss, or when you have intercourse? I never wanted to be with someone else, but there was a breaking point and I reached that. I remember calling a friend and telling her, "I'm about to go out to dinner with this guy," and she said, "Hey, you're allowed to go out with friends." And I said, "No, I'm about to go out with him in a different way." And I started crying, because I knew I was going to do something—I was at that point. I started crying because I felt so guilty. I loved my husband, I knew what I was about to do was wrong; it was contrary to everything I believed in, but, still I did it.

It turned into a big lie. On the weekends, I'd go to Washington or Josh would come here. During the week, when Josh was away, I was with Arnie most nights. And, the thing is, it's not like me—it's not my personality. It just wasn't something I ever thought I'd do. The affair didn't last long—maybe six months.

Hailey and Josh clearly did not consider the strain on their marriage Josh's new job would create. Had they done so, they might have decided not to undertake a long-distance relationship in the first place. They divorced not long after the affair ended. In retrospect, Hailey sees the affair with Arnie as a way of forcing into the open what, on some level, she already knew: that her marriage to Josh was over.

The divorce was inevitable. I think we both knew it for a while. The affair definitely didn't help but, for the most part, it was just because we weren't compatible. The two of us weren't satisfied with one another. You can add all of the
reasons together and get the same answer. But I don't think the affair was the
primary reason. I just think that I knew that Josh and I weren't going to be
together, but you don't know how to get out of it—so you just wiggle your way
out of it.

Despite her belief that her marriage was essentially over when she
initiated the affair, Hailey has suffered much remorse and anguish over
what she did:

I wouldn't ever want to go through it again. It's not comfortable to feel that way
about yourself, to look back and think, "I'm not an awful person, but I did an
awful thing to myself and to someone else." In a sense, something good came out
of it: I realized what I was lacking in my marriage and what I really needed, but I
got it the wrong way.

Hailey's story illustrates a common reason for infidelity among those
who believe that cheating is wrong. For people like Hailey, an affair is
the way they end a relationship that, on some level, they know is over.
Of the people we surveyed who had cheated in a committed relationship, 15 percent fell into this category. Unlike Hailey, the majority of
them expressed little regret about having an affair. It is as if they are
no longer married or otherwise committed; the paperwork may not be
complete, perhaps not even begun, but their *feelings* are already disen-
gaged. Their problem is that they don't know how to be fully honest
and direct about how they feel, both with their existing partner and
with themselves. Many people unintentionally inflict tremendous pain
on their partners because they can't admit what their secret sexual self
is telling them—that they no longer want to be in the relationship.
Ironically, in wanting to spare their partners the pain of a breakup, they
often end up inflicting far more pain by being unfaithful—and *then*
breaking up. The sexually intelligent person, in these circumstances,
recognizes these feelings and speaks about them candidly with his or
her partner, avoiding inflicting the added pain of infidelity on their
partner, and possibly even saving the relationship.

Sometimes people make the wrong choices, sometimes a relationship that seemed like "the one" changes over time—or the people do—and it is no longer viable. Ending a relationship that is not working may be inevitable, though regrettable. Having an affair, however, is not the most sexually intelligent way to do it. It causes terrible pain to the partner who is betrayed and can also leave the unfaithful partner with tremendous guilt, regret, and sorrow. As Hailey put it:

> It seems so obvious to me now, in retrospect. I could have saved both Josh and myself untold pain if I had just been more honest with myself. If you want to cheat on someone, you can say, "Hey, I don't want to be in a committed relationship."

You're Not Meeting My Needs

In our study, 29 percent of the people who had cheated on a partner did so out of frustration that their needs weren't being met or that they couldn't communicate with their partner. The two are often related; when people can't talk together about their expectations, desires, and disappointments, there is little hope that their needs will ever be met in the relationship. And when that happens, chances are that they will go elsewhere to satisfy them.

As we discussed earlier, people are sometimes sexually attracted to another person based on unmet emotional needs: we think we've finally met the person who will supply the affection, attention, and approval that we never received. Or it may be that we meet a person who frustrates us in a very familiar way and thus becomes an almost irresistible challenge, a chance to finally get it right. In fact, our partners can't heal long-standing emotional needs from the past, and it is unreasonable to expect them to be able to. But many of us do; we're inevitably disappointed and frustrated, and blame them for not making us happy—at the same time that they may be blaming us for not meeting *their* deep-seated emotional needs. When we have difficulty in communicating what we want from our partners and keeping informed of their needs in the relationship, we automatically put ourselves at a much higher risk of being unfaithful.

Shelby, a forty-seven-year-old divorced market analyst, told us a sad, but all too common story of infidelity. She has struggled with low self-esteem all her life. On the questionnaire item that asked "What do you think it is about you that makes you attractive to others?" Shelby's answer was "nothing." She went into marriage with a long-standing, unrequited longing to feel valued and loved, and, perhaps not surprisingly, she chose as a partner a man who was unable to show her even minimal affection or caring:

> My husband was like a robot. I felt like I could have been anyone or anything. A piece of furniture, a chair. I felt unloved and I needed to feel good. I was pursued by someone at work, and my self-esteem was so low that I eventually succumbed. I felt validated for a while by another man's interest in me. I found out eventually that the "other man" was much less honorable than I fantasized. He had a wife, which he never told me.

When Shelby discovered that her lover was actually married, she broke off the affair and divorced her husband. She went back to school to get her degree and has since been working, living alone, and trying to come to terms with what happened. She told us:

> I would never cheat again. Never sleep with someone, just to think I would be happier. I don't think I would ever do that again. I hope to God I wouldn't. It was an awful feeling, using someone else sexually, in a way. It didn't match up with values that I had about myself. Basically . . . it was compensating for something else.

Ben, a twenty-five-year-old business major, experienced similar difficulties in his relationship. For the first time in his life, he was with a woman he loved and felt loved by. Everything was going well until his girlfriend was under stress at work and frequently coming home preoccupied. That's when Ben cheated on her:

> I almost lost my girlfriend. I justified what I did at the time because I felt like my girlfriend was acting cold and aloof. She was just preoccupied with this stuff that was going down at work, but I got lonely and I needed affection. I just lost myself. I met a girl that I almost fell for. She was a nice person. I was honest with her and told her I had a girlfriend. She said she was involved with someone, too. The whole thing drove me crazy. Finally, I told the other girl, "Listen, I'm sorry, I don't love you, I don't really like you." She got really hurt.

I went to my wallet and took out a hundred-dollar bill and threw it at her. It was the most fucked-up thing I ever did in my life. I don't know what I was thinking.

Ben scored very high on the scale of sexual addiction, having had twenty-five to thirty partners in his lifetime. He attempts to substitute sex for the closeness and affection that he has craved all of his life. His current girlfriend is the first woman he's been able to establish an intimate connection with. No wonder he threw a hundred-dollar bill at the woman he cheated with; it was his way, it seems, of assuring himself that his primary relationship was a committed and intimate one—not just sex. Ben assumed that his episode of infidelity would fill the void left by his girlfriend's preoccupation with her work. But those unmet emotional needs run so deep and so far into his past that no committed relationship—and certainly no one-night stand—has the power to satiate them.

MacKenzie, a strikingly beautiful model in her twenties, shares with Ben and Shelby a legacy of unmet emotional needs. The difference is that MacKenzie has never cheated on her partner in a committed relationship. She's always "the other woman." The man MacKenzie is currently involved with, however, presents a unique and terrifying problem; he left his girlfriend for MacKenzie:

I seem to keep falling for married people, or people who are in relationships. And now the man I've been seeing broke up with his girlfriend. I mean, they had broken up several times while I was seeing him. But this time he actually left, which, I guess, I'm more concerned about. I don't know, it's kind of like, when they're in a relationship, there are no worries, because you already know where you stand. But when they're not in a relationship, it's kind of like where do you fall? I just don't want to get hurt. When you're the other woman, you know you'll never be the main one that's getting hurt.

MacKenzie is most comfortable in a sexual relationship that she knows can never lead to a commitment, but not because she doesn't want a committed relationship. For her, the pain of knowing from the beginning that she's going to be left is easier to accept than the pain of believing in the possibility of a real commitment that may end in disappointment. If that seems like crazy logic, it makes perfect sense, in the context of MacKenzie's earlier life.

When MacKenzie was growing up, her mother told her nothing about sex, for reasons of her own:

> I think that she was hurt a lot by it, so she didn't really want me to get into sex before I was ready. I think that's why she held off on everything, and didn't give me information. When she got pregnant with me, my father left and never looked back. And then when she tried to give him pictures of me, he'd be like, "Don't show me anything, I don't want to know."

When she was eighteen, MacKenzie went looking for the father she had never known and actually found him. She discovered that, after abandoning her and her mother, he had married and raised three children. MacKenzie had always secretly hoped and believed that her father loved her and that he would someday be a real father to her. Their meeting proved devastating for her, ending those hopes forever and confirming the sense of abandonment that she had lived with since childhood:

> When I found my father, he told me he didn't want to talk to me. He told me I was his mistake, and he would never tell his other family I existed. He didn't want anything to do with me.

It's not hard to see why, after careful examination of their circumstances, these people cheated on their partners. The problem is not that they were unhappy, but rather that they did not have the sexual intelligence to realize exactly why they were not completely satisfied with the relationship, and to communicate their needs in detail to their partners. Had they done so, they might not have resorted to infidelity and may have even been able to salvage a relationship that had taken a turn for the worse.

When Couples Can't Communicate

Besides the unreasonable expectations that people often bring to a committed relationship, there are also reasonable expectations for companionship, respect, caring, honesty, and a satisfying sex life. These expectations, too, are often disappointed, for a variety of reasons: often the demands of everyday life leave precious little time for being together or having a satisfying sex life. For most people today, just meeting these demands—going to work, doing the laundry, walking the dog, helping the kids with homework—add up to more than a full day. It's difficult for two people to maintain the connection they once felt—emotional, intellectual, and sexual—with all of these competing demands. Then it's easy to think that the solution is to search for that connection elsewhere.

That's what James did. At forty-nine, James is alone. His wife divorced him, and his children will have nothing to do with him. He's paid a very heavy price for one mistake, a mistake that might have been avoidable if he and his wife had known how to communicate better with each other. James didn't even cheat on his wife. He just came close.

James is a violin-maker, who supplements his income by giving private lessons and by playing in a community orchestra. His ex-wife was also a musician—she played the flute, semiprofessionally, until the demands of three children and a household took over her time. For the family to get by financially, she had to take a part-time job doing public relations for a local orchestra. Between the demands of their jobs, the needs of their children, and sheer exhaustion, James and his wife rarely had any time together for themselves—to have sex or even to talk.

James keenly felt the lack of connection they had once shared—the concerts they had gone to together, the conversations about music, art, politics. When that connection disappeared, James saw it as a deficiency in his wife, rather than a condition of the demands of family life. He told us: "I needed more intellectual stimulation than my wife could provide."

James thought he had found what was missing in his life with one of his students. Beautiful, intelligent, young, and enthusiastic, Gabrielle had lived in several European countries and grown up in a musical family. Though only nineteen, she was cultured, sophisticated, and already showed great promise as a violinist. As James put it:

One thing led to another. She initiated it, but just the way you'd expect a nineteen-year-old to initiate anything; it was very innocent when it started. Then it led to kissing. I was with her twice a week for an hour and a half—for her lessons. And there were all these points where I should have said, "No, no, no," and I just continued not to.

It was wrong on every possible level. This girl was nineteen, I was forty-four,

> she was my student. It's very hard to say "No," in those situations, but you still
> need to. I knew that, it wasn't anything I didn't know, I just didn't follow it
> through.
>
> I actually went to a motel with her but when it came time to go through with
> it, I just looked at her and said, "I'm sorry, I can't go through with this." I went
> home and told my wife the situation, and she filed for divorce.
>
> I'm embarrassed and sad about the relationship now. I felt pretty guilty about
> it. It was the worst mistake I've made in my life—maybe the stupidest thing
> anyone has ever done.

Though it would come as no comfort to James, what he did, while
lacking in sexual intelligence, is far from unique. Many couples don't
talk about their legitimate needs for time together, for a continuing
emotional and intellectual connection, and for a satisfying sex life. As a
result, one or both end up frustrated and may look elsewhere, thinking
sex with someone new is the answer. That's why it is so important to
continue to talk honestly about your sexual feelings and needs with
your partner.

It's clear that good communication not only helps to prevent problems, but actually contributes to a satisfying sex life. In a 1998 study,
Jeffrey Larson and his colleagues at Brigham Young University in
Provo, Utah, examined how various premarital factors influenced marital satisfaction in seventy couples aged seventeen to forty-eight years
old. Larson found that one of the best predictors of wives' sexual satisfaction was their husband's ability to communicate in an empathic
way.[155]

Couples who can talk together about the inroads of daily life on their
sex lives stand a much better chance of being faithful. Take the case of
Debbie and her husband, Phil. They've been married for ten years, but
they are committed to maintaining a satisfying sex life, and they talk
about their needs:

> We've been married for going on ten years. It's not always the way that it was
> before, where all he had to do was touch me and I'd get turned on. I don't know,
> but it's something that as time goes on, your relationship changes and becomes
> not so hot. It becomes a closer, intimate relationship. It's still captivating, but it
> is sort of like friendship and sort of like lovers at the same time. So the negative
> would be that it takes away from that hot passion that you get when everything

is new and exciting. Sometimes while you're having sex you're thinking, "I have to fold the clothes." There are all these other things, and those aren't things I used to think about before, when we were playing around before marriage, or having sex after marriage.

Realistically, you can't just take life away and make the bedroom special and different from life. Because you have the stresses of life that are going to carry over, it just does. So I try to be realistic, but at the same time I don't want to give up; I really want to strive for it to be more pleasurable, strive to make it special so you don't have to have life and stresses carrying over.

We've both agreed that's something we don't want to ever have happen— where sex gets lost because of all the other stuff. And we tell each other what we need. Yeah, I'll tell him right away "I need more time," or "I need you to touch me more." I'll tell him we need to change positions or we need to even wait, and then I'll try to please him in different ways so that he's being fulfilled. So that we're both having our needs met.

Accidental Infidelity

The largest proportion of people who had cheated on their partners in our study (45 percent) did so not because their relationship was ending, not because they had any complaints about a lack of communication with their partner or frustration about not getting their needs met. They just cheated. Their infidelity was something that "just happened" spontaneously. It's not that they didn't care about their partner or their relationship: 74 percent of this group—far more people than in the other groups—felt terrible regret for what they had done.

How do you "just happen" to have sex with someone other than your spouse or partner? People who said they cheated spontaneously scored very low on awareness of their secret sexual self—as did all of the people who had been unfaithful in a committed relationship. But, compared with those who cheated because they felt their relationship was essentially over or those who cheated because they felt their needs weren't being met, the spontaneous cheaters scored lower on the *cognitive* component of sexual intelligence—Scientific Knowledge. Much lower.

The cognitive component of sexual intelligence, you'll remember, represents both knowledge about human sexuality and the ability to act on that knowledge. What is it that spontaneous cheaters don't know about human sexuality that other people do? One hint comes from Sydney's experience.

A very successful stockbroker and a stunning woman—slim, grace-ful, with beautiful dark eyes and classic features reminiscent of Audrey Hepburn, Sydney came to us depressed and confused. Despite the fact that she was married—and loved her husband—when Sydney was out of town on business, she would inevitably pick up a man in a bar and sleep with him. She felt terribly guilty about her behavior, but it was as if she never saw temptation coming until it was too late. Had Sydney been more sexually intelligent, she would have been able to avoid those situations in which spontaneous infidelity seemed almost a foregone conclusion.

How to Stay Out of Temptation's Way

One reason why people who don't believe in cheating end up doing so anyway, may have to do with situational factors—temptations—that people never see coming. We asked the people in our study, "If you were in a committed relationship, how likely do you think it is that you would ever stray?" The vast majority—83 percent—assured us that they would *never* cheat or it was very unlikely. Only 15 percent said that it might depend on the situation. The situation, it turns out, may be more important than people believe.

In the early 1980s, psychologist James Hassett, a faculty member at Boston University, conducted a survey asking people about their ethical standards as opposed to their actual behavior. The survey was pub-lished in *Psychology Today* and he received over 24,000 completed questionnaires from readers of the magazine. What was new and fasci-nating about his study is that, unlike previous research—for example, Lawrence Kohlberg's, which focused on hypothetical moral dilemmas most people never encounter—Hassett asked about very ordinary situa-tions. For example, he asked respondents whether, having accidentally scraped another car backing out of a parking lot, they would leave their name and phone number or simply drive away. For each of these every-day situations, Hassett asked respondents whether they had ever com-mitted the unethical behavior, whether they believed the behavior was wrong, and whether, in certain circumstances—for example, if they were unlikely to be found out—they would commit the misdeed in the future.

When it came to marital infidelity, Hassett discovered that more people reported cheating on their spouses than on their tax returns. Here are his shocking findings:

- Forty-five percent of those polled said they had at one time cheated on their spouses.
- The majority of respondents (68 percent) believed that infidelity is wrong, yet a sizable proportion (37 percent) said they would do it again under the right circumstances (for example, if far from home and unlikely to see the person again).
- Even more people (42 percent) said they would be more likely to cheat under those circumstances if they were fairly certain they wouldn't get caught.
- And a whopping 50 percent said they'd cheat if the person were particularly attractive.[156]

It's easy to conclude that people are hypocrites or morally deficient—they do what they themselves condemn and they would do it again if they could. But we don't see it that way. We have always been fascinated by Jim Hassett's findings because they provide information that sexually intelligent people can use to help them behave in the way they wish. If you know what circumstances are most likely to lead you to stray, you have valuable information at your disposal and are less likely to spontaneously cheat on a partner. Thus, it is critical to take some time to think of the situations in which you would be tempted. Perhaps you, like Sydney, find that when you're lonely in a strange place, you're apt to behave in ways you normally wouldn't. In that case, staying in touch with your partner by phone, arranging to go out after business with a friend or relative who lives in the area, or even renting a good movie might be wise. By knowing as much as possible about your own susceptibility to temptation, you can adjust your lifestyle accordingly, and decrease the chances of ever becoming unfaithful.

There is an even more powerful way to resist temptation: develop sexual empathy.

Sexual Empathy

One important finding that came out of the Sexual Intelligence Project regarding infidelity is that people tend to act on sexual feelings without understanding fully what the impact may be on themselves and on their relationships. If people could clearly envision the devastating sense of betrayal cheating would be likely to produce and the damage it would probably cause to their relationships, they would be less apt to act on their sexual feelings. The failure to be sexually intelligent in this way, the failure to anticipate how one's sexual actions will affect others, can lead to devastating pain for ourselves and for those we love the most.

While it's important to be aware of situations in which any one of us might be tempted to cheat, perhaps the most important way to avoid unintentionally inflicting pain on your partner as well as yourself and possibly destroying your relationship, is to develop sexual empathy. Sexual empathy is the ability to imagine—vividly—how your partner would feel in certain sexual situations. It is based on knowledge of your partner's secret sexual self and it applies to more than just situations involving infidelity. For example, if you know your partner was sexually abused in childhood, having sexual empathy for him or her means being able to imagine his or her feelings—terror, rage, confusion—in situations that remind him or her of the past.

In many cases when people cheat, they presumably know, on an intellectual level, that their partner isn't going to be particularly happy about it. But what we've heard from person after person is that they never imagined the full impact of their infidelity on their partner—the terrible pain, the sense of betrayal, the loss of trust—until *after* the damage was inflicted. And to many people, it comes as a surprise when their partner ends the relationship over one infidelity.

As we've seen, the best predictor of whether or not people will stray in a committed relationship is their level of sexual intelligence. The people in our study who were most sexually intelligent were able to imagine vividly the effect of cheating on their partners—that is, they possessed sexual empathy. One of the questions we asked people was what they had done in the past when they had been tempted to cheat. Fully 20 percent said either they never gave any real thought to how their partner would feel or they assumed that, if they were caught, their partner would accept their infidelity. Not surprisingly, these people scored very low on sexual intelligence, on average a D. The people who scored highest were those who said they would agonize about cheating, knowing how devastated their partner might be.

Maria is a good example of one those sexually intelligent people.

Petite, with black ringlets and an infectious smile, Maria came in for the interview in surgical scrubs, having come straight from her work as an emergency-room nurse in a large hospital in Boston. She is twenty-eight years old and has been married for just a year and a half. Her green eyes swelling with tears, Maria described how close she came to having an affair early in her marriage:

> I had only been married for about six months. Now, you have to understand, my husband, Keith, was the first man I was ever with who treated me well, who really loved me, and, with him, you know, it meant something. It was real. I was working in the emergency room and there was a young doctor who had just started—a gorgeous guy, very seductive. He was one of these guys who, two days after he's started on the job, every woman there is in love with him. That was Jeff. I would laugh sometimes about these women who were suddenly wearing push-up bras to work, but, as it turned out, I wasn't immune.
>
> I got sucked in emotionally, first. It was a game, definitely, and he was in control of it. You know those relationships where you get just enough, just enough of what you need or want to get hooked, but not enough to ever sustain a relationship? It was based on an illusion with him. There would be a moment here or there—after a particularly bad trauma like a shooting or a car accident, he'd come find me in the coffee room and ask, "Are you all right?" Or, if I was coming down with something or tired, he'd come over and rub my shoulders. And there were soulful looks and hints that I was the only one who understood him—his wife didn't.
>
> I became obsessed with him. I thought about him all the time, I had dreams about him at night. Once or twice, I went out with him after work for drinks. It was the most powerful attraction—I came very, very close to having sex with him, and probably destroying my marriage.
>
> What it finally came down to was the thought of what it would do to Keith. I was lucky to have a good friendship with my husband. When it came right down to it, I just couldn't hurt my friend.

The importance of empathy in sexual relationships, and the relationship between empathy and adultery, was brought home by a 1997 study of 107 married couples aged seventeen to forty-one, conducted by psychologists David Buss and Todd Shackelford at the University of Texas at Austin.[157] These researchers examined public records of marriage licenses and sent a letter to couples who had been married within a six-month period, inviting them to participate in the study. Participants in this study completed a series of personality questionnaires at home, and then came to a laboratory-testing situation. To preserve the confidentiality of their responses, the husband and wife were separated and independently asked additional questions, particularly relating to their own likelihood to engage in six forms of extramarital behavior. These behaviors included flirting, passionately kissing, going on a romantic date, having a one-night stand, having a brief affair, and having a serious affair. They also rated the likelihood of their partner engaging in the same behaviors.

The results of the study found that personality factors were strong and consistent predictors of susceptibility to infidelity, and that the strongest of these indications was narcissism. The chief characteristic of narcissistic people is that they consistently lack empathy for others.[158]

Sexual empathy is also an important factor that protects people from situational temptations, as one of our participants made clear. Jerry, a fifty-six-year-old truck driver, spends a lot of time on the road, away from home, where he could cheat without being found out. He told us why he has never cheated on Lorrie, his wife of thirty-five years:

Knowing the pain I'd cause someone who is so good to me outweighs the sexual fulfillment of a short-term fling. I've been strong, and when I've been weak . . . I've been lucky!!!

We asked people what they would do if they knew they could cheat on their partner without getting caught. Those who said they'd definitely cheat scored on average just barely above an F in sexual intelligence. Those who said they would still consider the effect that cheating might have on their relationship scored highest on sexual intelligence. They were more knowledgeable about human sexuality, they were more aware of their secret sexual self, and they had more of the social skills, such as talking with their partner, required to avoid the lack of communication and frustration that can lead to infidelity.

Having the sexual empathy to be able to vividly imagine the effect of an affair on your partner is an important component of sexual intelligence, one that many people lack. In fact, it's even more important than religious values. On two questions assessing people's attitudes toward cheating—the questions asking people what they've done in the past when tempted and whether they would cheat in the future if they were sure they wouldn't get caught—approximately a third of our respondents told us they would never cheat, under any circumstances, because it is a sin. Interestingly enough, they scored lower on sexual intelligence than people who said they would consider the effect of cheating on their partner. Since sexual intelligence is the best predictor of whether people will commit infidelity, these individuals—despite their belief that cheating is a sin—are at higher risk than people who possess sexual empathy. Perhaps it's no surprise that so many conservative Christian preachers—for example, Jimmy Swaggart, Jim Bakker—preached rigid adherence to moral values that condemned adultery and nonetheless committed it themselves.

Consequences of an Affair

What happens when people do stray? Is an affair necessarily the end of a marriage? We've seen that some marriages do end in the wake of an affair: Hailey's marriage, for one. In a national telephone survey of 1,051 adults in September of 1997, 31 percent of the respondents said they would get a divorce if their spouse committed adultery; 54 percent said they would stay and try to work it out. More men (34 percent) than women (29 percent) said they would choose divorce.[159]

An affair doesn't have to ruin a marriage, and the end result of an affair can be very positive for both the individuals involved in a relationship, as well as the relationship itself. This, of course, is not to say that an affair is good for a marriage. When one partner in a relationship has an affair, it may be a warning sign that there are problems in the relationship. And this does not mean that it is just a problem with the individual who has been unfaithful. When one person has sex outside the relationship, it may be a message that his or her needs are not being met. In some cases, the person who cheats may have unrealistic expectations that a partner can assuage long-standing unmet needs, but it can also mean that his or her partner is not meeting needs that are realistic—for companionship, honesty, respect, and caring. The problem may, in many cases, be some combination of the two. Either way, it presents an opportunity for partners to talk about and confront problems in the relationship, as well as personally confronting each of their needs and expectations, including emotional needs that are unmet in the relationship. When people can do this, however painful infidelity is, it may prove the turning point for a better relationship. As Hailey, the architect who succumbed to an affair when her husband, Josh, took a job that kept him out of town all week, put it:

> I feel that extramarital affairs are a symptom of the problem, not the problem itself. People's insecurities and egos sometimes get in the way of working out a problem because they can't see past "the act of infidelity." While I don't support infidelity, I try to understand that there are reasons behind it besides the obvious. I feel that although infidelity greatly hurts the marriage in the sense that it causes a lot of pain, there are times when it is necessary to produce a change in the relationship, to force people to face what is really going on in their relationship. "Necessary" is not an accurate word—I don't think infidelity is necessary—but we as humans are prone to being weak at times and rather than choose to communicate, we choose infidelity. At best it leads to a chain reaction toward a better understanding. At worst it causes a lot of pain and heartache.

Turning the Tables: Revenge

One of the most destructive things people can do when they discover that their partner has had an affair is to have one themselves, "to get back at him (or her)." In a relationship, when one person "wins"—gets revenge—while the other loses—is "paid back"—in the long run, neither wins. It can lead to the end of the relationship. Plus, "winning" by getting revenge often doesn't feel that good.

Courtney, a twenty-year-old student, discovered that when she decided to get back at her boyfriend for cheating on her:

> It was maybe two years into our relationship. My boyfriend had cheated on me and I found out. Of course I was devastated; I didn't have a lot of close girlfriends. I hung out with him most of the time. I wasn't close to my family at the time, because I was a teenager . . . you know. He was really my only source of emotional support, and I just felt awful.
>
> We ended up reconciling, and then I decided to cheat on him as a way to put the mark straight. I had his car. He was gone in the National Guard for two weeks, and it was fairly shortly after he had cheated on me. There was this boy

who liked me, and there was a dance at school, and I had the car, and I gave him a ride home, and we went parking. We were kissing, and he tried to put his hand up my shirt, and I just couldn't go through with it—I was just overwrought with guilt. I guess I thought that cheating on my boyfriend would make me feel better, and it didn't.

Not only is revenge seldom sweet, it can also leave people feeling a great deal of guilt themselves—even though they weren't the first to cheat—and create additional damage to a relationship.

Take Ed's case. He is a forty-eight-year-old surgeon. He and his wife, Carrie, have been married for twenty-five years and have four children. Ed describes himself as a man who, in his twenties and thirties, was "addicted to achieving—at any cost." He was at the hospital, or in his research lab, more than he was at home. His wife cheated on him early in their relationship, and Ed went looking for revenge:

Very early on in the marriage, I was unable to distinguish between sex and emotional closeness. She felt emotionally abandoned with me. She sought comfort—sex—with someone else for about three months, primarily for emotional reasons. At first, I thought it was all about sex and I wanted to go kill this guy.

I felt neglected, betrayed, and vengeful, and went actively looking for another relationship.

Ed had an affair for about a year, one that his wife has never found out about. Finally, he ended it when he realized that having sex with someone else was not the solution to his and Carrie's problems.

Interestingly, *Carrie's* affair Ed has forgiven, although it took him a long time to do so, and to understand why she went looking elsewhere for the emotional closeness he couldn't give her at the time. It's his *own* infidelity that Ed still struggles with:

I never told my wife. It has really bothered me, but I didn't want to cleanse my soul at her expense. It was a mistake I made that I wouldn't repeat.

In retrospect, some seventeen years later, I take no pride in what happened. It did create a gap in the relationship that I feel has never completely closed.

Ed continues to feel guilt about his affair and feels that it continues to haunt his marriage to this day.

Ed's experience raises the difficult question of whether or not to confess infidelity to your partner. He himself expresses one opinion: that telling your partner can be a way of trying to relieve your own conscience at somebody else's expense. On the other hand, keeping infidelity a secret can mean being gnawed at by guilt for a lifetime. Keeping the secret also means that the two of you have no chance to confront—and solve—problems in the relationship that may have precipitated cheating. There is one more reason why keeping infidelity a secret can be destructive: sexually transmitted diseases. Condoms break, and HIV can be contracted from a single exposure. Cheating on our partners without telling them can, these days, be like holding a gun to someone's head and pulling the trigger.

High-Tech Sex

In this chapter we have seen couples who have succumbed to infidelity and others who have used sexual intelligence to avoid the pitfalls that lead to straying. Talking about your needs with your partner and avoiding "high-risk" situations are the surest ways to stay out of bed with someone who only *seems* to hold the promise of meeting your needs. But what if you don't jump into someone else's bed to find sexual, and emotional, connection—what if you log on to the computer and have a "cybersex" relationship that may not involve physical contact? Computers and the Internet have made available a whole new world of virtual relationships. Because relationships initiated on the Internet run the gamut from fleeting flirtation with a pen pal to deeply personal, and sexual, exchanges sustained over a long period of time, they raise a host of new questions about what constitutes fidelity within a committed relationship, even about what constitutes *sex*. For example, take Jared, a graduate student in his thirties we spoke to, who has been married for a number of years. He has been maintaining a computer relationship with a woman for most of the past year:

I've been corresponding by e-mail with this woman for months. I find it to be a wonderful relationship, because we can talk about anything. I have no intention of ever meeting her, and our conversations are not sexual at all. Even so, I haven't told my wife about it. I'm not sure how she'd feel.

Jared's hesitation in telling his wife reveals the hidden and potentially addictive nature of Internet relationships. He may not be sleeping around but he is committing emotional infidelity—sharing aspects of his life with another person that he can't share with his wife and feeling guilt about it. If he didn't feel that this relationship was a potential threat to the intimacy of his relationship with his wife, he would tell her. Jared seems to be using his Internet relationship to find intimacy that may be lacking in his relationship, or he may, in fact, be using the Internet as a "safe" way of exploring intimacy—one that has few consequences in the real world. Either way, he is acting in a less than intelligent way by not being honest with his wife—not so much by not telling her about his e-mail correspondence, but by not sharing with her the aspects of himself that he shares with his Internet correspondent. This Internet relationship has the potential to grow into something much more explosive that could ultimately rock the foundations of his marriage.

We all know that the Internet is here to stay—it is a fact of life, though we have found not many people use the Internet for "sexual" relationships. Five percent of the people who participated in the Sexual Intelligence Project admitted to having a romantic or a sexual relationship on the Internet, though a higher percentage did say they used the Internet to access pornography. Six percent of the respondents said Internet sex was fine because there was no physical contact involved, 12 percent said it was fine as a supplement to a committed, real-life sexual relationship, 43 percent said the Internet was a distraction that can cause problems in a relationship, and 40 percent thought that Internet sex was a form of adultery. Those people who claimed that Internet sex isn't adultery because it doesn't include sexual contact were significantly lower in sexual intelligence than those who saw it as a distraction that could hurt a committed relationship.

From Marleen's story, it is easy to see that Internet relationships are, indeed, a distraction that can hurt a marriage. She is an attractive brunette in her late forties who is married with two adult children:

I tried out responding to some personal ads and said to myself, "This e-mail stuff is kind of fun, but I could get in trouble by being with someone close by," so I actually read some personals and responded to someone who lived a thousand

miles away from me. And we maintained, for almost a year, a very intimate relationship that wasn't just about sex, although there was some steamy sex talk,
but we got to be confidants of each other. The relationship was a secret. I just
kind of thought we would grow old together, "virtually." I was very satisfied
with it, I was real happy. Then came the business trip that took me quite near
where he lived, the unanticipated random thing. I knew this was going to happen
in advance, so we wrote about it and talked about it and what we were going to
do. We decided that we would meet in a place where we could be intimate, though
we weren't clear whether or not we were going to have intercourse or not. Well,
that all happened. We met, and we went to a motel room. It was just incredible. I
had no idea ahead of time what he looked like. We had not exchanged pictures,
and it wasn't important. The physical side was never going to have anything to do
with our relationship, so who cared? But we felt instantly comfortable with each
other. Again, we knew each other intimately. I didn't really care what he looked
like. He was good-looking and everything, but it was just like I knew him already.
We probably had four hours together in the motel room. We undressed, were
naked together, and kissed and hugged, all that kind of stuff. We did not have
intercourse. But we explored each other.

Marleen talked about the reasons for her decision:

I guess, everybody draws their line somewhere, and that's where we decided to
draw our line. And we hadn't said ahead of time, "We'll do everything except
intercourse." But we had talked about it. "We could do this, we could do that, we
could have intercourse." And we had both said, "I could be in a motel room with
you naked and not have intercourse. Let's see what happens. Maybe it will be
that way, maybe we actually will." But we didn't.
    He was married as well as me. I guess that played a real part in our decision.
It's tough to say what goes into these things. It's not like we had this incredible
passionate desire or lust for each other, but we wanted to be able to be intimate
with each other, and that's what we did.

Marleen's relationship with her Internet lover took some unexpected
turns, when her husband found out:

Well, he went home, and I went home, and nothing bad happened. Lightning
didn't strike us down, and our e-mail relationship continued. Not a whole lot different. It was a really neat experience that we could refer to. But it did come out.

Who's to say whether it was an accident or on purpose, but I left something out on my desk that was not something about him, but it was a printout of a page from an Internet relationship site. I didn't really think that it was a big deal leaving it out, but my husband saw it and said, "Oh, this is about Internet relationships. Do you have Internet relationships?" And I could have at that time just said, "Oh, no, I just thought it was a neat idea," or whatever. But I just said, "I do." And I decided I would say everything, and I did.

What was my motivation? That's a tough one. I'm an articulate, self-aware woman, but I don't have an easy answer for that one. I was not feeling guilty in the sense that I didn't feel that I did something by my own standards that I felt all that bad about. But I knew that if my husband knew about it, he wouldn't be real pleased. I have a very close and communicative relationship with my husband, and I'm not used to there being major things that I'm doing that we don't talk about. So I guess I just wanted to talk to him about it. And in my own mind, I didn't feel like I had done something so bad that I was going to be in the doghouse forever and would end up having to get divorced.

Well, what happened was, he was really, really upset. He was personally hurt, and I just . . . it was stupid of me, but I was, "In my mind, this doesn't have anything to do with <u>you</u>." We have our relationship, and it is what it is, and I'm really happy with it, and I have every intention of staying married to my husband forever. I love him, and I love our relationship, and there are limitations to it, but that's how life is. So I just sort of thought it was about <u>me</u>, wanting to have another kind of experience, and it's only natural. No one can provide all experiences, and I wanted to do it. That obviously wasn't the way he saw it. He saw it as a statement on my part of him being not enough and inadequate, and he felt hurt and humiliated.

I still feel the same way that I said to you before that I didn't do anything that broke my own standards that I felt I could live with. But I see it now . . . I wasn't looking at it from his eyes, I was only looking at it through my eyes. And I get that that wasn't the way to be looking at it. So I feel different now in the sense that I have incorporated his perspective on such behavior in my view of things.

Marleen then talked about the extent to which the Internet relationships she has had are related to what she is not getting in her marital relationship:

My sex life with my husband is intimate, and we feel great with each other when we are through, and all that kind of stuff. But when you wake up beside someone for twenty-six years, that kind of thing. There was an exciting quality that the steamy, talking dirty supplied me that I had not experienced with my husband, and I kind of wanted to experience that, and I liked it. My husband and I had talked about this kind of stuff. I had even years before brought up stuff like, "Do you want to do role-playing stuff where we'll pretend like I'm a hitchhiker and you pick me up and we do it?" He just was not going to go there.

To finish up on that particular relationship, it ended. For a while we didn't write much at all, and then we wrote some. I guess, to make a long story short, we now write in the kind of "old friends" category. The whole thing lasted for maybe a year, and it was probably over three years ago, and in the last three years we might have exchanged four e-mails.

At this point . . . you know it's kind of ironic . . . my relationship with my husband is better than it's ever been. I think my revealing my Internet experience to him, despite the pain that it caused, brought us closer together. But I still have a lot of temptation to explore some new Internet relationships. It's something I struggle with.

Marleen's experiences sound a lot like the stories earlier in the chapter from couples who have experienced infidelity in their relationships. While the Internet is new and provides us with different ways to seek emotional and sexual support outside of a committed relationship (and makes it easier to justify doing so because our contacts may not be "physical"), in essence the Internet just puts a cyberface on the same old sexual issues that individuals and couples have always confronted: How willing am I to commit to this relationship? To what extent is my interest in other relationships a result of dissatisfaction with my current relationship? What are the consequences for my partner—how will my partner *feel*—if I pursue an Internet relationship? It is clear that Marleen did not enter into this Internet relationship in a sexually intelligent way. She was not aware of her own unmet sexual needs, and that she should have pushed harder to achieve a higher level of communication with her partner to meet those needs rather than look for someone outside of the relationship. And she did not envision the pain it would cause her husband—as we discussed earlier, sexually intelligent people act with empathy. Marleen justified her Internet relationship by not having "sex," not thinking that her husband would be hurt greatly by the fact that she was expending a lot of time and energy sharing her intimate life with another person (not to mention getting naked with him in a motel room!).

Marleen was fortunate that they were able to use this experience as a way to address communication problems in their marriage and go on to achieve a greater level of intimacy. But acting with sexual intelligence from the start is the best way to avoid the pain and guilt that affairs, virtual or otherwise, cause a relationship. Before you enter into an Internet relationship ask yourself why you are doing so, particularly if you are already in a committed relationship. What am I lacking in my existing love life? Am I sexually frustrated, or emotionally frustrated, or both? Is there a way that I can address these needs within my current relationship? Asking intelligent questions like this will prevent you from looking for love, and sex, in all the wrong places, online or off.

Many people might hesitate to have sex outside of marriage or a committed relationship if they understood how devastating the consequences could be for themselves, their partner, and the relationship. The problem is that people don't always weigh the consequences before acting. Sexually intelligent people are aware of their secret sexual self, including any long-standing needs that it is unrealistic to expect a partner to meet. They are also realistic about the power of temptation and know what sorts of situations to avoid in order to resist it. Finally, a key component of sexual intelligence is the ability to imagine fully how our partners would feel if we betrayed them. Sexually intelligent people talk to their partners about problems in their relationship—complaints, resentments, unmet needs—before they sleep with someone else.

How Sexually Intelligent Are You?

Consider what you would do in the following situation:

Imagine that five years ago you had a passionate affair with a man or woman who was the best lover you've ever had. The affair ended when he or she left town with no explanation. In the meantime, you married or entered a committed relationship with someone who is wonderful—a person who represents everything you've ever wanted in a committed relationship. Despite the fact that your current partner is very attractive and the sex is generally satisfying, there has never been the same chemistry you had with your ex-lover. In fact, lately you and your partner are going through one of those periods when the relationship—

and the sex—feel stale, in a rut. Imagine your old flame called, out of the blue, and suggested that you get together—just for coffee.

Questions to Consider

1. Would you meet your old flame?
2. Would you tell your partner that you were meeting an old flame?
3. What if you met your ex for coffee and the same chemistry was there— the sort of attraction that makes you feel alive for the first time in a long time. Would you have sex with him or her?
4. What would you do if your former lover told you that not marrying you was the biggest mistake of his or her life—and clearly was willing to remedy that? Would you consider leaving your current partner?

Bear in mind the following principles.

Scientific Knowledge

Nearly a third of married people consider cheating a reason for divorce.

Be skeptical of media images that suggest everyone is unfaithful all the time—with no consequences.

If your sexual life with your partner is stale, you're more at risk for infidelity because your sexual desire is high.

The vast majority of people cheat on their partners without really wanting to or intending to—and later feel terrible regret.

Awareness of the Secret Sexual Self

Respect the power of temptation, and anticipate high-risk situations that encourage infidelity—being alone with an old flame where the two of you aren't likely to be caught, for instance.

Remember that having the courage to examine your secret sexual self and develop awareness of your own sexuality is a much better protection against being unfaithful than simply telling yourself that cheating is a "sin" and you would never do it.

Ask yourself whether you are measuring your current sexual relationship against a mythic ideal of effortless great sex all the time.

Connecting with Others

Consider whether staleness in your current relationship might be a result of an underlying conflict or frustration that you and your partner aren't talking about.

Mobilize your sexual empathy and your knowledge of your partner's secret sexual self to imagine—vividly—how he or she would feel if you were unfaithful and what the consequences would be for your relationship.

Before you embark on an affair, turn the tables and imagine how you would feel if your partner were unfaithful.

Ask yourself whether the relationship with your partner is over in your mind—and, if so, end the relationship before entering an affair.

Epilogue: *A Sexually Intelligent Generation*

We started this book by sharing the dream of a thirty-two-year-old woman who participated in our Sexual Intelligence Project. If you remember, Lorraine had had vivid dreams of liv-

> **If you think education is expensive, try ignorance.**
> —Anonymous

ing in a small, dark, cramped apartment where she felt hopeless and alone, only to discover on the other side of a door in her apartment a series of beautiful, spacious rooms that promised freedom and fulfillment. Lorraine was mired in an unsatisfying sex life—she was married to a man whom she loved, but their sex life was lackluster. She was at the verge of despair, ready to divorce her husband, knowing that a fulfilling life was somewhere around the corner but not having a clue how to get there.

We were deeply moved by Lorraine's story, and by the hundreds of other stories we encountered in our research. While we did hear from some people who had vibrant, enjoyable sex lives, we were struck again and again by how frustrated the majority of the men and women who participated in our study felt. Some were in relationships like Lorraine's—they loved their partners but couldn't figure out how to bring passion back to their sex lives. Some were like Sydney, who cheated on her husband continually with men she met at clubs as a way to avoid dealing with her problems. And then there were people like Frank, who was so burned by the first woman he slept with that he gave up on women, sex, and, ultimately, happiness.

Throughout this book, we hope we have made it clear how important it is to have a fulfilling sex life. Sex should not be an afterthought—it is intimately connected to all parts of our lives, from our self-esteem to our physical health to the strength of our relationships with others. Our health and happiness are directly linked to our sexuality. We hope that this book has provided the means to understand what sexual intelligence is, why we must find ways to nurture this intelligence in ourselves, and specific ways to develop these skills. By sharing the stories of our research participants we have tried to demonstrate, on a practical level, the actions of people who are sexually intelligent and those who aren't, so we can better understand the three components of sexual intelligence: replacing cultural myths with scientific information about human sexuality; being aware of the secret sexual self; and creating and maintaining sexual connections with others. The good news that has come out of our research is that sexual intelligence is the key to a satisfying sex life, and it is something that can be measured, quantified, and developed.

But understanding the principles of sexual intelligence and how to put these principles into practice for ourselves is only part of the story. For we all have a chance to create a new world where people will already have the knowledge and tools to take control of their sex lives, a world in which our children don't have to suffer in silence or learn lessons the hard way, through years of trial and error and hard work, or even worse—never learn at all. While people can acquire an understanding of what sexual intelligence is and the tools to live a sexually intelligent life (or we wouldn't have written this book!), we have a dream of a generation of young people *already raised in a sexually intelligent manner.* If children are raised to understand the importance of sex, if they are taught about sexuality in a way that doesn't include scare tactics, then the chance is much greater that they will become sexually intelligent adults.

As a society we can't run away from our duty to educate our children—we wouldn't dream of not teaching them about the benefits of living in a democracy, about the dangers of smoking and doing drugs, about the importance of not cheating and stealing, about the need to eat healthy foods and exercise regularly. Likewise, we can't run away from the duty to educate them about sexuality, however difficult or embarrassing it might seem at first. As we saw in the chapter on first sexual experiences, young people not only know about sex but are engaging in sexual relations at an early age, with negative consequences for their sexual intelligence. People who gave more conscious thought to the meaning of sex had more positive first sexual experiences and also scored higher in sexual intelligence. Young teens have not developed emotional insight into their own likes, dislikes, and motivations and lack an awareness of social influences such as media messages and peer pressure to have sex. So when they do decide to have sex, they are ill prepared for the emotional ramifications of the act. And even if they delay having sex until they are older, we have found in our research that most families—and even society at large—do not give them the tools to understand the meaning behind their actions.

So how do we lay the foundation for creating a future generation of sexually intelligent adults? How do we encourage our children to delay becoming sexually active until they are emotionally ready, whatever that age may be? How do we prevent the problems and frustrations we have seen among the people in our study? The answer lies primarily within the family.

The Importance of Communication

We have shared many research findings in this book, but one of the most stunning to emerge from our study is the finding that only 7 percent of the people we talked to had had meaningful conversations with their parents about sex. This is particularly tragic, because parental communication is so directly tied to sexual intelligence—people who reported a lack of communication with their parents scored lower in sexual intelligence.

We asked the participants in our research what they thought their parents could have done differently, to better prepare them for a healthy adult sex life. Many of the responses were terribly poignant:

- "They could have been more open and honest about the subject, so then I wouldn't feel so afraid and unsure about the whole thing."
- "Talked to me about sex—told me that it's a natural thing—that I'm not a bad person for doing it."
- "Acted as if sex was a normal part of life."
- "Given me more self-confidence to be able to say no and mean it."
- "Had one themselves."

Parents need to play a significant role in the development of their children's sexual intelligence. This does not mean, however, that parents should try to control their children's sexual activity; neither does it mean they should be permissive. Rather, parents need to be involved in their children's lives, know what they are doing, communicate with their children about their own beliefs and values concerning sexuality, and help their children develop a sense of autonomy and awareness of their own sexual and emotional life.

Our research found that individuals who support open communication between parents and teens about sexuality are higher in their own levels of sexual intelligence. Our Sexual Intelligence Test included an item, "Parents should keep quiet about mistakes they have made in their own sexual life—after all, teenagers do what we do, not what we say." Respondents who agree that you shouldn't talk about your own sexual mistakes were significantly lower in sexual intelligence than those who felt you should share your mistakes with your teenage children. Parents who can be open and honest about their own sexual mistakes (this doesn't mean sharing all the gory details) can deepen their relationship with their children and help them develop in a sexually intelligent way.

We also asked, "When it comes to talking to teenagers about sex, which of the following approaches would you choose?" The only respondents whose sexual intelligence was above the D level were those who answered, "Ask them what they think about teenage sexuality and discuss what you know." Individuals who said, "tell them to abstain from sex, since the dangers of HIV are so high," were the lowest in sexual intelligence, scoring on average a D. Other, slightly more sexually intelligent, responses—but still in the D range—were "tell them to pay careful attention in their sex education class in school" and "tell them about safe sex and then avoid asking them anything about their private life."

Communication about sexuality should be a discussion, not a lecture, and attempts to manipulate teens' sexual behavior through guilt should be avoided. A research study published in 1999 examined the impact of parents' monitoring of their children and their use of guilt to try to prevent teenagers from engaging in risky sexual behavior. Kathleen Rodgers, a professor in the Department of Human Development at Washington State University in Pullman, Washington, surveyed 375 male and female high school students in Wisconsin who reported that they had had voluntary sexual intercourse.[160] She was particularly interested in whether these parental behaviors increased or decreased the likelihood of teenagers engaging in risky sexual behavior. Risky behaviors included having multiple sexual partners, not using contraception, or using ineffective methods of contraception such as withdrawal.

Professor Rodgers found that teenagers whose parents monitored them, that is, who knew where they were going and what they were doing, were significantly less likely to engage in sexual risk taking. However, she also found that teenage girls whose parents used a lot of guilt to control their behavior were substantially *more* likely to engage in risky behavior, particularly if it was their mothers who used this control tactic. These results are consistent with our own research and further reinforce our opinion that open and *honest* communication, rather than attempts at control, fosters sexual intelligence.

Telling teenagers to "wait until marriage" before having sexual intercourse doesn't work. In our sample, 64 percent of the respondents who said their parents told them to abstain from sex until marriage did not wait. We heard this story again and again from our interview participants. For example, Susan, who first had sex at fourteen, told us:

My mom just stressed abstinence. She got married when she was really young. She had a lot of kids when she was young, and then my sister had a child when she was young. I don't feel real comfortable talking to her about it. We have a good relationship, but I don't like talking about it with her.

People in our study whose parents preached a message of sexual abstinence were the lowest in sexual intelligence, lower even than respondents whose parents told them "nothing" about sex. Both of these groups were significantly lower in sexual intelligence than those whose parents gave them more comprehensive information about sexuality. Not only is an abstinence-only message ineffective, it may work against the development of sexual intelligence.

There is no reason not to start teaching our children the lessons of sexual intelligence early, and no reason not to develop these skills throughout life. Many of the skills that provide a foundation for sexual intelligence can be taught to children, at an early age, even before talking about sex directly. For example, sexually intelligent people know what they feel, what they like or don't like—not only when it comes to sexual behavior, but in general. We can teach our children to listen to their instincts, to be aware of their preferences, beliefs, and values and to respect those values in the face of peer pressure. Sexually intelligent people have empathy for their partners; we can certainly teach children at an early age to consider how others feel and to anticipate the effect of their behavior on other people.

Once our children are older, we not only can provide them with accurate scientific knowledge, share our experiences with them, and listen to them, we also can help them to understand the emotional impact of sexual experiences. That may be the biggest favor we can do them. Nathan, a twenty-year-old student, told us, for example:

> **If only my parents had talked about sex in a good way, openly and honestly, that's all I wish they had done with me. Instead of finding out on my own, and being like . . . because for me it was a terrifying experience, and it didn't have to be.**
>
> **I didn't even know the facts, all I knew was that if you are going to have sex, use a condom, which I certainly believe in anyway. But there are feelings and emotions that go along with it that nobody talked about either. You should be comfortable when you have sex, and if you have any worries, or if you are apprehensive in any way, then you shouldn't do it. Or if you do, then talk about why you are so apprehensive. I didn't have anybody to talk to about it.**
>
> **I think if my dad had told me about the emotional involvement, I might have waited. I guess he could have made me more comfortable with my sexuality, by . . . just talking to me.**

Nathan's father, like any loving parent, probably would have done anything to spare Nathan from feeling so alone and unprepared for an important part of adult life—if only he had known how.

Our children needn't go through what Nathan did, what we did—learning about sex on our own by trial and error.

Consider Liv, a young woman in her early twenties, studying to be a social worker. Her parents were Roman Catholics and had strong beliefs about sexual behavior before marriage:

My family is Catholic. I grew up in the Church and, you know, the Church is adamant about no sex before marriage. Especially our priest—it was a thing with him—practically every Sunday, you heard it. And I know that my parents got married first—they waited. Maybe they're right—because I know so many people are unhappily married who have sex, and I think that's just as bad . . . but that's kind of where their views are on that.

Despite her parents' views on sexuality, and the difficulty she has with reconciling her behavior with her own religious beliefs—she herself is a Catholic—Liv is currently involved in a sexual relationship with a man she cares for very much. A number of parents have a very hard time with this, and their relationship with their children often suffers.

But Liv was lucky. While her mother clearly articulated her values about sex, she was open to talking with her daughter, did not use guilt, and did not shame her.

I didn't originally talk to my mom, but actually within the past two to three months I finally decided "Okay, I can have an adult conversation with my mom" and I sat down and talked with her. And actually, I'm so glad I did—it was a big relief, and a weight off my shoulders. But, for the longest time, I wouldn't, not because I was afraid of her, but because I was really mad at myself for what I had done.

Finally, Liv overcame her own anger and opened up to her mother:

I finally sat down with her and said, "Mom, I just want to tell you, I have had sex before marriage." She knew before this conversation that I had had a bad situation when I was seventeen. And she knew about that kind of, but she didn't know anything after that, and I was like, "Listen, I'm in a situation now, I have had sex, and I've enjoyed it, and it's not been a scary experience. I've been on birth control pills." I told her, "I can't keep on hiding this, and I want you to know." And I sat down and I spent . . . Oh, God. We spent four or five hours just talking. And getting to know each other better, and I found out a lot of things about my mom that I never knew, that made me feel better, and stuff like that. It turned out to be a really good experience that I was happy about.

She shared with me things that I had never known, like that she was married before she met my dad. The marriage only lasted a year or so, and then they got an annulment. I had never known that. She hadn't said anything about it. She hadn't had children or anything like that, but at the same time, she's explaining, you know, the reason she got married the first time was because she had had sex before she was married, and she thought the only way to make that better was to get married. And I was like, "Wow, I never knew that." And I thought, "My goodness, my mom's a human." (laughs) She made a mistake. So, it was just a really good experience to find that out about her, and realize that I wasn't alone in making mistakes. Even though she didn't agree that I should be having sex before I was married, she was very happy in some ways that I wasn't afraid and that it wasn't a situation that I was scared and stuff like that. So that was good. I'm lucky, I know.

While Liv's mother was able to see beyond her own beliefs that people should wait until marriage to have sex, not everyone has parents who are so open to discussion. As we've stressed, it is vitally important to talk to our children about sex, but it is equally important to listen to what they have to say and to discuss sexuality in a positive, healthy way that encompasses the complexities of living in this modern age.

By cultivating in ourselves, and teaching our children, the skills of sexual intelligence, the richness and beauty of a satisfying sex life—for many of us unsuspected, though there all along—can be theirs from the start.

How Sexually Intelligent Are You?

Try out your sexual intelligence skills on this dilemma:

Imagine that your fourteen-year-old daughter or son attends a sleepover at a friend's house. Several days later you accidentally overhear him or her talking on the phone about what happened that night—there was a party at which the girls took turns pairing up with different boys and giving them oral sex.

Questions to Consider
1. How would you handle this situation?
2. What would your immediate feelings be?
3. What would you be tempted to do or say in the heat of the moment? How likely do you think it is that that behavior would help the situation?
4. Would you feel differently if it was your daughter rather than your son?

5. Whom would you go to in order to talk about the problem and get advice in handling it?
6. How, when, and where would you initiate a conversation about the party with your child?
7. What would you say to your child?
8. How would you find out whether or not your child understands the risks of sexually transmitted diseases from unprotected oral sex?
9. How would you talk to your child about the psychological risks of engaging in this behavior?
10. How much would you tell your child about some of your own sexual experiences in adolescence?
11. How could you tell whether or not what you've said will have any impact on your child's behavior?
12. What could you do in the future to safeguard your child from destructive sexual experimentation?

Bear in mind the following principles.

Scientific Knowledge

The vast majority of young people say they've never had a meaningful conversation with their parents about sex.

Rigid, extreme measures to prevent your child from being sexual—such as forbidding dating, and so on—are likely to backfire.

Parental neglect and lack of involvement often lead children to become sexual before they're ready.

Counseling abstinence without supplying other sexuality information doesn't work.

Awareness of the Secret Sexual Self

Be aware that children partly take their cue about sexual matters from watching their parents' behavior.

Remember your own first experiences with sex and how you felt and confront any conflicts about sexuality that you may still be dealing with.

Connecting with Others

Explore with your child the emotional needs and conflicts and the social pressures that may lead them to engage in substitute sex.

Don't lecture your children. Ask them what they think about sexuality and listen.

Talk to your teens openly about all aspects of sex, including the emotional and social consequences, as well as facts about diseases and reproductive biology.

Talk to other parents about what their kids are doing sexually, and how they are coping.

Don't make the mistake of communicating to your child that sex is dirty or dangerous in and of itself.

Counteract media portrayals of consequence-free sex by talking to your child about the reality as opposed to the fantasy.

Don't be afraid to share with your teens the things you've learned from painful experience—it is not the case that they will necessarily do what you did and it may even keep them from the same mistakes.

Appendix

The following questions are designed to measure your sexual intelligence, based on the research we discuss in our book.

Test Your Sexual Intelligence

For each question, choose the answer you feel best reflects your opinion, feelings, or behavior.

1. In your current relationship (or in your last long-term relationship), approximately how often do you (did you) talk with your partner about your sex life?
   a) Once a week
   b) Once a month
   c) Once every six months
   d) Never

2. How would you rate your current sex life, compared to most other people's sex lives?
   a) Not nearly as exciting as most people's
   b) About the same as most people's
   c) More exciting than most people's
   d) I'm not currently in a sexual relationship

3. If a problem came up in your sex life with your partner, what would you be most likely to do?

   a) Bring it up directly with my partner

   b) Approach the topic indirectly

   c) Give it some time and hope things would change

   d) Look for a more compatible partner

4. If a problem came up in your sex life with your partner, how would you feel about talking with a close friend or a confidante (e.g., a therapist).

   a) I would never feel comfortable talking with an outsider about my sex life.

   b) I might talk with someone about my sex life, but only as a last resort.

   c) I would be comfortable talking to a friend or confidante about my sex life.

5. Have you ever kept a sexual secret from a partner over a long period of time?

   a) No, never

   b) Once or twice

   c) Several times

   d) Frequently

6. If your partner wanted to engage in a sexual behavior that you find uncomfortable, what would you do?

   a) Go ahead and engage in the behavior anyway

   b) Investigate why the behavior interests my partner, but makes me uncomfortable

   c) Tell my partner that the behavior is off limits, period

   d) Consider ending the relationship

7. Compared to the effort you put into the various tasks of daily life (e.g., shopping, cleaning, hobbies), how much effort do you put into securing an active, satisfying sex life?

   a) Much of the time, I am thinking about how to have more sex.

   b) To me, a satisfying sex life is at least as important as my hobbies and daily chores.

   c) By the time I'm done with the tasks of daily living, I don't have either the time or energy to think about improving my sex life.

d) I'm embarrassed by how bad my sex life is, so I try not to think about it at all.

8. The only way to safeguard oneself from inappropriate behavior in the workplace is to adopt a completely sexless persona.

a) True

b) False

9. To what extent would you say you are particularly masculine (or feminine)?

a) I'm extremely masculine (or feminine) compared to other people.

b) I'm fairly masculine (or feminine) compared to other people.

c) I have and value both masculine and feminine traits.

d) I have both, but am trying to act more masculine (or feminine).

10. When a man and a woman encounter a problem in their sexual relationship, it's most likely because

a) men and women just want different things in bed.

b) they haven't talked sufficiently about their needs and desires.

c) they are not really right for each other.

d) the psychology of men and women are polar opposites.

11. How likely are you to assume that great sex is a sign of true love?

a) I believe having great sex doesn't necessarily have anything to do with being in love.

b) I believe having great sex likely means that a couple is meant to be together.

c) I believe having great sex practically guarantees being in love.

12. In the past, when you had a conflict, how often have you had sex instead of talking?

a) I've never substituted having sex for talking about a problem.

b) A few times I have used sex to try to avoid a problem temporarily.

c) I think sex is a good way to decrease the level of conflict in a relationship.

d) I always solve a problem first and then have sex.

13. If you had just met someone you liked a lot and wanted a serious relationship with, would you typically have sex very early on in the relationship?

    a) If it was someone I like a lot, I would wait to have sex until I knew them better.

    b) A few times I've had sex with someone before I got to know them well.

    c) I would definitely have sex with someone I didn't know well if I liked them a lot.

14. Do you ever feel that your current sex life is not as exciting as the sex lives of the people on TV and in the movies?

    a) The sex I'm having is disappointing, compared to the passion I see on the screen.

    b) I have once or twice in my life had sex that passionate.

    c) It's hard to compare on-screen passionate encounters to a real-life relationship.

15. How many times in your teenage years did you have a meaningful conversation with one or both of your parents about sex?

    a) I never talked with my parents about sex.

    b) They lectured me about sex.

    c) We had open and positive conversations about sex.

16. How do you feel about the content of the sexual fantasy you have most often or find most arousing?

    a) I'd be horrified if anyone knew the content.

    b) I'd be embarrassed if my partner knew the kind of fantasies I have.

    c) I might be a little hesitant but also find it exciting to share the content with my sexual partner.

    d) I talk to my closest friends about my fantasies.

17. How would you compare your sexual fantasies with those of most people?

    a) I'd bet a lot of people have fantasies like mine.

    b) I don't really know what other people fantasize about.

    c) I think my fantasies are abnormal, compared to other people's.

18. When you are sexually aroused, how aware are you of whether you are feeling a mostly physical urge as opposed to, say, feelings of affection or a need to be close?
  a) I never really distinguish between physical and emotional urges.
  b) Sometimes I'm aware of what feels like a purely physical urge to have sex.
  c) Sometimes I'm aware that I want to be emotionally close more than I'm physically aroused.
  d) When I am aroused, it is always a combination of physical and emotional urges.

19. How often have you initiated sex when you were feeling bad about yourself or upset about something in your life, like work?
  a) I rarely initiate sex when I'm feeling bad or upset about something.
  b) There have been times when I had sex to try to feel better about myself or my life.
  c) I often want sex when I'm feeling bad about myself or what's going on in my life.

20. In the past, when I've been tempted to cheat on a spouse or partner in a committed relationship
  a) I agonized over cheating, knowing how hurt and betrayed my partner would feel.
  b) I didn't really give any thought to how my partner would feel.
  c) I would never cheat on my partner because it would be a sin.
  d) I thought about my partner but assumed he or she would accept it if they found out.

21. If your partner revealed fantasies about having sex with someone who is the opposite sex to you, what would you conclude?
  a) My partner is latently gay (or if you are gay, "my partner is actually straight").
  b) He or she has psychological problems.
  c) He or she no longer finds me attractive.
  d) He or she is not so different from many people.

22. How aware are you of the physical characteristics that constitute your "type"?

a) I'm immediately drawn to people who look a certain way.

b) I'm attracted to individuals who look a certain way, but I don't always choose to be in a relationship with them.

c) I'm attracted to many different physical types.

d) I've never given any thought to the "type" of person I'm attracted to.

23. If you knew you could cheat without getting caught, what would you do?

a) I would definitely cheat.

b) I would still consider the effect of cheating on my relationship.

c) Cheating is a sin; I would never do it.

24. When you think about yourself as becoming elderly (over age 70), how likely is it that you would continue to have sex?

a) I can't imagine myself having sex at that age.

b) It's pretty unlikely that I will still be sexually active then.

c) I hope to be sexually active in my 70s.

d) I plan to do everything I can to remain sexually active into my 70s.

25. When you think about your use of the Internet to access sexual material, how important would you estimate it is in your life?

a) I would never consider Internet sex.

b) Internet sex is one way I might consider obtaining sexual gratification.

c) Internet sex is an important part of my sexual life.

d) I couldn't imagine not having access to sex on the Internet.

26. Under which of the following circumstances would you be most likely to go online for a sexual encounter?

a) If I were temporarily unattached

b) If I were having a fight with my current partner

c) To experience things I've never done

27. How often have you felt powerless to control or stop your sexual behavior?

a) I'm totally in control of my sexual feelings and behaviors.

b) I sometimes have sexual desires that feel overwhelming, but I don't necessarily act on them.

c) I frequently feel that my sexual behavior is out of control.

28. How comfortable do you feel with your sexual behavior?

a) Although some people might be concerned about my sexual behavior, I see no reason to change.

b) I frequently promise myself to stop a certain behavior, but then I do it anyway.

c) I've never had any reason to be concerned about my sexual behavior.

29. How often do you try to escape your problems using sex?

a) If it weren't for sex, my problems would overwhelm me.

b) Occasionally I use sex to deliberately escape my problems.

c) I never use sex for that purpose.

30. How do you typically feel after you have sex?

a) I often feel depressed.

b) I sometimes feel depressed.

c) I usually feel content and satisfied.

d) I feel nothing.

31. Have you ever gotten someone to have sex by, for example, holding their arms down, making threats, or ignoring when the person said "No" or "Stop"?

a) Never

b) Once

c) Occasionally

d) Frequently

32. Would you say that having been sexually coerced or traumatized earlier in life has any influence on a person's later enjoyment of sex?

a) Not if several years have passed without a negative experience

b) If one's current partner is nonthreatening, it's very unlikely

c) Only if the person dwells on it too much

d) In many cases, it's very possible

33. When it comes to talking to teenagers about sex, which of the following approaches would you choose?

a) Tell them to abstain from sex, since the dangers of HIV are so high

b) Tell them about safe sex and then avoid asking them anything about their private life

c) Tell them to pay careful attention in their sex education class in school

d) Ask them what they think about teenage sexuality and discuss what you know

34. One way to help your teenage daughter (or son) to avoid getting into a date-rape situation would be to

a) not allow them to date until they are at least sixteen.

b) only allow them to go out in groups.

c) encourage them to pay attention to feelings of uneasiness or fear.

d) make sure they are not dating the wrong kind of people.

35. Parents should keep quiet about mistakes they have made in their own sexual life—after all, teenagers do what we do, not what we say.

a) True

b) False

36. Would you agree with the statement "A good sex life is not something you can work at—it either happens or it doesn't"?

a) Definitely

b) Maybe

c) Not at all

37. To what extent do you agree with the statement "There is always a price to pay, sometimes a very high price, for sexual passion"?

a) Strongly agree

b) Agree

c) Disagree

d) Strongly disagree

38. Do you ever feel shame about some of your sexual desires or behavior?

a) Frequently

b) Sometimes

c) Never

39. On the average, how often do you have sex?

a) A few times a year or less

b) Once or twice a month

c) Once or twice a week

d) Three times a week

e) Four times a week or more

40. When a woman acts friendly toward a man she has just met

a) it's likely she is interested in having sex with him.

b) she is probably the type of woman who behaves seductively toward men.

c) she probably is just being friendly.

41. On a date, men should

a) act like gentlemen, open doors for their date, etc.

b) not feel constrained to do those typically male behaviors.

c) actively avoid traditionally male behaviors like opening doors, etc.

42. How often have you had sex when you don't want to, just to please your partner?

a) Never

b) A couple of times

c) Occasionally

d) Fairly often

43. How does your weight affect your feelings toward having sex?

a) Not at all.

b) I could be somewhat happier with my body.

c) I'm too overweight to have a good sex life.

d) I'm not muscular enough to have a good sex life.

44. How does your appearance affect your feelings toward having sex?
   a) I'm not attractive enough to have a good sex life.
   b) It affects my chances for a good sex life somewhat.
   c) No effect—I'm quite happy with my appearance.

45. How do you feel about individuals who identify themselves as "gay"?
   a) Homosexuality is morally wrong.
   b) Homosexuality is okay, but it shouldn't be flaunted.
   c) It would be wrong for them to deny their sexual identity.

46. Although they may deny it, many women really want to be taken sexually by force.
   a) True
   b) False

47. How do you feel about someone who is in a committed relationship secretly having sex with someone on the Internet?
   a) It is fine because there is no physical contact.
   b) It is okay as an (innocent) supplement.
   c) It is a big distraction and it can contribute to problems in a relationship.
   d) It is a form of adultery and thus is problematic because it happens behind your partner's back.

48. If you were not happy with your physical appearance or with your body, who would you be most likely to talk to about it?
   a) A friend
   b) My sexual partner
   c) A professional
   d) Nobody

49. Do you think that having sex, like exercising and having good nutrition, can actually make you more healthy and live longer?
   a) No, sex has nothing to do with physical health.
   b) Maybe, but science hasn't proved that sex is healthy.
   c) Yes, science shows that sex is good for you.

50. Do you make a conscious effort to have safe sex?

a) No, I don't have to because my partner and I have been tested for AIDS and we know each other well enough to trust each other's commitment to monogamy.

b) No, I don't have to because I am heterosexual and heterosexual people hardly ever get AIDS.

c) No, because none of the people I sleep with look sick.

d) Yes, whenever at risk I take precautions.

51. How often have you felt ashamed about not being "masculine" or "feminine" enough?

a) I often feel ashamed about that.

b) I sometimes feel ashamed about that.

c) I never feel ashamed about that.

52. How much do you feel you understand the behavior of the opposite sex?

a) There are times when I don't completely understand the behavior of the opposite sex.

b) The behavior of the opposite sex makes no sense to me.

c) I don't think that men and women behave differently from one another.

Scoring the Sexual Intelligence Test

Scoring

Below are the points for each answer. We've indicated some questions that are particularly good indicators of your skills in the three areas of sexual intelligence: *Scientific Knowledge, Awareness of the Secret Sexual Self,* and *Connecting with Others.* Total up the points you received for each question, add 118 to your score and divide by 264. This is your SI (Sexual Intelligence) score. If your SI score is 90 or above, you earned an "A." This is very good. If your SI is 80–89, you got a "B," still pretty good. If your SI score is between 70–79, you got a "C"; this is about average. If you scored between 60–69 you got a "D," and if your SI is below 60, this would be an "F."

1. [Connecting with Others] Talking with one's sexual partner about sex is very important, although many people do not do so.
   a) 3 points
   b) 2 points
   c) 1 point
   d) −3 points

2. Many people assume their sex life is bad compared to most people, when in fact the level of sexual dysfunction in the United States is very high.
   a) −2 points
   b) 3 points
   c) 0 points
   d) 0 points

3. Being willing to talk to your partner about your sex life is an important aspect of sexual intelligence.
   a) 3 points
   b) 2 points
   c) 0 points
   d) −3 points

4. Seeking help with problems is the intelligent thing to do.
   a) −3 points
   b) 1 point
   c) 3 points

5. [Awareness of the Inner Sexual Self] While no one shares everything about themselves with their partner, keeping secrets from your partner often does not reflect sexual intelligence.
   a) 3 points
   b) 1 point
   c) −1 point
   d) −3 points

6. Considering sexual behavior that makes you uncomfortable, particularly behavior that interests your partner, helps you to understand your secret sexual self.

  a) −1 point
  b) 3 points
  c) −1 point
  d) −3 points

7. [Connecting with Others] Effort is necessary to achieve a satisfying, regular sex life.

  a) −1 point
  b) 3 points
  c) −1 point
  d) −2 points

8. [Scientific Knowledge] Sexuality is a part of who we are, so trying to be "sexless" denies that part of our secret sexual selves.

  a) 0 points
  b) 3 points

9. Rigid adherence to gender-role stereotypes reduces one's sexual intelligence and increases the likelihood of conflict in intimate relationships.

  a) −3 points
  b) 0 points
  c) 3 points
  d) −1 point

10. Gender differences in sexual preferences can lead to problems if individuals are not open to talking about their own and their partner's needs and desires.

  a) 0 points
  b) 3 points
  c) 0 points
  d) −2 points

11. [Scientific Knowledge] Being sexually intelligent means recognizing that sex is just one aspect of a relationship that sometimes can give the illusion of emotional intimacy.
   a) 3 points
   b) 0 points
   c) −3 points

12. Using sex to avoid emotional conflicts does not reflect sexual intelligence.
   a) 3 points
   b) 1 point
   c) −3 points
   d) 3 points

13. Having sex early in a relationship can give the illusion of emotional intimacy when the basis of real intimacy in terms of shared experience and emotional sharing is not present.
   a) 3 points
   b) 1 point
   c) −3 points

14. A sexually intelligent person recognizes that the sex lives of characters on TV and in the movies represent distorted images of what a healthy and intelligent sex life should be.
   a) 0 points
   b) 1 point
   c) 3 points

15. Being able to communicate in a meaningful way about sexuality with one's parents is an important aid in the development of sexual intelligence.
   a) −1 point
   b) −2 points
   c) 3 points

16. Being sexually intelligent means embracing our sexual fantasies as an important part of our secret sexual selves.

   a) −2 points

   b) −1 point

   c) 3 points

   d) 2 points

17. Most people have very similar fantasies, and characterizing them as "abnormal" or "healthy" is not productive.

   a) 3 points

   b) 0 point

   c) −2 points

18. Being sexually intelligent means being aware of the causes of one's sexual desire.

   a) −1 point

   b) 1 point

   c) 1 point

   d) 1 point

19. Trying to use sex as a way of feeling better may work in the short-term, but it avoids the real emotional issue and can lead to sexual compulsivity.

   a) 3 points

   b) 0 points

   c) −3 points

20. [Awareness of the Secret Sexual Self] A sexually intelligent person considers the impact that his or her sexual behavior is likely to have on a partner, rather than simply assuming he or she will never be tempted to stray because of moral considerations.

   a) 3 points

   b) −3 points

   c) −1 point

   d) −2 points

21. Homosexual fantasies among straight people are very common, as are heterosexual fantasies among gay people.

    a) −2 points

    b) −1 point

    c) −1 point

    d) 3 points

22. Since the type of person that individuals are attracted to is related to a variety of life experiences, including our parental and sibling relationships from childhood, being sexually intelligent means having an awareness of how these experiences influence the type of person that appeals to us.

    a) 0 points

    b) 1 point

    c) 3 points

    d) 0 points

23. Most people would be tempted in this situation, and a sexually intelligent person is aware of this important situational influence.

    a) −2 points

    b) 3 points

    c) 1 point

24. [Connecting with Others] A high percentage of elderly people continue to have satisfying sexual lives.

    a) −1 point

    b) −1 point

    c) 1 point

    d) 3 points

25. Using the Internet as an important source of sexual gratification can weaken one's capacity to sustain an emotional and sexual relationship with a partner, a relationship that ultimately is more satisfying.

    a) 0 points

    b) 1 point

c) −1 point
d) −3 points

26. Using the Internet to avoid emotional issues in a relationship can be very destructive.
a) 1 point
b) −3 points
c) 1 point

27. Being unable to control one's sexual behavior is a sign of a sexual compulsion.
a) −1 point
b) 3 points
c) −3 points

28. Being concerned about your sexual behavior and trying to stop it is a sign of a sexual compulsion.
a) −3 points
b) −3 points
c) 0 points

29. [Awareness of the Secret Sexual Self] Being sexually intelligent means recognizing that sex is not a solution to emotional problems.
a) −3 points
b) 0 points
c) 2 points

30. Feeling depressed after you have sex is a sign of problems such as a history of sexual trauma or current relationship problems.
a) −3 points
b) −1 point
c) 3 points
d) −1 point

31. Compelling another person to have sex against their will is a crime, and it is extremely destructive of a relationship.
   a) 3 points
   b) −1 point
   c) −2 points
   d) −3 points

32. [Scientific Knowledge] Having a history of sexual trauma will almost certainly interfere with an individual's capacity to enjoy sex later in life.
   a) −2 points
   b) 0 points
   c) −2 points
   d) 3 points

33. [Scientific Knowledge] Lecturing teenagers is a fairly ineffective way of changing teenagers' behavior; trying to engage them in a conversation about it can help to increase their sexual intelligence.
   a) −2 points
   b) 0 points
   c) 0 points
   d) 3 points

34. Teenagers need to learn to recognize their emotional reactions can be important warning signals to them that they should not ignore.
   a) 0 points
   b) 0 points
   c) 3 points
   d) 0 points

35. Sharing your mistakes, and the emotional pain that they produced, with your teenager can help create an emotional bond with him/her and increase the likelihood that they will behave in a sexually intelligent way.
   a) −3 points
   b) 3 points

36. [Scientific Knowledge] People need to work at having a good sex life.

a) −2 points

a) 0 points

c) 3 points

37. [Scientific Knowledge] Sex is not in itself dangerous; it is an important part of a healthy life.

a) −1 point

b) 0 points

c) 1 point

d) 3 points

38. [Awareness of the Secret Sexual Self] It is less than sexually intelligent to engage in behaviors that you would need to feel shame about—such as forcing someone else to have sex; it is also unhealthy to feel shame about sexual behavior that is not harmful to yourself or others or nonconsensual.

a) −3 points

b) 0 points

c) 3 points

39. [Connecting with Others] Researchers have found that the greatest health benefits seem to be associated with having sex weekly; more than three times a week may be an indication of sexual compulsivity or of relationship problems.

a) 0 points

b) 1 point

c) 2 points

d) 3 points

e) 2 points

40. While men often take friendliness as a sign of a woman's sexual interest in them, it is often simply friendliness.

a) −3 points

b) −1 point

c) 3 points

41. Studies suggest that stereotypes about how men and women should behave can actually be damaging to male-female relationships.

a) 0 points

b) 3 points

c) 0 points

42. [Awareness of the Secret Sexual Self] Having sex to please a partner when you don't actually want to have sex is less than sexually intelligent.

a) 3 points

b) 0 points

c) −1 point

d) −3 points

43. Body image has an important influence on many people's sexual life, even though many people—both women and men—have very distorted body images, believing themselves either too fat or not muscular enough to be attractive.

a) 3 points

b) 0 points

c) −3 points

d) −3 points

44. Many people have negative views about their own sexual attractiveness that interfere with having a satisfying sex life.

a) −3 points

b) −1 point

c) 3 points

45. There is nothing malevolent about sexual desire toward members of the same sex—we need to honor others' sexual choices as long as they do not harm others.

a) −3 points

b) −1 point

c) 3 points

46. It is a myth that women want to be raped.
   a) −3 points
   b) 3 points

47. Using the Internet for sex can contribute to relationship problems.
   a) −3 points
   b) 0 points
   c) 3 points
   d) 2 points

48. It is important to talk about issues that affect your feelings toward your sexuality, particularly with your partner.
   a) 1 point
   b) 3 points
   c) 2 points
   d) −3 points

49. Research shows that sex definitely has a wide range of health benefits.
   a) −3 points
   b) 0 points
   c) 3 points

50. Taking precautions is very important.
   a) 1 point
   b) −3 points
   c) −3 points
   d) 3 points

51. Sex-role stereotypes that inculcate shame in people are very destructive.
   a) −3 points
   b) −1 point
   c) 3 points

52. Men and women do, in fact, behave differently, largely as a result of differential socialization, and where there are real gender differences, it is important to know about them. On the other hand, men and women are much more alike than many people assume.

    a) 3 points

    b) 0 points

    c) 0 points

Endnotes

CHAPTER 1

1. All of the personal stories are from interviews conducted as part of our Sexual Intelligence Project. The names of the participants, as well as identifying characteristics such as their occupation, ethnicity, and age, have been changed to protect their anonymity. In some cases, individual stories are compilations of two or more similar individuals.

2. Harris, L. (1989). Harris Survey no. 892046. Harris Data Archive, Institute for Research in the Social Sciences, University of North Carolina, Chapel Hill. Question no. MH1: "How important is it to you to have a satisfying sex life?"; *USA Today.* (1987). Survey no. 3008. Institute for Research in the Social Sciences, University of North Carolina, Chapel Hill. Question no. 58B. Sex as a source of stress in life. Question no. 15B. Concerns about having sex more regularly.

3. Wypijewski, J. (July 1998). The secret sharer: Sex, race, and denial in an American small town. *Harper's Magazine, 297,* 35–54.

4. Laumann, E. O., Paik, A., & Rosen, R. C. (1999). Sexual dysfunction in the United States: Prevalence and predictors. *Journal of the American Medical Association, 281*(6), 537–544. For full text on the web, see: http://jama.ama-assn.org/issues/v281n6/full/joc80785.html.

5. Conrad, S. D., Milburn, M. A. (2001). Sexual intelligence: A predictor of sexual satisfaction and sexual dysfunction. Paper presented at the

Eastern Region Annual Conference of the Society for the Scientific Study of Sexuality, Portsmouth, Virginia, April 1, 2001.

6. We by no means want to deny the usefulness of therapy, in general, or in dealing with sexual dysfunctions. There are many different types of therapy, and many of them can be used to develop the specific behaviors and attitudes that distinguish sexually intelligent people from the less sexually intelligent.

CHAPTER 3

7. Forty-one percent of the people we talked to agreed to one extent or another that "masturbation should not be practiced." Forty-three percent agreed to some extent with the statement "masturbation is wrong and will ruin you." Thirty-seven percent believed that "masturbation is a form of self-destruction." Thirty-eight percent agreed that "masturbation is wrong and a sin."

8. Michael Cirigliano, M.D., Assistant Professor of Medicine at the University of Pennsylvania School of Medicine, and Karen Donahey, Ph.D., director of the Sex and Marital Therapy Program at Northwestern University Medical Center, quoted in O'Neill, Hugh, & McGrath, Tom. (November 1997). Love is the drug. *Men's Health, 12*, 104.

9. Karen Donahey, Ph.D., director of the Sex and Marital Therapy Program at Northwestern University Medical Center, quoted in *Men's Health, 12*, O'Neill & McGrath, Love is the drug, 104.

10. Psychologists Carl Charnetski and Frank Brennan of Wilkes University in Wilkes-Barre, Pennsylvania, presented these results in a paper presented at the Eastern Psychological Association April 1999 meeting in Providence, Rhode Island, reported in *New Scientist*, April 17, 1999.

11. Progesterone and DHEA are the precursors, or pro-drugs, for more specialized steroid hormones, including cortisol, aldosterone, estrogen, and testosterone. "Tamoxifen, toremifene, DHEA, and vorozole inhibit tumor growth in rodent mammary carcinoma models and are promising chemotherapeutic agents for use against breast cancer development." (See Nephew, K. P., Osborne, E., Lubet, R. A., Grubbs, C. J., & Khan, S. A. [2000]. Effects of oral administration of tamoxifen, toremifene, dehy-

droepiandrosterone, and vorozole on uterine histomorphology in the rat. *Proceedings of the Society for Experimental Biology and Medicine, 23,* 288–294). Improve cognition, see: Bastianetto, S., Ramassamy, C., Poirier, J., & Quirion, R. (1999). Dehydroepiandrosterone (DHEA) protects hippocampal cells from oxidative stress-induced damage. *Molecular Brain Research, 66*(1–2), 35–41. Immune system functioning, see Cheng, G. F., & Tseng, J. (2000). Regulation of murine interleukin-10 production by dehydroepiandrosterone. *Interferon Cytokine Reseach, 20*(5): 471–478. Bone growth, see Chiu, K. M., Keller, E. T., Crenshaw, T. D., & Gravenstein, S. (1999). Carnitine and dehydroepiandrosterone sulfate induce protein synthesis in porcine primary osteoblast-like cells. *Calcified Tissue International, 64*(6), 527–533). Depression, see Cyr, M., Calon, F., Morissette, M., Grandbois, M., Di Paolo, T., & Callier S. (2000). Drugs with estrogen-like potency and brain activity: Potential therapeutic application for the CNS. *Current Pharmaceutical Design, 6*(12), 1287–1312.

12. Dr. Theresa Crenshaw, sex researcher and retired director of the Crenshaw Clinic, quoted in O'Neill & McGrath, Love is the drug, *Men's Health, 12,* 104. Also see Vermeulen, A. (1983). Androgen secretion after age 50 in both sexes. *Hormone Research, 18*(1–3), 37–42.

13. Jansson, J. H., Nilsson, T. K., & Johnson, O. (1998). Von Willebrand factor, tissue plasminogen activator, and dehydroepiandrosterone sulphate predict cardiovascular death in a 10-year follow up of survivors of acute myocardial infarction. *Heart, 80*(4), 334–337.

14. Davey Smith, G., Frankel, S., & Yarnell, J. (1997). Sex and death: Are they related? Findings from the Caerphilly cohort study. *British Medical Journal, 315*(7123), 1641–1644.

15. Khalkhali-Ellis, Z., Moore, T. L., & Hendrix, M. J. (1998). Reduced levels of testosterone and dehydroepiandrosterone sulphate in the serum and synovial fluid of juvenile rheumatoid arthritis patients correlates with disease severity. *Clinical and Experimental Rheumatology, 16*(6):753–776. See also Sowers, M. F., Hochberg, M., Crabbe, J. P., Muhich, A., Crutchfield, M., & Updike, S. (1996). Association of bone mineral density and sex hormone levels with osteoarthritis of the hand and knee in premenopausal women. *American Journal of Epidemiology, 143*(1), 38–47.

16. Hawkes, C. H. (1992). Endorphins: The basis of pleasure? *Journal of Neurology, Neurosurgery & Psychiatry, 55,* 247–251; Nicoli, R. M., & Nicoli, J. M. (1995). Biochemistry of eros. *Contraception, Fertilité, Sexualité, 23*(2), 137–144. On the role of oxytocin, see Young, L. J., Wang, Z., & Insel, T. R. (1998). Neuroendocrine bases of monogamy. *Trends in Neurosciences, 21,* 71–75. Benefits of marriage, see Steinhauer, J. Studies find big benefits in marriage. *The New York Times,* April 10, 1995, section A, p. 10, col. 4, reporting on research by Dr. Linda Waite, professor of sociology at the University of Chicago, presented at the Population Association of America.

17. Ventegodt, S. (1998). Sex and the quality of life in Denmark. *Archives of Sexual Behavior, 27,* 295–307.

18. A 1998 study of 240 Australian college students by Marita McCabe and Robert Cummins of the School of Psychology at Deakin University in Burwood, Australia, found that sexual experience was strongly related to the quality of life reported by the participants in the study. McCabe had reported earlier, in a study in the Winter 1997 issue of the *Journal of Sex and Marital Therapy,* that, in a sample of the general public, both men and women with sexual problems, such as the inability to reach orgasm, lack of arousal, premature ejaculation, inability to maintain an erection, or lack of sexual desire, had a significantly lower quality of life than did people without such problems. See McCabe, M. P., & Cummins, R. A. (1998). Sexuality and quality of life among young people. *Adolescence, 33,* 761–773; McCabe, M. P. (1997). Intimacy and quality of life among sexually dysfunctional men and women. *Journal of Sex and Marital Therapy, 23,* 276–290.

19. Matthias, R. E., Lubben, J. E., Atchison, K. A., & Schweitzer, S. O. (1997). Sexual activity and satisfaction among very old adults: Results from a community-dwelling medicare population survey. *Gerontologist, 37,* 6–14.

20. See Steinhauer, Studies find big benefits in marriage, section A, p. 10, col. 4, reporting on research by Dr. Linda Waite, professor of sociology at the University of Chicago, presented at the Population Association of America.

CHAPTER 4

21. Gribble, J. N., Miller, H. G., Rogers, S. M., & Turner, C. F. (Research Triangle Institute, Washington, D.C.) (1999). Interview mode and measurement of sexual behaviors: Methodological issues. *The Journal of Sex Research, 36,* 16–24.

22. King, B. M., & Lorusso, J. (1997). Discussions in the home about sex: Recollections by parents and children. *Journal of Sex and Marital Therapy, 23* (1), 52–60, 59.

23. Ibid., 59.

24. Miller, B. C., McCoy, J. K., Olson, T. D., & Wallace, C. M. (1986). Parental discipline and control attempts in relation to adolescent sexual attitudes and behavior. *Journal of Marriage and the Family, 48,* 503–512.

25. Metzler, C. W., Noell, J., Biglan, A., Ary, D., et al. (1994). The social context for risky sexual behavior among adolescents. *Journal of Behavioral Medicine, 17*(4), 419–438.

26. Milburn, M. A., & Conrad, S. D. (1996). *The politics of denial.* Cambridge, MA: MIT Press.

27. Donnelly, J., Duncan, D. F., Goldfarb, E., & Eadie, C. (1999). Sexuality attitudes and behaviors of self-described very religious urban students in middle school. *Psychological Reports, 85*(2), 607–610.

28. Pluhar, E., Frongillo, E. A., Jr., Stycos, J. M., & Dempster-McClain, D. (1998). Understanding the relationship between religion and the sexual attitudes and behaviors of college students. *Journal of Sex Education and Therapy, 23,* 288–296.

29. Tschann, J. M., & Adler, N. E. (1997). Sexual self-acceptance, communication with partner, and contraceptive use among adolescent females: A longitudinal study. *Journal of Research on Adolescence, 7*(4), 413–430.

30. Lexis-Nexis Roper Center at University of Connecticut Public Opinion Online, Accession number 0217158, June 15, 1994; Lexis-Nexis Roper Center at University of Connecticut Public Opinion Online, Accession number 0312297, October 14, 1998; Lexis-Nexis Roper Center at University of Connecticut Public Opinion Online, Accession number 0312296, October 14, 1998.

31. Telljohann, S. K., & Price, J. H. (1993). A qualitative examination of adolescent homosexuals' life experiences: Ramifications for secondary school personnel. *Journal of Homosexuality, 26*(1), 41–56.

32. Harris, M. B., & Bliss, G. K. (1997). Coming out in a school setting: Former students' experiences and opinions about disclosure. In M. B. Harris, et al. (Eds.), *School experiences of gay and lesbian youth: The invisible minority* (pp. 85–100). New York: Harrington Park Press/The Haworth Press.

33. Hershberger, S. L., Pilkington, N. W., & D'Augelli, A. R. (1997). Predictors of suicide attempts among gay, lesbian, and bisexual youth. *Journal of Adolescent Research, 12*(4), 477–497.

34. Boxer, A. M., Cook, J. A., & Herdt, G, (1999). Experiences of coming out among gay and lesbian youth: Adolescents alone? In J. Blustein, C. Levine, et al. (Eds.), *The adolescent alone: Decision making in health care in the United States* (pp. 121–138). New York: Cambridge University Press.

CHAPTER 5

35. Henry K. Kaiser Family Foundation. Sex on TV: Content and Context: A Biennial Report to the Kaiser Family Foundation. http://www.kff.org/content/archive/1458/.

36. Lexis-Nexis Roper Center at University of Connecticut Public Opinion Online, Accession number 0011243, January 16, 1987.

37. Zillmann, D., & Bryant, J. Pornography's impact on sexual satisfaction. *Journal of Applied Social Psychology, 18*(5), 438–453.

38. *Glamour* (2000, April).

39. Ogden, J., & Mundray, K. (1996) The effect of the media on body satisfaction: The role of gender and size. *European Eating Disorders Review, 4*(3),171–182.

40. Harrison, K., & Cantor, J. (1997).The relationship between media consumption and eating disorders. *Journal of Communication, 47*(1), 40–67.

41. Pope, H. G. Jr., Phillips, K. A., & Olivardia, R. (2000). *The Adonis complex: The secret crisis of male body obsession.* New York: Free Press.

42. Zillmann, D., Weaver, J. B. Pornography and men's sexual callousness toward women. In Zillmann, D., & Bryant, J. (Eds.). (1989). *Pornography: Research advances and policy considerations* (pp. 95–125). Hillsdale, NJ: Erlbaum.

43. Zillmann, D., & Bryant, J. Shifting preferences in pornography consumption. *Communication Research, 13*(4), 560–578.

44. Milburn, M. A., Mather, R., & Conrad, S. D. (2000). The effects of viewing R-rated movie scenes that objectify women on perceptions of date rape. *Sex Roles, 43*, 379–398.

CHAPTER 6

45. This is a paraphrase. The original comes from *Tom Sawyer Abroad:* "The person that had took a bull by the tail once had learnt sixty or seventy times as much as a person that hadn't, and said a person that started in to carry a cat home by the tail was getting knowledge that was always going to be useful to him, and warn't ever going to grow dim or doubtful. Chances are, he isn't likely to carry the cat that way again, either. But if he wants to, I say let him!"

46. For example, see Sawyer, R. G., & Smith, N. G. (1996). A survey of situational factors at first intercourse among college students. *American Journal of Health Behavior, 20*, 208–217, as well as Guggino, J. M., & Ponzetti, J. J., Jr. (1997). Gender differences in affective reactions to first coitus. *Journal of Adolescence, 20*, 189–200. Also see Sprecher, S., Barbee, A., & Schwartz, P. (1995). Was it good for you, too?: Gender differences in first sexual intercourse experiences. *Journal of Sex Research, 32*, 3–15.

47. In addition to the references listed in endnote 46, see also Rosenthal, D. A., Smith, A. M. A., & de Visser, R. (1999). Personal and social factors influencing age at first sexual intercourse. *Archives of Sexual Behavior, 28*, 319–333.

48. Betty Chewning and Richard Van Koningsveld at the University of Wisconsin–Madison Sonderegger Research Center recently reported a study based on Koningsveld, R. V. (1998). Predicting adolescents' initiation of

intercourse and contraceptive use. *Journal of Applied Social Psychology*, *28*, 1245–1285.

49. Sawyer, R. G., & Smith, N. G. (1996). A survey of situational factors at first intercourse among college students. *American Journal of Health Behavior*, *20*, 208–217.

50. Rosenthal, D. A., Smith, A. M. A., & de Visser, R. (1999). Personal and social factors influencing age at first sexual intercourse. *Archives of Sexual Behavior*, *28*, 319–333; Chewning, B., & Koningsveld, R. V. (1998). Predicting adolescents' initiation of intercourse and contraceptive use. *Journal of Applied Social Psychology*, *28*, 1245–1285; and Capaldi, D. M., Crosby, L., & Stoolmiller, M. (1996). Predicting the timing of first sexual intercourse for at-risk adolescent males. *Child Development*, *67*, 344–359.

CHAPTER 7

51. For example, see Basson, R. (1999). Androgen replacement for women. *Canadian Family Physician*, *45*, 2100–2107; and Marumo, K., Baba, S., & Murai, M. (1999). Erectile function and nocturnal penile tumescence in patients with prostate cancer undergoing luteinizing hormone-releasing hormone agonist therapy. *International Journal of Urology*, *6*(1), 19–23.

52. Liebowitz, M. R. (1983). *The chemistry of love*. Boston: Little, Brown.

53. See Carmichael, M. S., Humbert, R., Dixen, J., Palmisano, G., Greenleaf, W., & Davidson, J. M. (1987). Plasma oxytocin increases in the human sexual response. *Journal of Clinical Endocrinology and Metabolism*, *64*, 27–31; and Murphy, M. R., Seckl, J. R., Burton, S., Checkley, S. A., & Lightman, S. (1987). Changes in oxytocin and vasopressin secretion during sexual activity in men. *Journal of Clinical Endocrinology and Metabolism*, *65*, 738–741.

54. Young, L. J., Wang, Z., & Insel, T. R. (1998). Neuroendocrine bases of monogamy. *Trends in Neuroscience*, *21*, 71–75.

55. Fisher, H. (1995). The nature and evolution of romantic love. In W. Jankowiak (Ed.), *Romantic passion* (pp. 23–41). New York: Columbia University Press.

56. Bermant, G. (1995). To speak in chords about sexuality. *Neuroscience and Biobehavioral Reviews, 19,* 343–348.

57. Peplau, L., Rubin, Z., & Hill, C. (1977). Sexual intimacy in dating relationships. *Journal of Social Issues, 33,* 86–109.

58. Sternberg, R. J. (1988). *The psychology of love.* New Haven, CT: Yale University Press.

59. Nelson, E. S., Hill-Barlow, D., & Benedict, J. O. (1994). Addiction versus intimacy as related to sexual involvement in a relationship. *Journal of Sex and Marital Therapy, 20,* 35–45.

60. Pert, C. B. (1997). *Molecules of emotion: Why you feel the way you feel.* New York: Scribner.

CHAPTER 8

61. However, there are some sexual behaviors called "paraphilias" that we and many other psychologists define as pathological. A behavior is considered among the paraphilias if it involves: (1) sexual urges or fantasies that are repeated and intense; (2) centered on inanimate objects or those who cannot consent (such as children and animals); or (3) it involves suffering or humiliation experienced by oneself or inflicted on one's partner.

62. Kinsey, A. C., Pomeroy, W. B., & Martin, C. E. (1948). *Sexual behavior in the human male.* Philadelphia: W. B. Saunders. See also The staff of the Institute for Sex Research, Indiana University (Alfred C. Kinsey et al.) (1953). *Sexual behavior in the human female,* Philadelphia: Saunders.

63. Our results comparing men and women exclude three male "outliers" who reported 50, 75, and 150 partners. Research has shown that outliers such as these bias the mean or average scores calculated for a sample. Using this procedure, other researchers have found comparable results

to ours. A comparison with national figures suggests that our data are roughly comparable, though there are some differences that are likely due to the average age of our participants and the way we conducted our research: for example, nationally representative data collected between 1988 and 1990 by the General Social Surveys, done by the National Opinion Research Center at the University of Chicago. On the 1990 survey, they found that a substantial number of adults (37 percent) reported having sex once a month or less. Forty percent of their sample said they had sex once a week or more, while more than 20 percent reported having sex at least twice a week. Compare that figure to Edward Laumann's finding (Laumann, E. O., Gagnon, J. H., Michael, R. T., & Michaels, S. [1994]. *The social organization of sexuality: Sexual practices in the United States.* Chicago, IL: The Univ. of Chicago Press.) that roughly one-third of people claimed to have sex twice a week, the results of a national survey in France that found both men and women on average have sex twice a week, and our own finding that 50 percent of our respondents have sex two times a week. (Aldhous, P. [1992]. French venture where U.S. fears to tread. *Science, 257,* 25.) The GSS survey (Smith, T. W. [February 1992]. A methodological analysis of the sexual behavior questions on the GSS [Methodological Report #65]. University of Chicago: National Opinion Research Center [see also a revised version of this report in *Journal of Official Statistics, 8* (1992), 309–326.]) done in 1989 found that the average number of lifetime sexual partners reported by men and women (heterosexuals only) differed very significantly. On average, men claimed 9.36 partners and women claimed 3.02 partners, a difference of over 3 to 1. Different studies have found widely varying results in the numbers of partners claimed, however, and, in particular, there is reason to doubt that the discrepancy between men and women in their lifetime number of partners is as large as the GSS survey suggests. See, for example, Einon, D. (1994). Are men more promiscuous than women? *Ethology and Sociobiology, 15,* 131–143.

64. See Person, E. S., Terestman, N., Myers, W. A., Goldberg, E. L., & Salvadori, C. (1989). Gender differences in sexual behaviors and fantasies in a college population. *Journal of Sex and Marital Therapy, 15*(3), 187–198; and Hsu, B., Kling, A., Kessler, C., Knapke, K., Diefenbach, P., &

Elias, J. E. (1994). Gender differences in sexual fantasy and behavior in a college population: A ten-year replication. *Journal of Sex and Marital Therapy, 20*, 103–118.

65. Kaplan, H. S. (1979). *The new sex therapy.* New York: Brunner/Mazel.

66. Byrne, D., & Osland, J. A. (2000). Sexual fantasy and erotica/pornography: Internal and external imagery. In L. T. Szuchman & F. Muscarella (Eds.), *Psychological perspectives on human sexuality.* (pp. 283–305) New York: John Wiley & Sons.

67. Strassberg, D. S., & Lockerd, L. K. (August 1998). Force in women's sexual fantasies. *Archives of Sexual Behavior, 27*(4), 403–414.

68. Bond, S. B., & Mosher, D. L. (May 1986). Guided imagery of rape: Fantasy, reality, and the willing victim myth. *Journal of Sex Research, 22*(2), 162–183.

69. Moore, N. B., & Davidson, J. K., Sr. (1997). Guilt about first intercourse: An antecedent of sexual dissatisfaction among college women. *Journal of Sex and Marital Therapy, 23*, 29–46.

70. Hurlbert, D. F. (1993). A comparative study using orgasm consistency training in the treatment of women reporting hypoactive sexual desire. *Journal of Sex and Marital Therapy, 19*, 41–55.

CHAPTER 9

71. Hendrick, S. S., & Hendrick, C. (1995). Gender differences and similarities in sex and love. *Personal Relationships, 2*(1), 55–65. See also Oliver, M. B., & Hyde, J. S. (1993). Gender differences in sexuality: A meta-analysis. *Psychological Bulletin, 114*(1), 29–51.

72. Note, however, that it was mostly men (in fact twice as many men as women) who said they believed there are "no differences" in the levels of desire between the two sexes.

73. Smith, T. W. (February 1992). *A methodological analysis of the sexual behavior questions on the GSS* (Methodological Report #65). University of Chicago: National Opinion Research Center. See also a revised

version of this report in *Journal of Official Statistics,* 8 (1992), 309–326; and Einon, D. (1994). Are men more promiscuous than women? *Ethology and Sociobiology, 15,* 131–143.

74. Oliver, M. B., & Hyde, J. S. (1993). Gender differences in sexuality: A meta-analysis. *Psychological Bulletin, 114*(1), 29–51.

75. Differences in disclosure are reported in Hatfield, E., & Rapson, R. L. (1993). *Love, sex, and intimacy: Their psychology, biology, and history.* New York: HarperCollins College Publishers; the longitudinal study was conducted by Rubin, Z., Hill, C. T., & Peplau, L. A. (1980). Self-disclosure in dating couples: Sex-roles and the ethic of openness. *Journal of Marriage and the Family, 42*(2), 305–317.

76. See Hendrick & Hendrick, Gender differences and similarities in sex and love, *Personal Relationships, 2,* 55–65.

77. Barba, J. F. (1998). Sexual orientation and capacity for intimacy. *Dissertation Abstracts International: Section B: The Sciences & Engineering, 58*(10-B), 5635.

78. Kelly, J. A., O'Brien, G. G., &., Hosford, R. (1981). Sex-roles and social skills considerations for interpersonal adjustment. *Psychology of Women Quarterly, 5,* 758–766.

79. Tanwar, S., & Sethi, A. S. (September 1986). The relationship of sex-role orientation, locus of control, and achievement motivation to self-esteem among college females. *Journal of Psychological Researches, 30*(3), 121–128; and Quackenbush, R. L. (1990). Sex roles and social-sexual effectiveness. *Social Behavior and Personality, 18*(1), 35–39.

80. Walfish, S., & Myerson, M. (1980). Sex-role identity and attitudes toward sexuality. *Archives of Sexual Behavior, 9*(3), 199–203; see also Johnson, M. E. (1989). Sex-role orientation and attitudes toward sexual expression. *Psychological Reports, 64*(3, Pt 2), 1064.

81. Rosenzweig, J. M., & Dailey, D. M. (1989). Dyadic adjustment/sexual satisfaction in women and men as a function of psychological sex role self-perception. *Journal of Sex and Marital Therapy, 15*(1), 42–56.

82. Spencer, S. L., & Zeiss, A. M. (1987). Sex roles and sexual dysfunction in college students. *Journal of Sex Research, 23*(3), 338–347.

83. Radlove, S. (1983). Sexual response and gender roles. In E. All-

geier & N. B. McCormack (Eds.), *Changing boundaries: Gender roles and sexual behavior* (pp. 87–105). Palo Alto: Mayfield.

84. Ray, A. L, & Gold, S. G. (1996). Gender roles, aggression, and alcohol use in dating relationships. *Journal of Sex Research, 33,* 47–55.

85. Bernard, J. L., Bernard, S. L., & Bernard, M. L. (1985). Courtship violence and sex-typing. *Family Relations: Journal of Applied Family and Child Studies, 34*(4), 573–576.

86. Coleman, M., Ganong, L. H. (1985). Love and sex role stereotypes: Do macho men and feminine women make better lovers? *Journal of Personality & Social Psychology, 49*(1), 170–176. See also Zammichieli, M. E., Gilroy, F. D., & Sherman, M. F. (1988). Relation between sex-role orientation and marital satisfaction. *Personality and Social Psychology Bulletin, 14*(4), 747–754.

CHAPTER 10

87. Walser, R. D., & Kern, J. M. (1996). Relationships among childhood sexual abuse, sex guilt, and sexual behavior in adult clinical samples. *Journal of Sex Research, 33*(4), 321–326.

88. Fleming J., Mullen, P. E., Sibthorpe, B., & Bammer, G. (1999). The long-term impact of childhood sexual abuse in Australian women. *Child Abuse and Neglect, 23*(2):145–159.

89. Herman, J. L. (1981). *Father-daughter incest.* Cambridge, MA: Harvard University Press.

90. Courtois, C. (1988). *Healing the incest wound: Adult survivors in therapy.* New York: Norton.

91. See Blume, E. S. (1990). *Secret survivors: Uncovering incest and its aftereffects in women.* New York: John Wiley & Sons; Browne, A., & Finkelhor, D. (1986). Impact of child sexual abuse: A review of the research. *Psychological Bulletin, 99*(1), 66–77; Meiselman, K. (1978). *Incest: A psychological study of the causes and effects with treatment implications.* San Francisco: Jossey-Bass; Briere, J. (April 1984). The effects of childhood sexual abuse on later psychological functioning: Defining a "post-sexual-abuse syndrome." Paper presented at the Third National

Conference of Sexual Victimization of Children, Washington, D.C.; and Courtois, C. (1979). The incest experience and its aftermath. *Victimology: An International Journal, 4,* 337–347.

92. Perlman, D., & Fehr, B. (1987). The development of intimate relationships. In D. Perlman & S. Duck (Eds.), *Intimate relationships: Development, dynamics, and deterioration.* Thousand Oaks, CA: Sage.

93. Ibid.

94. Fleming, Mullen, Sibthorpe, & Bammer. The long-term impact of childhood sexual abuse in Australian women.

95. Psychologists often consider sex between a person under sixteen and someone at least four or five years older to be abuse, since the older person, by virtue of the age difference, has a great deal more power, and the sex is unlikely to be completely consensual.

96. Lisak, D., & Roth, S. (1990). Motives and psychodynamics of self-reported, unincarcerated rapists. *American Journal of Orthopsychiatry, 60*(2), 268–280; and Lisak, D., & Roth, S. (1988). Motivational factors in nonincarcerated sexually aggressive men. *Journal of Personality and Social Psychology, 55*(5), 795–802.

97. Griffin, S. E. (1995). Adolescent sex and relationship addicts. *Sexual Addiction and Compulsivity, 2,* 112–127.

98. Carnes, P. (1991). *Don't call it love: Recovery from sexual addiction.* New York: Bantam Books.

99. Pitman, R. K., van der Kolk, B., Orr, S. P., & Greenberg, M. S. (1990). Naloxone-reversible analgesic response to combat related stimuli in Post-traumatic Stress Disorder. *Archives of General Psychiatry, 47,* 541–544.

100. Carnes, P. J. (1998). The case for sexual anorexia: An interim report on 144 patients with sexual disorders. *Sexual Addiction and Compulsion, 5,* 293–309.

CHAPTER 11

101. Feingold, A. (1992). Good-looking people are not what we think. *Psychological Bulletin, 111,* 304–341.

102. Anderson, S. M., & Bem, S. L. (1981). Sex typing and androgyny in dyadic interaction: Individual differences in responsiveness to physical attractiveness. *Journal of Personality and Social Psychology, 41,* 74–86.

103. Cutler, W. B. (1999). Human sex-attractant pheromones: Discovery, research, development, and application in sex therapy. *Psychiatric Annals, 29*(1), 54–59.

104. Maugham, W. S. (1949). *A writer's notebook.* Garden City, NY: Doubleday.

105. See Zebrowitz, L. A., Olson, K., & Hoffman, K. (1993). Stability of baby-faceness and attractiveness across the life span. *Journal of Personality and Social Psychology, 64,* 453–466; Langlois, J. H., & Roggman, L. A. (1990). Attractive faces are only average. *Psychological Science, 1,* 115–121; Thornhill, R., & Gangestad, S. W. (1993). Human facial beauty: Averageness, symmetry, and parasite resistance. *Human Nature, 4,* 237–269; and Buss, D. M., et al. (1990). International preferences in selecting mates: A study in 37 cultures. *Journal of Cross-Cultural Psychology, 21*(1), 5–47.

106. Kalick, S. M., Zebrowitz, L. A., Langlois, J. H., & Johnson, R. M. (1998). Does human facial attractiveness honestly advertise health? Longitudinal data on an evolutionary question. *Psychological Science, 9*(1), 8–13.

107. See Kenrick, D. T., & Gutierres, S. E. (1980). Contrast effects and judgments of physical attractiveness: When beauty becomes a social problem. *Journal of Personality and Social Psychology, 38*(1), 131–140.

108. See Zillmann, D. & Bryant, J. (1988). Pornography impact on sexual satisfaction. *Journal of Applied Social Psychology, 18*(5), 438–453; and Weaver, J. B., Masland, J. L., & Zillmann, D. (1984). Effect of erotica on young men's aesthetic perception of their female sexual partners. *Perceptual and Motor Skills, 58*(3) 929–930.

109. Howard W. Odum Institute for Research in Social Science Louis Harris Data Archive, Institute for Research in the Social Sciences Study Number S884019, November 1988; Lexis-Nexis Roper Center at University of Connecticut Public Opinion Online, Accession Number 0260288, March 14, 1996.

110. Kendrick, K. M., Hinton, M. R., Atkins, K., et al. (1998). Mothers determine sexual preferences. *Nature, 395*(6699), 229–230.

111. See Ainsworth, M. D. S., & Bowlby, J. (1991). An ethological approach to personality development. *American Psychologist, 46,* 333–341.

112. Hazan, C., & Shaver, P. (1987). Romantic love conceptualized as an attachment process. *Journal of Personality and Social Psychology, 52*(3) 511–524; and Shaver, P., & Hazan, C. (1987). Being lonely, falling in love: Perspectives from attachment theory. *Journal of Social Behavior and Personality, 2*(2), 105–124.

CHAPTER 12

113. Gutek, B. A. (1985). *Sex and the workplace.* San Francisco: Jossey-Bass.

114. Powell, G. N., & Foley, S. (1999). Romantic relationships in organizational settings: Something to talk about. In G. N. Powell, et al. (Eds.), *Handbook of gender and work* (pp. 281–304). Thousand Oaks, CA: Sage.

115. Pierce, C. A., Byrne, D., & Aguinis, H. (1996). Attraction in organizations: A model of workplace romance. *Journal of Organizational Behavior, 17,* 5–32.

116. Ibid.

117. Quinn, R. E. (1977). Coping with Cupid: The formation, impact, and management of romantic relationships in organizations. *Administrative Science Quarterly, 22*(1), 30–45.

118. Anderson, C. I., & Hunsaker, P. L. (February 1985). Why there's romancing at the office and why it's everybody's problem. *Personnel,* 57–63.

119. Mainiero, L. A. (1989). *Office romance: Love, power, and sex in the workplace.* New York: Rawson Associates.

120. Ibid.

121. Powell & Foley, *Handbook of gender and work.*

122. Williams, C. L., Giuffre, P. A., & Dellinger, K. (1999). Sexuality

in the workplace: Organizational control, sexual harassment, and the pursuit of pleasure. *Annual Review of Sociology, 25,* 73–93.

123. Powell & Foley, *Handbook of gender and work.*

124. Williams, Giuffre, & Dellinger, Sexuality in the workplace.

125. Pierce, Byrne, & Aguinis. Attraction in organizations.

126. Williams, Giuffre, & Dellinger, Sexuality in the workplace.

127. Powell & Foley, *Handbook of gender and work.*

128. Pierce, Byrne, & Aguinis, Attraction in organizations.

129. Powell & Foley, *Handbook of gender and work.*

130. Ibid.

131. Mainiero, *Office romance.*

132. Powell & Foley, *Handbook of gender and work.*

133. Pierce, Byrne, & Aguinis, Attraction in organizations.

134. Dillard, J. P. (1987). Close relationships at work: Perceptions of the motives and performance of relational participants. *Journal of Social and Personal Relationships, 4,* 179–193.

135. Pierce, Byrne, & Aguinis, Attraction in organizations.

136. 9-zip! I love it! (November 22, 1993). *Time, 142*(22), 44–46.

137. See Tangri, S. S., Burt, M. R., & Johnson, L. B. (1982). Sexual harassment at work: Three explanatory models. *Journal of Social Issues, 38,* 33–54; and Wide harassment of women working for U.S. is reported. (July 1, 1998). *New York Times,* B6.

138. Ragins, B. R., & Scandura, T. A. (1995). Antecedents and work-related correlates of reported sexual harassment: An empirical investigation of competing hypotheses. *Sex Roles, 32*(7–8), 429–455.

139. Williams, Giuffre, & Dellinger, Sexuality in the workplace.

140. Ibid.

141. Ibid.

142. See Abbey, A. (1987). Misperceptions of friendly behavior as sexual interest: A survey of naturally occurring incidents. *Psychology of Women Quarterly, 11*(2), 173–194; and Abbey, A. (1991). Acquaintance rape and alcohol consumption on college campuses: How are they linked? *Journal of American College Health, 39*(4), 165–169.

143. Studies have found that males and females generally agree on

what constitutes sexual harassment, such as uninvited sexual behavior, quid pro quo situations, or sexual assault, bribery, or coercion. See Collins, E. G. C., & Blodgett, T. B. (1981). Sexual harassment: Some see it . . . some won't. *Harvard Business Review, 59,* 76–95; Merit System Protection Board. (1981). *Sexual harassment in the federal workplace: Is it a problem?* Washington, DC: U.S. Government Printing Office; and Tata, J. (1993). The structure and phenomenon of sexual harassment: Impact of category of sexually harassing behavior, gender, and hierarchical level. *Journal of Applied Social Psychology, 23,* 199–211.

144. See Fiske, S., & Glick, P. (1995). Ambivalence and stereotypes cause sexual harassment: A theory with implications for organizational change. *Journal of Social Issues, 51*(1), 97–115; and Glick, P., & Fiske, S. (1996). The ambivalent sexism inventory: Differentiating hostile and benevolent sexism. *Journal of Personality and Social Psychology, 70*(3), 491–512.

145. Glick, P., & Fiske, S. (1997). Hostile and benevolent sexism: Measuring ambivalent sexist attitudes toward women. *Psychology of Women Quarterly, 21,* 119–135.

146. Begany, J. J., & Milburn, M. A. (In press). Psychological predictors of sexual harassment: Authoritarianism, hostile sexism, and rape myths. *Psychology of Man and Masculinity.*

147. See Milburn, M. A., & Conrad, S. D. (Winter 1996). The politics of denial. *Journal of Psychohistory, 23*(3), 238–251; and Milburn, M. A., Conrad, S. D., Sala, F., & Carberry, S. (1995). Childhood punishment, denial, and political attitudes. *Political Psychology, 16*(3), 447–478.

148. Adorno, T. W., Frenkel-Brunswik, E., Levinson, D. L., & Sanford, R. N. (1950). *The authoritarian personality.* New York: Harper.

149. Altemeyer, R. (1988). *Enemies of freedom: Understanding right-wing authoritarianism.* San Francisco, London: Jossey-Bass.

150. See Ou, T. Y. (1996). Are abusive men different? And can we predict their behavior? Honors thesis, Department of Psychology, Harvard-Radcliffe College, Cambridge, MA; Petty, G. M., & Dawson, B. (1989). Sexual aggression in normal men: Incidence, beliefs, and personality characteristics. *Personality and Individual Differences, 10*(3), 355–362; and

Walker, W. D., Rowe, R. C., & Quinsey, V. L. (1993). Authoritarianism and sexual harassment. *Journal of Personality and Social Psychology*, 65(5), 1036–1045.

151. Because of the fact that the University of Massachusetts–Boston is a public, urban university that serves many nontraditional students, the men were a diverse group, both in terms of age and ethnic background. They ranged in age from eighteen to seventy-four, with 19 percent over the age of forty and 29 percent over the age of thirty. The group included Caucasians; Latino-Americans; African-Americans; Asian-Americans; recent immigrants from Haiti, Southeast Asia, Russia, and Europe; and one Native American.

CHAPTER 13

152. Wiederman, M. W. (1997). Extramarital sex: Prevalence and correlates in a national survey. *The Journal of Sex Research*, 34(2), 167–174.

153. Lexis-Nexis Roper Center at University of Connecticut Public Opinion Online, Accession number 0282090, June 6, 1997.

154. See Wiederman, Extramarital sex; and Lexis-Nexis Roper Center at University of Connecticut Public Opinion Online, Accession number 0293042, February 11, 1998.

155. Larson, J. H., Anderson, S. M., Holman, T. B., & Niemann, B. K. (1998). A longitudinal study of the effects of premarital communication, relationship stability, and self-esteem on sexual satisfaction in the first year of marriage. *Journal of Sex and Marital Therapy*, 24(3), 193–206.

156. See Hassett, J. (June 1981). Is it right? An inquiry into everyday ethics. *Psychology Today*, 15, 49–56; and Hassett, J. (November 1981). But that would be wrong. *Psychology Today*, 15, 34–53.

157. Buss, D. M., & Shackelford, T. K. (1997). Susceptibility to infidelity in the first year of marriage. *Journal of Research in Personality*, 31(2), 193–221.

158. Brown, N. W. (1998). *The destructive narcissistic pattern*. Westport, CT: Praeger.

159. Lexis-Nexis Roper Center at University of Connecticut Public Opinion Online, Accession number 0285888, September 18, 1997.

EPILOGUE

160. Rodgers, K. B. (February 1999). Parenting processes related to sexual risk-taking behaviors of adolescent males and females. *Journal of Marriage and the Family, 61*(1), 99–109.

Index

Religion:
    beliefs that do not match
        behavior, 74–75
    case studies of faith, fear, and
        sex, 75–79
    and fear of sex, 72–74
    and homosexuality, 80
Reproduction, 128, 213
Research Triangle Institute
    (Washington, D.C.), 63
Rodgers, Kathleen, 280, 281
Roman Catholic Church, 73, 81,
    282–83
Romantic love, 135–36, 220
Roth, Susan, 197

S

Safe sex, 91
Sawyer, Robin, 117
Scientific information, 15–16, 17,
    61–62
    on child abuse, 203
    on fantasies, 160
    on gender, 182
    on infidelity, 259, 274
    on pornography, 106
    on reasons for sex, 56, 144
    on sexual attraction, 222–23
    on workplace attractions, 247
Secret sexual self, 10–11, 31–43
    abandoning, 185–204
    awareness of, 16–17, 56, 57,
        107, 144, 160, 182–83, 203,
        223, 247, 274
    and cultural norms, 38–41
    and gender, 181, 182–83
    and infidelity, 274
    and painful past, 34–36,
        188–89
    and reasons for sex, 142
    and sexual attraction, 223
    and unmet emotional needs,
        36–38
    and workplace attractions, 247
Self-knowledge. See Secret sexual
    self
Self-mutilation, 201

Serotonin, 133
Sex education, 70, 117, 278,
    281–82, 285
Sex life:
    commitment to satisfying,
        51–52
    dissatisfaction with, 94
    hard work needed for
        satisfying, 14, 91
    importance of satisfying, 278
    and pornography, 93–94
    reasons for, 45–57, 127–44
    stumbling blocks to, 61–69
    talking about, 17–18
Sex roles. See Gender stereotypes
Sex-typing. See Gender
    stereotypes
Sexual addiction, 186, 197–201
Sexual aggression, 170
Sexual arousal, 132, 156
Sexual attraction, 15, 16, 207–24
    immediate, 209–10
    and looks, 210–12
    and opposite-sex parent,
        215–16, 217
    to some rather than others,
        212–16
    in workplace, 225–39
Sexual Aversion Disorder, 201
Sexual behavior, 147–52
Sexual desire, 147
    case studies, 7–8, 40–41, 153
    gender stereotypes about, 167,
        169–71
    looking into one's own, 152–56
    and past experiences, 16
Sexual drive. See Sexual desire
Sexual dysfunction, 50, 94, 186,
    193–94, 310n.6
Sexual empathy, 250, 261–65
Sexual frequency, 46, 317n.63
Sexual harassment. See
    Workplace harassment
"Sexual Healing" (song), 99
Sexual history, 42–43
Sexual intelligence, 278, 281–82
    on child abuse, 202
    components of, 14–18, 20

About the Authors

SHEREE DUKES CONRAD is an assistant professor of social psychology at the University of Massachusetts at Boston. She received a B.A. in psychology from Wesleyan University and a Ph.D. in personality psychology from Boston University. She is the author, with Michael Milburn, of *The Politics of Denial* (MIT Press, 1996), based on their award-winning research on the link between childhood punishment and adult political and social attitudes, for example, on abortion.

Dr. Conrad also conducts research on the long-term cognitive, emotional, and interpersonal effects of childhood sexual and physical abuse, as well as the determinants of domestic violence. She is a member of the International Society for the Study of Dissociation and the International Society of Political Psychology.

MICHAEL A. MILBURN is professor of psychology at the University of Massachusetts at Boston. He received an A.B. in psychology from Stanford University and a Ph.D. in social psychology from Harvard University. He is the author of dozens of published articles and two books, *Persuasion and Politics: The Social Psychology of Public Opinion* (Wadsworth, 1991) and, with Sheree D. Conrad, of *The Politics of Denial* (MIT Press, 1996). In addition to his research on public opinion and public policy, Dr. Milburn conducts research on the effects of the mass media. He is a member of the International Society of Political Psychology and the Society for the Scientific Study of Sexuality.